How To Get
Your Child Into
Commercials
And Modeling

How To Get Your Child Into Commercials And Modeling

Jane Gassner Patrick

Doubleday & Company, Inc., Garden City, New York
1981

Library of Congress Cataloging in Publication Data

Patrick, Jane Gassner.
How to get your child into commercials and
modeling.

Includes index.
1. Acting for television—Vocational guidance.
2. Children as actors. 3. Television advertising.
4. Models, Fashion—Vocational guidance. I. Title
PN1992.8.A3P3   791.45′028′023
ISBN: 0-385-15317-1
Library of Congress Catalog Card Number 79–8031
Copyright © 1981 by Jane Gassner Patrick

Acknowledgments

A novel may be written in a vacuum; nonfiction never is. Thanks must go to all those people, mentioned by name and not, who interrupted their lives to share their experience with me. But my deepest gratitude is for a small group of people, without whom this book just would not be.

To Sheila Manning, Paula Mehr, and Sandra Firestone, for introducing me to the world of children in commercials.

To Christopher Keane, for the example, encouragement, and occasional kick in the pants.

To Shelly Hutter, for teaching me about onions and logjams, and giving me the tools to deal with both.

To Marlene Adler Marks, who was, is, and will always, but always, be there.

And to Trevor Valentine, who had to read every page and put up with me through it all.

Dedication

To my parents, Harold and Lee Gassner—
For all the things, big and small, that have
made up their loving, a lifetime of dedications
would still fall short.

Contents

Preface

Several years ago I approached *Los Angeles* magazine with an idea for an article on child actors. I had recently seen a little girl called Natasha Ryan pull out all the stops playing a four-year-old battered child in a TV movie called *Mary Jane Harper Cried Last Night.* I couldn't believe a small child could give such a varied emotional performance on her own. Surely, I thought, there was a director pulling puppet strings behind her. I knew of the tricks directors of old had used to get heart-rending performances from the child stars of the thirties and forties. Baby Leroy laughed because they poured water on his mother's head. Shirley Temple cried because they sent her mother from the set. Were directors still manipulating emotions from child actors with such unsophisticated ploys? Or were they benefiting from our vast knowledge of child psychology and using more Machiavellian techniques?

Those were the questions I proposed to answer in my article. But *Los Angeles* wasn't interested. Rather, they asked me to do a business-oriented article on children who act in commercials. There was big money being made from and by these kids; *Los Angeles* wanted to know how and how much.

So I did the research and wrote the article their way. I got the statistics: More than a thousand child actors on the West Coast are represented by some fifty agents, appearing in many of the two thousand or more commercials turned out yearly by a hundred

Los Angeles production companies, each spot earning countless millions for the advertiser, upward of $10,000 to $20,000 for the producers, and anywhere from $1,000 to $15,000 for the child.

And from interviewing those involved—agents, casting directors, producers, ad agency people, and the kids and their parents—I put together a picture of what makes a child "commercial," how these children move into and through the business, and how, in fact, they are marketed.

When the article appeared, the response amazed both *Los Angeles* and me. It wasn't the business-minded who called in and wrote the magazine; it was parents. The article had been titled "Hey, Little Boy—Ya Wanna Be in a Commercial?" The answer was an overwhelming "Yes."

Most of the parents merely wanted the names and phone numbers of agents who handle children. Those calls were easy enough to satisfy. But a few asked for more than that. "I've always thought my son would be perfect for commercials," one mother wrote. "But I don't know if I'm right or how to go about finding out. Could you tell me what I should know about the business before I decide whether to get him into it. Also, I'm sure there is a wrong way and a right way of going about it—or maybe there's just a best way. If so, I'd like to learn what it is so I don't make a mess of things just because I did not know."

I put that letter aside, planning to write a long reply. "Dear Mrs. Smith," I would say. "You're very wise to want to learn about the business before you start your son off in it. You're also very rare. Most parents just grab hold of their dream to have a commercial kid and then run with it, regardless of the consequences. They hear about the money a child can make and they think about the fame, but they never stop to learn about the risks, sacrifices, and heartbreaks involved for children and parents in the business. Having a child in commercials is a career for both of you. Like any other career, one has to consider beforehand not just whether your child is right for commercials, but are commercials right for your child?

"And, yes, there is a wrong way, a right way, and a best way of getting into the field. Commercial-making is a complicated business; there are a lot of ins and outs, pitfalls and props that you should know about before you even start. I wish I could lay them out for you, map, in fact, a step-by-step course for the best way to get and keep your son successfully in the business. But it would take pages and pages to do that . . ."

It would, in fact, take a book. Which is why I never answered that letter. Until now.

How To Get
Your Child Into
Commercials
And Modeling

1

The Pros and the Cons: <u>Should</u> Your Child Do Commercials?

In the best of all possible worlds, this is how it happens.

Once upon a time there was a family called Lee, who lived in a tract house on a large development forty-five miles east of Los Angeles. They were a typical American family. Bob Lee, a broad-shouldered man in his thirties, was a salesman who raced cars as a hobby. Dark, slim Elaine Lee was a housewife with three young children to care for. And those three kids—Bobby, Mike, and Gary—were happy, wholesome children whose lives were the normal round of school, Little League, and bike-riding on the block with the neighborhood kids.

Until one afternoon when Elaine Lee got a phone call. It was from a friend of one of Bob's racing buddies, a woman who worked for a top Hollywood agent.

"We've just had a call for blond, four-year-old boys to do a Clairol commercial, and we don't have anyone on our books to send," she said. "But I remember Gary, and he'd be just perfect for it. Would you consider bringing him in?"

Would she? Elaine's thoughts ran fast in opposite directions: yes, no, maybe. She was proud and flattered. Sure, she'd love to see her son do a commercial. Even to be thought of as good enough—well, what mother could turn that down? But no, what about all those Hollywood stories? The ones that told of a business that took young children, chewed them up, and spit them out as hopeless neurotics, scarred forever by the sights they'd seen, the fame they'd had, the rejection they'd suffered. What mother would let her child in for that? But wait, maybe those tales weren't all true. And think what an opportunity this was. Could there be any real harm in just trying it, this once only?

Elaine asked the agent, listing her fears as they came up. For an hour they talked, going over the pros and cons, the reality and fiction of kids who do commercials. That night, Elaine and Bob sat down and she told him what she'd learned. Together they thrashed it out and decided that, providing Gary was in agreement, Elaine would take him down to this one audition. If he liked it, fine. If not, they'd just forget the whole thing.

They brought Gary in and explained to him in four-year-old language just what was going to happen the next day. He'd have to go by himself into a room of strange people, which would be scary. But all they wanted to do was talk with him, just like he talked with everyone else. It wasn't a test or anything that meant he was good or bad, or that they liked him or didn't like him. And then, maybe, if the color of his hair was the color they were looking for, he would get to be in a commercial. Just like the kids he saw on TV. How did all that sound?

Just fine, Gary thought. The next day, this cheerful little boy walked into the interview—and into the beginning of a career that now, five years later, has seen him in commercials for most of the major advertisers. His brothers soon joined him, and the three of them earn upward of $50,000 a year.

Gary's entry into commercials is a child's version of the Lana Turner/Schwab's Drugstore discovery scene. It's a rare happening, one that parents dream of but rarely see realized. However, its uncommonness is not the main reason Gary's story represents the best of all possible worlds. Rather, it is Elaine and Bob Lee's careful consideration of the consequences, both good and bad, of putting Gary into commercials that makes his story so unique.

Most parents never stop to think of what's ahead when they start planning a commercial career for their child. They see only the pot at the end of the rainbow—the money, the glamour, the thrill of success. They don't realize or recognize that with a rainbow comes rain, and in the case of commercial kids, the downpour can be a deluge leaving in its wake a battered child and a torn family. And, as with a flood, you never know the extent of the damage until long afterward.

On the other hand, the rain before a rainbow is just as often a sprinkle, bringing blue skies and tall, green grass. So too can a commercial career nurture a child and his family, providing them with benefits they might never have known.

Sprinkle or downpour, you can only know which will be true for your child if you know what to expect from the business. There are some definite negatives; there are some definite positives; and there are some aspects that you alone can tip to one side or the other.

To parents outside the business, the biggest lure for putting a child in commercials is the money. Make that MONEY, printed in big, black letters. Read or hear about a kid who does commercials and there will be the child's income, the string of zeros after a nice fat number enticingly marching across the page, followed by talk of trust funds for college, European vacations, and new houses with swimming pools and maids to keep them clean.

Parents in the business know better. True, a child can make a small fortune acting in commercials. The flat fee for a commercial shooting session is $275. The big money comes from residuals, a commission of sorts that is based on where and how often the commercial is shown. Experts say that the average commercial earns a child between $1,000 and $5,000 a year. Experts also say that the average successful child can make twelve to twenty commercials a year. Multiply those figures and you get a very attractive income.

However, considering the thousands of kids on agents' books as commercial actors, it is the rare one who nets such an income.

The ones we read about are the unique success stories—which is why, after all, they get into the news. Never mentioned are those other children who make maybe just one commercial a year, say a local one with no residuals, which pays just the flat session fee.

Also never mentioned is the fact that in the commercial business, like many others, it takes money to make money. There is a host of expenses that can eat into or up any profit a child may make. Some of them are obvious, others hidden; but all are necessary to ensure a child's success.

Take photographs, for instance. The composite or head shot accompanied by a résumé is the only sales tool an agent has in promoting talent. It's handed out to every person even remotely associated with commercial casting. In fact, many agents maintain huge looseleaf notebooks filled with photos of their clients in offices of all the casting directors, advertising agencies, production companies, and the like in their city. For the child, these photos are the calling cards of the profession. Every time a child goes on an interview, he hands over a composite for the commercial-maker to keep.

These photographs are so crucial to a child's success that they must be professionally done. School pictures or the $1.98 specials from Thrifty's rarely can be used, because they almost never capture the natural essence of the child. Even more expensive portrait photographers tend to pose the child in stiff, cutesy positions. As one agent says, "What looks nice on the mantelpiece is absolutely *not* what we want in a commercial composite."

Consequently, agents recommend that you have your child's professional pictures taken by photographers who specialize in commercial casting photography. These experts know exactly how best to display your child. And they charge for that expertise— sometimes as much as $100 a sitting. That does not include the duplication of the photograph, usually done by lithograph, which will run to another $100.

And don't count on these pictures being a one-time expense. As your child grows and changes, new pictures must be taken to reflect that. "There's nothing worse," says one director, "than seeing a tall, slim ten-year-old you really like in a casting session, and then later, when you go to show his picture to the advertiser for a final okay, you're faced with a portrait of a chubby little six-year-old who is absolutely wrong for the part."

Another continuing expense is union dues. The two unions children in commercials belong to are the Screen Actors Guild (SAG) and the American Federation of Television and Radio Artists (AFTRA). If a child's commercials have been shot on film, he must join SAG; if they're done on videotape, AFTRA is his union. Often the child who works frequently does commercials in both media and ends up belonging to both SAG and AFTRA.

Each union charges one-time initiation fees as well as biannual dues. Initiation into SAG costs a hefty $525; for AFTRA, it's $300. The biannual dues vary according to which local branch the child belongs to and what his income was in the past year. In Los Angeles, for example, the minimum for a child who earned under $2,500 is $25 every six months for SAG and $22 for AFTRA. Those dues slide up to $287.50 and $200 for kids in the top income bracket.

True, you don't have to worry about union fees until *after* your child has done the first commercial. "But it's a funny thing how parents tend to forget about them," says Janice Borovay, the young woman who heads the children's department at the Ann Wright Agency in Los Angeles. "The child does the first commercial, the parents get some money, and they're happy. But with the second commercial, they have to join the union and they *never* want to put out that $525 or $300 in dues."

Borovay is a former actress with a gentle manner and soft voice that hide her no-nonsense attitude toward parents. A look of disapproval comes over her face as she adds, "I tell parents from the start: 'Put the money you get from the first commercial away and save it so that when the second comes along and you have to join the union, the money is there. I don't want to get into any problems in that area and I'm certainly *not* going to pay the dues for you."

Photographs and union dues are the only charges that the business absolutely demands of you. However, there are a number of other expenses that no one talks about but that are there all the same.

Transportation is probably the biggest of these. Commercial interviews are held five days a week, and the child with an active commercial career is often going on two or three interviews each day. Sometimes they're all in one area, sometimes they're at opposite ends of the town. Somehow or other, the child must get to all of them. Public transportation, taxi, a car—they all cost money. Elaine Lee, for example, ferries her boys ninety to a hundred miles round trip to Los Angeles for their interviews. At today's prices, her gas bill alone is considerable, not to mention the cost of wear and tear on her car. Obviously it is worth it to Elaine Lee to pay the price for her sons' careers. And it may be for you too —eventually. But at the beginning, before your child has gotten any work, make sure you have ready cash set aside for all the chauffeuring you're going to have to do.

You should also have a kitty for what I call "appearance incidentals." Included in this category are things like haircuts, clothing, and cosmetics. Remember you now have a professional on your hands, one who makes money by looking good. Unless you're a prize haircutter, you're going to have to pay for frequent trims for your child, and good ones. Forget home permanents by the lady next door, or the biannual shaved head by the barber down the street. Have you ever seen a child on television whose hair didn't look great? Not too long, not too short, flattering to the face and very casual—that's the product of someone who *styles* hair, doesn't just cut it. You know what the going rate is for a salon trim in your area; expect to pay it every four to six weeks.

Keeping your child in properly fitting clothes for interviews is also a must. Many parents keep a special wardrobe just for interviews. But that isn't really necessary, since most agents prefer that your child wear normal school clothes. Unless, of course, you are the type who ensures that clothes last a year by patching knees, letting down hems, and turning a blind eye to tops that have been through the wash once too often. That simply won't do for interviews. Your child must have at least one outfit, be it jeans and T-shirt or a dress, that looks relatively new, is a bright, becoming color, and fits perfectly.

In the cosmetics category come things like blemish cover, sun tan cream, lip balm, and, for teenagers, complexion products. Again remember that your child will, as the saying goes, be making his fortune on his face. Commercial-makers look for perfection in the kids they cast. They will turn down the child with a facial imperfection that shows, no matter how temporary. If yours has a small scar or dark circles under his eyes, the blemish cream will cover it up. But there is nothing that can hide cracked lips or a peeling, sunburned face. Like Angie's. This bright little girl with a wide grin and huge brown eyes was perfect in every way for a part in a national toy commercial. Except for one thing: her freckled face still showed the ravages of a bad sunburn. "I adore her," cried the director at the casting session. "But how can I use her with those big spots all over her face? I just don't understand parents. We're talking about this child making at least $5,000 on this commercial. Couldn't her mother have put out just a dollar for some sun tan lotion!"

Because commercial-makers do demand an unmarred appearance in the children they cast, you can expect to spend more money on dentistry. Unmarred in this business means having a full set of straight, white teeth. Those cute gap-toothed grins mean only the Tooth Fairy is putting money in a child's coffers. Kids with missing teeth are *never* cast in food commercials and have a hard time getting other jobs as well. Since the age of toothlessness coincides with the age when a child is most in demand by commercial-makers, dentists have come up with a prosthetic device called a "flipper." This is a removable bridge in which are set the appropriate false teeth. It is molded to fit snugly over the child's growing-in teeth and must be altered periodically as more and more of the permanent tooth appears. Prices for a flipper vary, depending on where you live and how expensive the specific dentist is. Jerry Albus, a Los Angeles dentist who cares for a number of commercial kids, charges $85 for the flipper and $15 for each adjustment made as the new tooth grows in. You can multiply that base charge by two, because your child will need a flipper for both the upper and lower teeth. Now, you don't *have* to get flippers for your child; that's your choice. But you are severely limiting his career if you don't.

More difficult to deal with is the problem braces present. Children with wires on their teeth are rarely cast unless a commercial specifically calls for them. As Sandra Firestone, head of Studio V Management in New York, told one boy with a shiny grin, "I get about two calls a year for kids with braces. I'll put you in my special file and when that call comes in, I'll let you know. But don't wait for it. It might come tomorrow or it might be months away. But as soon as you know when your braces are coming off, I want you to come in to see me again and then we can really talk about your career."

There are some orthodontists, however, who have designed removable braces. They are more expensive than the normal, permanent type, but if your child is in the middle of a successful commercial career, such an investment might well be worth the money.

A few parents, knowing of commercial-makers' mania for perfection, will stop at no expense to ensure their child's career. Dr. Albus tells of one mother whose nine-year-old daughter was already a very successful commercial kid. But her mother fancied that there was something drastically wrong with her teeth. One day she called the dentist and demanded that he cap every one of her child's healthy teeth. Dr. Albus was appalled. "It was a ridiculous request and I absolutely refused to do it. But it's possible that she found another dentist who would."

In addition to the dentist, there is another health specialist much frequented by commercial kids: the dermatologist. While most teenagers grin and bear the years of acne, a commercial kid can't afford to. Even the mildest case must be brought under control and often only regular trips to the doctor will do that.

There is one expense that many parents mistakenly believe they must pay for: dancing, singing, and acting lessons. These classes can cost a pretty penny but, say some experts, add little or nothing to a child's potential or actual commercial career.

Considering the money involved in getting and keeping a child in commercials, it is not surprising that most families with commercial kids are in the middle income bracket. "It isn't only that these parents, generally midlevel executives, have the ready resources to implement their child's career," says James White, vice president of the Mary Ellen White agency in New York. "They are also the ones astute enough to see that there is money in this business and to program themselves to break through to success. However, the lower level of the population *will* put up with more privation to get their child into commercials."

So, if money isn't a problem for you, fine, you don't really have to worry about the cost of having a commercial kid. If you are on a strict budget, however, take the information here and think long and hard about whether you can, in fact, afford a commercial kid.

There is so much talk of money in the business of commercial-making that most outsiders see nothing but dollar signs when they think of the rewards of having a commercial kid. Actually, of far greater worth is the way a commercial career can strengthen and develop a child's character. Think of words like independence, discipline, confidence, reality—they are the true payoff a commercial kid walks away with.

Commercial-making is not an easy job. It demands a high level of discipline and professionalism from all who work at it. Including kids. Little, if any, allowance is made for the vagaries of childhood. "I don't want to" is an intolerable statement in an interview or on a set. If the director wants a scene repeated forty times before he's satisfied, the child must go through it forty times, *each time giving his best*. Is he tired, hot, hungry, bored, or desperate to go to the bathroom? No one's asking, no one's interested; there's a job to be done *now* and that's all that's important.

Remember the beautiful, dark-haired little girl on the Northern Tissue ads? That is Shelby Balik. She's been in the business since she was four, and at the ripe old age of eight now, she has a solid list of commercial credits behind her. See her now in a spot for a spray-on laundry product. One of three kids in the commercial, she has the messiest segment.

The scene is Shelby washing a dog—a very large dog that fills to overflowing an old wooden washtub. The set has been carefully contrived. Three giant bags of potting earth have been dumped on the green grass around the tub. A thorough hosing down has turned it into a circle of mud. It's a warm summer day (actually February in Los Angeles) and the sun shines through the branches of a tree overhead.

The action is simple: Shelby, with joyful, loving care, will scrub the huge, shaggy animal with a large floor brush. After a few seconds of this traditional child-and-dog scene, reality will break in. The dog will, as they always do, vigorously shake the water off its back, drenching Shelby and splattering mud on her pristine, pale-pink T-shirt. Suddenly, an off-camera voice will ask: "Oh no, what's your mom going to do?" A split-second reaction from Shelby, an "eech" look at her now-filthy shirt. But no worry, no fear—her mom's got that great stain remover and she'll just *"Shout* it out!"

It's late afternoon and the sun is fast falling; this segment *must* be shot and wrapped quickly. Enter Shelby. Enter the dog. The big animal is lifted into the water-filled tub by his trainer, who, pockets filled with some sort of doggy rewards, will stand by to coach him not to move. Now there are a lot of things this dog may be trained to do, but shaking on cue isn't one of them. That, the most crucial part of the shot, must be left to the dog's instincts.

Take one—camera rolls, Shelby scrubs, the dog doesn't move. Take two—the same. Take three, four, five, six, seven, eight . . . Everyone gets into the act: "Spray his head . . . throw water in his face . . . dry him off and put him in again . . . pet him . . . don't pet him . . ." Each is tried and each fails. The animal is stolid, only looking sadder and sadder, bedraggled, inching as far away from Shelby and the source of his sodden misery as he can. Again and again and again. The director keeps the camera rolling, continually cueing Shelby on her line. "Look at your shirt longer . . . say the product name louder . . . you're jumping your cue . . ."

The sun is fading and the trainer warns the dog can't take the water much longer, he's beginning to shiver. With each futile take, the tension grows. Suddenly, with no warning, the dog shakes. The perfect moment: Shelby is scrubbing, the director cues her, the line comes out with just the right emphasis, just the right smile, just the right look. And overhead a low-flying plane roars into the sound track. Cut. Try again. Damn the planes.

The whole performance begins again and finally, nineteen takes later, after several changes of T-shirt, one cold, wet dog and one still smiling, still enthusiastic, still happy Shelby manage to perform together on a perfect, planeless take. Cut. Print. That's a wrap.

"Shelby, you were terrific," the director tells her. "You really are a pro."

Nearby Shelby's mother, a beautiful woman who has spent the afternoon reading and sunning on a large blanket spread on the grass, gathers together her paraphernalia, ready to begin the long drive home. "I'm grateful for what this business has done for Shelby. The money means nothing. What is important is that she's learned to handle herself in any situation. She has a deep sense of responsibility; she keeps her school grades up, maintains her relationships with her peers, *and* does the best she can every time she goes out on an interview or a job. I had a lot of preformed negative opinions about this business. But I must say that through Shelby's experience in it, I've been pleasantly surprised. She's a neat child and I like her. And I credit her acting career with a lot of what she is."

Years ago, when the work ethic for children was still a part of our culture, kids learned those basic life lessons naturally. Every child was expected to pull his weight in the family structure. Being responsible for their own chores and animals and paper routes taught kids the truth of those adages: You want something, you work for it. If you say you're going to do something, do it. A job worth doing is worth doing well. A day's pay for a day's work. No one gets a free ride.

But somewhere along the line, most of us stopped demanding such effort from our children. Maybe it was when we decided that life is hard enough as it is for an adult; let kids enjoy themselves while they can. "One of the problems with growing up today in the United States is that we don't really know how to make our children bloom," said Arthur Swan, principal of the Professional Children's School in New York, in Jason Bonderoff's book, *The Solid Gold Sandbox.** "We waste so much of their potential by isolating them from the rest of society and overprotecting them. We prolong adolescence to the point where you can't even tell where it ends anymore. Performing is one of the few remaining things that children can do other than staying on the educational treadmill. I suspect in the future that will become more of a positive attribute than it seems now. There was a time when children were excused from school to help with farm jobs, or to work in their fathers' shops, but we don't have the equivalent of those things anymore. It's just not the custom today. Yet I think it must be something rather splendid for a child . . . to bring home a paycheck—and it's not just an ego trip, but something deeply gratifying . . . to be able to say 'Look what I can do!' "

Listen to Kara Olsen, an impish, freckle-faced blonde who at nine is a five-year veteran of the commercial business: "What I like best about being in commercials is the feeling of accomplishment I get at having done the job well. The hardest thing is having to do the same scene over and over again. Sometimes it's not my fault, but when it is, I feel droopy and sad. But then, finally when I've done it so many times and I *finally* get it right—boy, that is a really rewarding feeling."

But it isn't only confidence and perseverance and discipline that these children get from their careers; it is also learning that life is not always going to go their way. What Elaine Lee calls "learning the no's of life." At a time when a child's world revolves solely around him, when he believes above all in his own supremacy, the commercial kid is learning that reality means that he's not going to get everything he wants simply because he wants it.

"My kids learned quite early that they would be turned down for jobs simply because they weren't what the director was looking for," says Elaine Lee. "Maybe they had the wrong color hair.

* Bonderoff, Jason, *The Solid Gold Sandbox*, Pinnacle Books, © 1975 by Jay Bonderoff.

Or their faces didn't quite match with the rest of the 'family' in the commercial. But the boys know that just because they didn't get the part it does not mean there is anything wrong with them as people. They've learned, quite simply, reality."

Of course, there is another side to this coin, one which you must very carefully consider. Those aspects of commercial-making that instill all these fine qualities can, just as easily, prove the child's undoing.

That the Lee boys and others like them have learned to accept rejection as reality is a credit to their parents. But for some children, being turned down time after time is devastating. In fact, just walking into the interview room can, particularly for the shy child, be a terrible experience.

Evelyn Schultz, mother of twin commercial kids and head of the children's department at the Wormser, Helfond & Joseph agency in Los Angeles, knows the scene well. "Imagine the poor child, six years old and for the first time he's taken by the hand by his mother to a place where there's a whole bunch of strange people sitting out in a waiting room. Then he's called into this inner sanctum, *alone,* and as he walks in, there are three or four adults sitting around a table staring at him. Next thing he knows they've put a camera in his face, said 'What's your name?' and he's supposed to . . . Well, the poor child doesn't know what's happening."

Even kids who are veterans at the interview process talk about how scary it is. "When I go into that room and see all those men and the lights and big camera and all those other little girls around, I get nervous," says Kara Olsen. "And being nervous makes me mess up. I get all fidgety and then people think I'm too uptight. I have to keep reminding myself to relax and just be myself."

The pressure to perform, to be "on" and cute takes its toll after a while. You can see it in children who, despite years in the business, walk into the interview shaking. There is a desperation in their eyes born of a desire to please crossed by a sense of futility that they actually can. "It's when they start to get nervous where they never did before that you know they've had enough," says one mother. "It didn't happen to my daughter right away, but when it did, I took her out of the business. I knew the rejection was getting to her."

The tension and pressure don't stop even when a child has gotten a job. The casual atmosphere of the shooting set is deceptive. The pressures the adults are under to get the commercial done, on time and with a minimum of problems, pass down to the child. Take the commercial featuring Shelby Balik. It was a beautiful day, and while Shelby and the crew were shooting at the far end of the lawn, six or seven people were lounging on the patio, drinking beer and Perrier, having, it seemed, just a great day off. In fact, they all were, at least figuratively, chewing their nails. First, there were the men who worked for the company that manufactured the stain remover. They had flown out from the Midwest to oversee the shoot and make sure the commercial perfectly depicted their product. This was the second time they'd done this spot. The first commercial was rejected; would this one do any better? And if it didn't, whose head would roll? Where could they put the blame?

Maybe on the advertising agency men. The writer had gone back to Chicago after casting the commercial, but the account executive and the producer were still there, glad-handing the product men, keeping them happy, reassuring them but all the time worrying about staying on budget and on time, wondering how the pictures looked, and knowing that if they didn't get the spot right this time, they could lose the account.

The waves of worry passed over the lawn to the director, the man ultimately responsible for how the commercial turned out. He could control the shots, the set, the actor, but he couldn't do anything about those damn planes that kept swooping overhead, droning through dialogue and holding up shooting for minutes at a time. And that dog, how the hell to get that dog to perform *before* the light faded, *before* the trainer called a halt, *before* Shelby got too tired, *before* his state-mandated eight hours with her were up.

And finally, at the bottom of the pressure pecking order— Shelby. Wanting to do well, to get it right, to please, and understanding, even in an eight-year-old way, that a lot was riding on her ability to do the job. She had to coordinate everything the director told her, remember her actions, her line, her smile, so that it all came out right at exactly the moment the dog chose to shake.

The director of that commercial, Glen Swanson, is a big, easygoing man, calm and kind and terrific with kids. Other directors aren't so great. They're impatient, indifferent, or even downright nasty. Kara Olsen, for instance, remembers directors who have taken out their frustrations on her. "They say, 'Don't you *know* how to do this?' Or everytime something goes wrong in a take, they'll go, 'You've gotten it wrong *again!*'" Such an attitude can crush a child.

But even those directors with the best of intentions can forget what it's like to be a child. Chad Kraus is a six-year-old bundle of energy who's just beginning a commercial career in New York. His mother, Marla, is a dark-haired, exotic-looking woman who used to dance professionally. She remembers what it was like to be a child performer and would like to control Chad's career so he misses the bad parts. It doesn't always work out that way. "When Chad did his first commercial, we had a bit of a problem with the director. I knew it was going to be a long, tiring day for him—we had to be up at six in the morning—so I tried to get him to sleep early the night before. But no way, he was having none of it. He didn't get to bed until about 11 P.M. So little sleep is not the best way to start the day, that's for sure. Then we got to the set on time but nothing was ready. We had to sit around for a good two hours before they even started putting makeup on the kids.

"*Finally,* they started to shoot the scene Chad was in. Nothing major went wrong but there were little things and they kept doing it again and again and again. Everyone could tell that Chad was starting to get tired and so the director—well, he was a very sweet man but he just didn't think. He told Chad, 'Okay, this is the last time we're going to do it.' *He* knew it wasn't, but Chad really took it to heart. He really thought that if the guy said this was the last time, this *was* the last time. Then when it wasn't, Chad got upset.

I can understand it. He's only a little kid and the director just
didn't handle him well at all."

Whatever the business-oriented problems facing commercial
kids, they are often nothing compared to the hard time the outside
world gives them. At an age when conformity is mandatory for a
child to be accepted by his peers, the commercial kid pops up as
the odd one in the bunch. He gets to leave school early, even miss
whole days at a time. He's on TV, has oodles of money, knows fa-
mous people—maybe he's even a star! As a result, at the very
least, he is in for a fair amount of teasing; at the worst, he is totally ostracized.

Myra Unger is a Brooklyn housewife with two commercial kids,
Abe and Judy, whose success in the business took its toll at
school. "Both of my children have always done well in school.
They're bright, their test scores are high, and they never shirk any
responsibility. My husband and I went to a great deal of trouble
to explain to the school staff what the situation with the childrens'
careers was. We assured the teachers that Abe and Judy would do
any extra homework that was required. In return, it was agreed
that they would be allowed to leave school early for auditions or
jobs. But it didn't work out that way. The teachers were antagonistic and the other children were antagonistic. For the first time
since they were two and a half, my kids were unhappy at school.
They finally reached the point where they didn't want to leave acting but they didn't want to go to school either. Finally, we put
them in the Professional Children's School. Abe said it was like
going home."

There is only one problem with the Unger's solution: Abe and
Judy are now isolated from the so-called normal world of children. Other parents opt for a different way. They allow their kids
to fight it out for themselves among their peers. It's more or less a
sink or swim situation. One young veteran of more than eighty
commercials has, in her ten years, acquired a very philosophical
attitude. "I still get teased a lot at school, but I've gotten used to
it. And I've lost some friends, but I just figure they must not have
been my real friends to begin with. The kids are jealous, I know

that. I'd really like for them to just treat me as normal but they won't and there's nothing I can do about it."

At this point, you may be wondering how any child finishes a commercial career with his psyche intact. But the fact is that something on the order of survival of the fittest takes place with these kids. The ones who are not able to withstand the pressure and rejection generally drop out along the way; those who are healthy, well-adjusted, and strong are the ones who carry on.

But consider this: While a commercial career may suit your child, it may be terrible for your family. Your major sacrifice is time. Interviews are scheduled every afternoon; commercial shoots take up an entire day. "I tell mothers of kids I take, 'The commitment is yours, not your child's,' " says Janice Borovay. " 'I may not know until one o'clock that afternoon that your child has an interview. That means that when I call you, you have to drop what you're doing and take him to the interview. Then you have to sit there and wait with him. When he works, you have to take him to the set and sit with him all day. You're the one who is going to have to do all that schlepping, not me. If you miss an interview, I'll give you one more chance at it—unless there's been an illness or something like that. But if it's just that you don't feel like it or that you don't want to buck the traffic, then forget it. I won't call you again.' "

Accept the fact that the business, from your perspective, is a rat race. Many times agents give parents three and four interviews a day to get their kid to. You're racing to one, all the time knowing that you have a callback on another and suddenly you get stuck in traffic. Or a casting session is running late. In the latter case, you can't complain for fear of irritating the casting director. All you can do is leave and lose out on the job. With a traffic jam, you have no choice. You just sit there spinning your wheels and chewing your nails. It's nerve-wracking, frustrating, and, for some parents, ultimately just not worth it.

But even if you think you can take it, what about the rest of your family? Chad Kraus's little brother, Jeremy, is either dragged to auditions or left at home with a babysitter. How is that sort of

treatment going to affect your noncommercial kids? Will they be
able to cope with suddenly losing your attention, with taking second place to their commercial brother or sister?

And your spouse? Bob Lee comes home to an empty house and
no dinner when one of his three sons has an interview or job.
How would your spouse feel about that? It is not unknown for a
couple to divorce over their child's career. "I've seen it happen
again and again: If the kid becomes successful, the parents divorce," says Los Angeles agent Don Schwartz. "It has to do with
the father not being able to take the loss of the mother's attention.
And, too, many men can't take the fact that their child is now the
major breadwinner in the family."

In his book *The Solid Gold Sandbox,* Jason Bonderoff cites a
typical case. Warren and Claire Grant once were a happy couple,
living on his $12,000-a-year salary as a postal clerk in Newark,
New Jersey. When their daughter Wendy made her first commercial at the age of five, the Grants' marriage began the long road
downhill. Claire Grant's days suddenly became filled with a round
of Wendy's interviews, shooting sessions, singing lessons, dancing
lessons, or acting lessons, and her evenings were taken up with
phone calls to agents and casting directors. What dinner there
was, after Warren's hard day at work, often consisted of a pizza
picked up on Claire and Wendy's way home from New York.

According to Bonderoff, "It wasn't long before Warren reached
the breaking point. He was the kind of man who needed to feel 'in
control of things,' and as much as he resented his wife's absen-
teeism, he begrudged his daughter's financial success even more.
After two years in the television game, Wendy was bringing in
double the paycheck her father did. . . .

"The next step was inevitable—and when Wendy was eight, her
parents were divorced. . . . For a while, Warren came to visit
Wendy on Sunday afternoons; then the visits began to taper off.
Wendy was often too busy to socialize, anyway. Finally, he
stopped coming at all."

The Grants' story doesn't *have* to be the result of having a successful commercial kid, but you must realize that it *can* be. And if
you are now overwhelmed with the dangers inherent in putting

your child in the commercial business, you are right at the point where I've tried to get you.

Now you're ready to spend some time actually thinking about *why* you want your child to have this career. Is it for you—or for him? That is a loaded question, because there is only one correct answer. If it's for you—if you're looking to have your ego fulfilled, to have something to occupy your time, to escape from your loneliness, to bask in reflected glory, then I advise you to forget it right now. You're writing a death sentence for you, your family, and your child.

If, on the other hand, you want a commercial career for your child because *he* wants it, because it will be fun and profitable, because it will mold and strengthen him in a positive way, then you're on the right track.

Now, talk to your child and talk to your mate and talk to the other children in your family. If everybody, knowing all the pros and cons, agrees with your desire, then commercials are, in fact, right for your child.

And you're ready for the next question: Is your child right for commercials?

2
Talent / Temperament / Type: <u>Can</u> Your Child Do Commercials?

Sandra Firestone wasn't too impressed when she first saw Charlie Aiken's picture. As one of the top kids' managers in New York, she'd had many photographs come over her transom of cute little hopefuls who just weren't commercial material. Usually she made a quick phone call to the parent and, in her warm and friendly manner, said "No." But Charlie had been recommended by the mother of a boy Sandra's young son was in a film with. And so she felt an obligation to call him in.

She wasn't looking forward to the interview. A kind and gentle woman with a genuine caring for the feelings of others, she hates having to turn someone down in person. But a favor is a favor. So Charlie Aiken came in for his interview, sat in her small, plant-filled office on West Fifty-seventh Street, and talked. She spent more time with him than she'd anticipated, and by the time he

finally left, Sandra Firestone knew she had just seen her one and
only perfect commercial kid.

"He was twelve at the time," she remembers. "But he was very
small for his age. He had this terrific fresh, open, freckled face.
He was alive and alert and enthusiastic. Instinctively, he just did
everything right.

"I had him read a sample commercial *and* some dialogue from
a TV show. Now usually I have to have kids read this copy over
and over again and then I help them out along the way. Not
Charlie; he just picked it up and did it perfectly.

"He had everything going for him: His looks were right, his
ability was right, his attitude was right, and his enthusiasm was
right. I was absolutely stunned. When he left, I turned to my associate and all I could say was 'Wow!'

"I took him on, and in his first year in the business Charlie did
over forty on-camera commercials, plus some voiceovers, plus
some demo commercials. That's more than twice as much as my
best kid does now. But Charlie is a real rarity; I've never had any-
body else like him."

Ten years ago, perfect Charlie Aiken might have had no career
in commercials: he isn't pretty enough. In fact, until very recently, the most important determination of a child's potential in
commercials was looks. Commercial kids *had* to be beautiful. Not
only that, they had to be either blond, blue-eyed angels or
redheaded, freckled Huck Finn types. The reality of our melting
pot nation had no place in the commercial world; nor, in fact, did
the reality of childhood. Children in commercials then were man-
nequins who looked wonderful, smiled sweetly, and said little.

Today, however, due in no small measure to the upheaval of
the sixties, the faces of commercials have changed. Advertisers
want not the perfect little robot smiling out from their ads but a
real live kid, one both a mother and a child can relate to. Reality
has replaced beauty in determining whether a child is commercial,
and since the reality of America's children includes black and
white, pretty and plain, there is a career in commercials for almost
any kind of child.

There are, in fact, only two things your child *must* have in order to enter the field: commercial talent and a good temperament. Beauty, age, size, type—certainly they are important. But there are no absolutes in any of these areas that in and of themselves would prevent your child from pursuing a commercial career. Rather, each category has a range of acceptability, and within this range there are preferences (e.g., the best age, the best type, etc.); these factors, more than anything, indicate how much in demand your child will be, and therefore how frequently he will work.

Commercial Talent

Talent, for commercial kids, has little to do with the common definition of the word. It is, rather, a collection of specific personality traits, none of them particularly unique or difficult to find in children. Sandra Firestone was articulating some of them when she described Charlie Aiken as alive, alert, and enthusiastic. Other agents lump these traits under the general headings of "pizazz," "charisma," "sparkle," or just plain "super personality."

Those terms are ambiguous, arbitrary, and at one time or another (at least in a parent's eye) apply to most children. In short, they'll do you little good as criteria for determining if your child actually has commercial talent. So let's be a little more specific.

The commercially talented child is the one with a strong personality who is winning, warm, and outgoing. He's a charmer, the sort who stands out in a crowd, who draws people to him naturally and effortlessly.

His talent is not only this appeal but, more important, his ability to project his personality immediately. Commercial kids are essentially salespeople. They sell the product they represent not by outright huckstering but by creating an image that appeals to the buying public. But they only have, at most, thirty seconds in which to impress their audience. Consequently, their effect must be instantaneous, their high spirits and attractiveness such an integral part of them that it is immediately and clearly obvious.

Rodney Allen Rippy's sensational effect on the sales of Jack in

the Box hamburgers is a perfect example. After just six commercials featuring young Rodney manfully trying to shove that huge
hamburger into his baby mouth, Jack in the Box's sales increased
more than $140 million. The public didn't start buying Jack in the
Box in greater numbers because Rodney made them think the
hamburger tasted so great, but because they loved him and so
loved Jack in the Box. They remembered him, so they remembered Jack in the Box. And when they finally did come to that
choice between eating at Jack in the Box or at one of the competi-
tors, they went for the former simply because that was the kind
Rodney ate. His warmth, his appeal, his personality were all
transferred to Jack in the Box. It was a commercial-makers dream
—success by association.

Another keynote of commercial talent is naturalness. Commercials are slice-of-life vignettes, showing kids doing, as the song
says, what comes naturally. Rodney was just eating a hamburger.
Another success story, Mikey of Life cereal fame, was just having
breakfast. Think of a commercial, any commercial featuring a
child, and chances are you're thinking of a child brushing his
teeth, drinking milk, playing with a toy, sick in bed, or any of the
other normal activities of childhood.

However, while the effect of the commercial is reality, the process of making it is totally unreal. The commercial child at work is
playing a master game of Let's Pretend. Let's pretend this strange
woman is really my mother; let's pretend I've really just hurt myself; let's pretend this is my bedroom and I'm alone playing with
my own toys. In order to achieve this look of normalcy, the commercial child must have a powerful imagination. And it must be
an imagination uninhibited by an unfamiliar setting, numerous
spectators, and all the paraphernalia of filmmaking. The imagina-
tive child who withdraws in alien settings or when uncomfortable
is not commercially talented. The child who is independent, instantly at ease with adults, able to walk into any situation and in-
teract naturally without embarrassment or hesitation is.

Another element of commercial talent is a high energy level
along with a long attention span. Commercial-making is a tedious
job, involving hours of waiting and constant repetition. The com-

mercial child must be able to sustain concentration and energy at peak level throughout this eight- to twelve-hour day.

And finally, despite this independence, despite this high energy and strong personality, the commercial child is tractable. He pays attention, obeys orders, and is willingly guided by the adults in charge.

The child who exhibits all these qualities is, indeed, a talented commercial kid. Whether he can sing, dance, and emote like Olivier counts for little in commercials; that he is self-confident, secure, expressive, and animated counts for all.

You may instantly recognize your child from this detailing of commercial talent. But if you're not really sure, get out a pencil and paper and answer the following questions:

1. Does your child have a lot of friends?
2. Do teachers tell you your child is one of their favorite pupils?
3. Is your child one of those kids who constantly has to be reminded not to talk to strangers?
4. Is your child enthusiastic about trying new things and going new places?
5. Does your child get good grades?
6. Does your child play well alone?
7. Is your child happier drawing with plain paper and pencils than coloring in a coloring book?
8. Do strangers stop you on the street to tell you how cute your child is?
9. Does your child cry easily?
10. When your child is tired, does he or she get cranky and irritable?
11. Is your child exhausted after a couple of hours of shopping?
12. Is he or she a fearful child?
13. Does your child cry or make a fuss when you leave?
14. Does your child play with a toy for just ten or fifteen minutes before abandoning it for something new?
15. When playing with friends, is your child generally the

leader of the pack, the one the others look to for what to play,
when, and how?

16. When your friends come to visit, does your child disappear?

17. Is your child embarrassed if adults make him or her the
center of attention?

18. Are your child's citizenship marks in school ever less than
good or excellent?

19. Do you have to remind your child frequently to pick up
toys, do homework, and the like?

20. Is your child generally happy in school and at home?

Now for the correct answers:

1. YES. How many times have you known a popular kid who
wasn't secure and easy to get along with? Commercial-making is a
company business; kids in it must be capable of working in a
group. The child who is a loner rarely mixes well. In fact, that a
child has no friends is often a sign of deep-seated problems that
might become full-blown if he had a commercial career.

2. YES. If teachers like him, then your child is probably polite,
obedient, and tries to do his best at everything. Exactly the things
that will make commercial-makers like him.

3. YES. This is a sure sign that your child is confident and
secure that others will like him. A commercial kid's going to have
to talk to a lot of strangers in his career; it better be something he
enjoys doing.

4. YES. A good sign of a child's security—and curiosity—is
that he seeks out new experiences. The child who doesn't will be
lost in the commercial business, where every interview and job is
a totally new experience.

5. YES. Most commercial kids are very good students. They
are bright, hardworking, and eager to learn.

6. YES. In order to spend time happily alone, a child has to
have a good imagination.

7. YES. Kids who prefer coloring books generally don't like

to initiate action or create their own worlds—unless they're the type who color faces blue and grass red!

8. YES. If your child's appeal is so strong it is stopping people in the street, then it's exactly what commercial-makers are looking for.

9. NO. There's no place for the supersensitive child in commercial-making.

10. NO. There's no doubt that sometime during the long day on the set, a child will get tired. If he reacts by being cranky and irritable, no one will chance working with him again.

11. NO. If your child is dragging on your arm after just a few hours 'round the shopping center, she or he doesn't have the necessary stamina for commercial-making.

12. NO. The fearful child is usually the retiring child, not exactly the ebullient personality that's the keynote of commercial talent.

13. NO. Commercial kids *have* to be independent. The child who won't leave mother or father will not get to first base in commercial-making.

14. NO. If he or she does, his or her attention span is not long enough for a commercial-maker's needs.

15. YES. Then your child obviously has a strong personality and a natural winning way.

16. NO. If the child disappears, he or she is obviously intimidated by adults and will never get past the first interview for any commercial.

17. NO. The commercial kid must go through long periods of time when all eyes are on him or her.

18. NO. If you answered "yes," then your child may have a behavior problem and commercial-making is not the business for him or her.

19. NO. Good—that means your child listens and obeys. Which means commercial-makers will love your child.

20. YES. If your child is happy, he or she is secure. And if a child is secure, then he or she is most probably outgoing and animated, and perfect for commereials.

Give yourself five points for each correct answer and total them up. If your score is eighty or above, it's safe to say your child has commercial talent. If it's below eighty, he does not—at least for now.

There is a qualifier on that statement because many of the aspects of commercial talent can be developed in a child. Sometimes it happens naturally. Childrens' personalities do change from one age to the next. You may just find your shy, clinging six-year-old is outgoing and independent by the age of seven.

If you don't want to trust to nature, however, you can do something more active to make your child bloom. You can send him to dancing school. For years, parents of daughters have done this as a matter of course. Boys, however, are rarely given such an opportunity. But we're talking here not only of ballet—which needn't, incidentally, breed a leotard-clad sissy—but of jazz, disco, tap, and acrobatics. These classes are one of the best ways of turning a shy, awkward child into a lithe, confident one. Dancing classes teach a child grace, balance, and poise. The child learns how to move well, to feel sure of his body, to take direction, and to work in an ensemble. Moreover, mastering even the most basic step will give the child a sense of achievement and pride, both so necessary in gaining the security and sureness from which the other elements of commercial talent tend to follow.

Don't, however, fall prey to the Shirley Temple syndrome: grooming your child for stardom by enrolling him in every class available. The child whose after-school hours are a constant round of professional training is often over-trained for the naturalness commercials demand. "I can't stand the kids whose parents send them to ballet, tap, jazz, acrobatics, and baton-twirling classes," says one outspoken agent. "These kids don't know what it is to just play in the backyard. I'm looking for simplicity, for kids who are spontaneous and real. Not for some little darling who does ten dance routines and sings 'On the Good Ship Lollipop' complete with all those ridiculous hand motions."

You can avoid this by, first of all, limiting your child to one afternoon a week of dance. Also, you must be very particular about

the school you choose. Visit a class before you commit your child
to a series of lessons. Does the teacher strike you as a frustrated,
would-be star who is priming the children for a career in Hollywood? Are there photographs on the wall of last year's recital,
showing little kids in rouge and lipstick wearing satin and se-
quins? Is the classwork devoted to learning routines for this year's
performance? Are the young girls tottering around on toe shoes?
If the answers are "yes," leave immediately. As a fifteen-year veteran of all kinds of dancing schools, I can tell you that the worst
were the ones run by a Miss Trixie or Fifi, where I learned to be
an Autumn Leaf. The best was taught by a gym teacher who made
me sweat through the classical ballet positions and *only* held a recital the years she felt we students had something to show.

Another part of the Shirley Temple syndrome is singing and
acting lessons. The former are useless—unless, of course, your
child has ambitions to sing on the stage. Acting classes, while they
do engender poise and confidence, can easily make your child into
a stilted puppet. Shelby Balik, for example, took acting lessons for
a short time until her mother found directors complaining that she
was losing her spontaneity.

Classes in commercial acting are a different story. Run generally by casting directors, these short-term schools teach a child the
specifics of the commercial business. Sheila Manning, a Los Angeles commercial casting director, holds Saturday morning classes
for kids in her office. "I teach them how to read a script they've
never seen before and get them used to being videotaped. I want
them to know how not to be afraid, so I put them in every situation they might encounter. I have some guest directors in who I
know are nasty so that the kids get used to their manner. I don't
teach them how to act; I just develop their confidence so they can
project what is already there."

Temperament

There is nothing that will blackball a child from the commercial
business faster than a bad temperament. And temperament here

translates to just one word: discipline. Commercial-making is a very trying business. It involves long hours, many of which are spent waiting for a five-minute interview or a ten-second scene to be shot. Often that ten-second scene must be filmed over and over again, with the director trying different angles, interpretations, or bits of business. The child who can't sit still, who can't keep quiet, who won't listen and obey immediately, will not be tolerated by commercial-makers.

Agents do everything they can to identify in advance the child with such a behavior problem. "If children aren't well-behaved in this office," says Dorothy Day Otis, another former actress who is known as the Dean of the Los Angeles children's agents, "if we can't keep them seated, if they keep running to the window, jumping up and down, or talking out of turn, then I *know* it's not going to work for them. If they're not well-disciplined here, then we just won't sign them."

Sometimes it isn't a child's physical misbehavior that tips the agent off but his cockiness, a know-it-all precocious attitude that most agents, in the words of Sandra Firestone, ". . . can live without. I had one little boy whose mother is president of a society for gifted kids and, boy, that child certainly knew it. I'm sure I have other kids whose IQs are probably in the same range, but he was just too much aware of his. I told his mother, 'His attitude is smart-ass and it's not going to work. People in the business do not want a ten-year-old boy acting superior. He is good and he reads well, but he's going to get nowhere with that attitude.' "

Despite agents' watchfulness, such problem children do slip through the screening process. They've managed to behave themselves in the agent's office. Or the agent really isn't sure how bad a problem it is. "I was very doubtful about taking one little boy," remembers agent Evelyn Schultz. "He was a very precocious child to begin with, and he came into my office with his brother and a friend. Having an audience so stirred him up that I had to send the other kids out. I debated whether I should take him, because he was very bright and very small for his age, both good things. Also, he wasn't your average freckle-faced kid; there was something different and special about him.

"I decided to try him on a couple of interviews and see what happened. Well, I didn't get any feedback from the first one, but on the second, the casting director called me and said, 'I will *never* see that child again.' The child absolutely refused to cooperate on the interview. And what's more, he knew he was being bad, he knew he was just being smart. I'll try him one more time and see what happens. If he can't settle down, then that will be it; I just won't send him out anymore."

If any of this reminds you of your child, know that you can go a long way in settling him down enough to satisfy the demands of commercial-making. But first you must admit that it's a problem. "Mothers don't like to believe that their children are obnoxious on an interview," says Evelyn Schultz. "When I get bad feedback from a casting director, I call the mother in and tell her. A lot of times she'll bristle and say, 'What! My angel, my darling, quiet little boy who never says anything?'

"I got that from one mother, so I asked to talk to her son alone. I sat him down and said, 'How do you like going on interviews?'

"He stuck his face right up to mine and snarled at me, 'Sometimes I do and sometimes I don't!'

"His mother, like a lot of others, didn't want to believe that her child was anything but an angel. I tried to tell her so she could do something about it, but she wouldn't listen. Now I just won't send him out anymore, and one of these days the mother is going to call and ask, 'Why hasn't my son gone out on any interviews lately?' And once more I'll tell her exactly why."

This is not the place to give advice on your child's behavior problems. But note just one telling comment from a top commercial producer: "The successful commercial kids are those who understand their role in the business and know how to behave accordingly. And that really depends on how they're treated at home. Whether they're given responsibilities there, be it doing the dishes or taking care of a pet, and whether they're expected to carry out those chores no matter what. That kind of training at home develops the attitude and discipline we require here in the business."

There is, of course, a difference between the high-spirited child and the undisciplined, uncontrollable one. And sometimes when a child who has the energy, enthusiasm, and confidence commercial-makers demand goes into the high-pressure situation of an interview or shooting set, he can go right over the top and become irrepressible. Often, too, that difference between high energy and hyperactivity can be a very thin line, drawn by the personal preferences of the agent, casting person, or director involved.

Tami Lynn is a young woman who parlayed her knowledge of the commercial business, garnered through guiding the career of her son, Shane, into a thriving career for herself as Los Angeles' first children's manager. And if there is one thing she likes to see in the kids she handles, it's cockiness. "I had a dynamite little girl in here yesterday. She's only six years old, but she just walked in and knocked me over because she has a mouth on her that is so terrific. I love it, but some people think it's obnoxious. They take offense when a kid is chatty and outspoken. Like I sent her on two calls in one day. The first one, the casting director adored her. But the second, the casting director called up and told me, 'I hate this kid.' It really just depends on where the casting person is coming from."

The same situation is true of a feisty, little redhead who's been acting in commercials since he was four. Jason is a particular favorite of one top casting director who loves his bouncy, smart-aleck nature; she calls him in on every interview in his age and type range. Sometimes he's loved by the interviewers and sometimes he's hated.

Once, on an interview for a detergent commercial, he practically turned the session upside down. He swaggered into the interview room one hot summer day without even a hello to the six men seated at the long table there. Instead, he headed for the first thing that caught his eye—a microphone hanging precariously from the ceiling. He jumped up to grab it and pulled it down to his mouth. "Hello," he boomed in a gravel-voiced imitation of a news announcer. "My name is . . ."

"Wait a minute," interrupted Glen Swanson, the director, as mild-mannered as ever. "Let go of the mike, please."

"I thought it was to talk into," Jason shot back.

"It is, but you don't have to touch it," replied Swanson. "Just stand next to it, and we'll be able to hear you fine."

Jason wiggled off to the side with a disco two-step and immediately caught sight of his own image in the television monitor at the back of the room. He was magnetized, dancing and waving and winking for his one-eyed audience in the back. Finally, Swanson's assistant flicked off the monitor. Not missing a beat, Jason made a grab at the mike again. Swanson was losing patience. "C'mon, why don't you stand still for a minute. Tell us your name and how old you are."

"I'm six, six, six . . . ," Jason sang.

"Six going on thirty," muttered one of the other men.

"You know something," Jason flashed at him. "Your nose is pink and green. Yes it is. Yes it is."

The little room, cluttered with people and humming equipment, was hot. The six interviewers were sweating and annoyed. "All right, that's enough." Swanson's tone brooked no nonsense. "You're not listening to me, and I don't have time for that. Now tell us your name and age, then I'm going to give you your cue and I want you to say the line and nothing else."

Jason shrugged, resigned but not cowed. "Yeah, my mom always spanks me for not listening to her, too."

Everyone laughed, the tension broke, and Jason went on to give an excellent performance. But later, when the men were making their casting decisions, everyone agreed when Swanson said, "Jason was the best of all the boys we saw, but I wouldn't use him. That kid is practically wired for sound. You'd line up his shot and he'd be halfway down the street before the cameras rolled."

Jason lost out on that job, yet he is cast again and again by one of the major camera advertisers. Perhaps the director they use is more tolerant of his behavior. Or maybe he's not the nice guy Glen Swanson is.

Whatever the reason, don't count on your child's misbehavior being tolerated by anyone. Know that if you don't control and discipline him ahead of time, his wildness will probably ruin his chances for a successful commercial career.

Talent/personality and a good temperament are the only *essential* prerequisites for a commercial kid. However, a child needs more than that to be successful. He or she must also fit into the age, size, and type ranges.

Age

Any child between the ages of six months and eighteen years is at a good age for commercials. Better is between six and twelve, but the best age, called by some the Golden Years, is between six and ten.

To understand why this is so, you must realize that children are generally used in one of two ways in commercials. Either they are primary spokespeople for a product, or they appear as part of a family. In the first instance, the products themselves usually require children of the Golden Age. Toys, for example, are marketed mostly for six- to ten-year-olds, and their commercials must, by law, use children of the age group the product is made for.

In commercials where the kids are part of a family, the advertiser is generally aiming at the "average young American family." Statistics have determined that the children of this hypothetical family are usually between six and ten.

Children outside that age range are primarily used in commercials where no other age would be acceptable: Babies, for instance, *must* do the diaper spots, and no one but a teen could promote pimple creams. That is not to say that there aren't commercials where those outside the Golden Age are used as members of the "average family"; it just doesn't happen that often.

Even when given the choice, most commercial-makers prefer not to use the under-sixes or over-tens. Under six, "it's hit or miss," says one director, "whether the preschooler will perform on cue. I've been on a set with lights fixed, everyone's ready, and the take has been slated so the camera is already rolling, when the kid just says, 'I don't want to.' And no amount of bribery, sweet talk, or even getting angry will move him to change his mind.

"Also, you can't really count on getting a particular response out of young children. You can tell them what to do, but by the time you're rolling, chances are they've forgotten what you've said. And even getting their attention is hard. Really, with these young kids, it's just pot luck what you end up with."

In California, preschoolers have an even smaller chance of working than in other states. The legislature has passed very strict labor laws that control the number of hours a child can work. The maximum—four hours out of an eight-hour day on the set— applies only to kids over the age of six. Consequently, commercial-makers will not use a child under six years old unless they absolutely have to.

On the other side of the six-to-ten age range, there are problems of a different sort. Puberty arrives, and with it come cracking voices, pimples, and braces. All very normal, but not the perfection advertisers demand of the people representing their products. And too, kids who were cute and giggly and natural at nine and ten, easy to direct and willing to try anything, suddenly, as preteens, become stiff and constrained. Playacting is not natural to them anymore: It's silly kid stuff and embarrassing to boot. In short, all the qualities commercial-makers demand of children— spontaneity, enthusiasm, naturalness—tend to evaporate in those early teen years. The children who do keep working beyond the age of eleven are talented performers capable of acting the child, even when they're not.

This may sound grim for the hopeful parent whose child is outside the Golden Age; however, it is not an impossible situation. Remember that we're talking about *how much* not *whether* a child will work. Certainly every agent is always open to enquiries about the under-sixes. Most of them keep a "baby file" where they put photographs of the under-four-year-olds with potential, to wait for a call specifying that child's age and coloring.

For those entering the business at the ripe old age of thirteen or fourteen, things are a bit more difficult. There are some agents who won't even interview a child older than twelve unless he or she has had some experience in the business or comes with a "fantastic" recommendation. But there are other agencies, such as

Mary Ellen White, which have a separate program specifically for teens.

And there is one further factor that is heartening to parents of kids on the far side of the Golden Age. Commercial-makers don't really care how old your child actually is, only how old he *looks*. Remember Charlie Aiken, the perfect commercial kid? He was twelve when Sandra Firestone first saw him, and a good part of his "perfection" was that he looked much younger.

Size

"We're looking," says agent Don Schwartz, "for the kid with a mind two years older than his body."

In other words, small is best. Commercials are one place where the pip-squeak child is at an advantage and the hearty kid, big for his age, becomes the underdog.

The reason is clear if you think back to the age most commercials call for, and to the commercial-maker's problems in working with young children. It's just plain easier on everyone involved if the part of a young child can be played by a more mature one.

For instance, not that many six-year-olds can read well enough to handle many lines or complicated ones. Eight-year-olds generally can. Not that many seven-year-olds have the concentration or stamina to maintain performance level through twenty, thirty, or even forty takes. Nine-year-olds can. And how many eight-year-olds can understand the subtleties of giving varied line readings? Not as many as there are ten-year-olds who can. In short, the child who looks a couple of years younger than he actually is satisfies the advertisers' need for youth and the commercial-makers' need for maturity.

From the agents' point of view, small children are more welcome clients than the average-sized because they can do so many more commercials. They can play a wide range of parts, from their own age on down. So ask any agent about the first thing they look for in a child, and she will invariably answer, "a small one."

If you're not sure where your child stands in the rank of sizes for his age, ask his teacher. Is he one of the taller children in the class? Unless he stops growing when everyone else shoots up, his commercial chances are not very good. If he is average height, he won't be as desirable as a small child and probably won't work as often, but he still has a good chance for a career. If, however, yours is the littlest kid on the block, he is, at least size-wise, absolutely perfect for commercials.

"Smaller is better" also gives hope to parents of the child normally too old for a good start in the business. If your thirteen-year-old still looks only ten or eleven, you'll have few problems with agents turning him down because he's "too old."

Type

All parents with ambitions to put their child into commercials worry first about whether their kid is "the right type." Relax. According to most experts, there is no right—or wrong—type for kids. There are just some types who work a lot and some who work a little.

Agents refer to their client lists as "books." For children, because there are so many types, the agents' books are broken down into specific categories and subcategories. Generally, age is the primary category. Each age is then broken down by sex and coloring. Then there is a final breakdown into the specific types.

You really only have to be concerned with where your child fits into this when it comes to considering what his chances are for working. Already you know that as far as the age breakdown goes, the six- to ten-year-olds work the most. Statistically, both sexes work about the same amount. So the first cut comes with coloring.

The fair-haired child in commercials, as in fairy tales, is still the one who is filled with grace. From basic blond to sandy brown, these kids do get the most work in the business. They have what Janice Borovay calls "the basic, white bread, commercial look."

Second in success is the redhead. In fact, there was a time, particularly in New York, when it seemed that almost every commercial kid had red hair. With their smattering of freckles and turned-up noses, these kids, usually Irish, conjure up images of Huck Finn, presenting commercial-makers with just the right down-home, slightly naughty look they want.

There are, however, two factors that can limit redheaded children. First is the matter of freckles. Too many and the child stops looking average, thus limiting the number of commercials he can appear in. The rule, someone once said, is that boys can be gently freckled all over while girls can only have a trickle across their noses.

The other problem with red-haired children is that it's often hard to mix and match them with the actors chosen to play the parents in a commercial. There just don't seem to be as many redheaded adults as there are kids. Consequently, these children sometimes miss being cast in a family commercial simply because their coloring doesn't match the adult actors'.

At the bottom of the coloring list are brunettes. Commercial-makers, for some reason, just don't consider dark-haired children to be truly representative of the average American kid.

Once agents have classified children according to age, sex, and coloring, they divide them further into one of the two major type classifications: the Beautiful child and the Character child.

The Beautiful classification is relatively straightforward. Children of this type are those gorgeous kids with perfect, symmetrical faces, generally blond and blue-eyed and very, very WASP.

Beautiful kids were once the only type that worked in commercials. Sandra Dee and Tuesday Weld were the forerunners of this class. But then, in the Sixties, there was a massive swing of the pendulum from beauty to off-beat, which culminated with the popularity of kids like Mason Reese and Larry Bleidner. Their popularity was so great that agents who previously had refused to sign anyone but the average or extraordinarily pretty child were suddenly scouting for homely kids. "All the advertisers wanted was kids with freckles or the freaky look," remembers Tami Lynn. "It was the uglier, the better, and a lot of good-looking kids' careers were hurt then."

Even up until a few years ago, the situation for the Beautiful child was such that Monica Steward, an agent for the William Schuller Agency in New York, said, "There's not a child on a commercial today who you'd say is really gorgeous."

That statement is no longer true. In fact, there are now certain advertisers—Mattel, for example—who use Beautiful kids almost exclusively. However, it is doubtful whether the Beautiful child will ever again be in the forefront of commercial casting.

Defining the Character child is more difficult in that it seems to be a catch-all label for every kind of kid other than Beautiful. Moreover, the dividing line between Beautiful and Character is often only a matter of the particular agent's personal taste. "Sometimes I'll get a child who I think is a Character," says Dorothy Day Otis. "I'll send that child out on a Character call and the casting director will come back and say, 'That is a perfectly gorgeous child, not a Character type at all. Why'd you send him to me?' I've come to the conclusion that beauty really *is* in the eye of the beholder."

The extreme Character child, however, is easy to spot. The fat, the skinny, the very freckled, the off-beat—all of these are true Character kids. Your child doesn't have to be as unusual-looking as Mason Reese, with his chipmunk cheeks and raisin eyes, to be considered a true Character type; any deviation from what is considered "average-looking"—jug ears, a long nose, pudgy face—will put him in that category.

The heyday of this true Character type is, as we've said, now over. Instead of being the general rule in casting calls, these children are now being sent out only when there is a specific request for an off-beat type. But while agents are no longer beating the bushes for homely children, there is enough call for them to warrant carrying them in most age groups on an agent's book.

Also considered a Character child is the ethnic kid. Jewish, Italian, or any variation of Semitic or Mediterranean, these children, too, are not often sent for general casting calls. It's a sad but true fact that although we are a melting pot nation, there are those among that mass of consumers with the greatest buying power who can't stand Jews, Italians, blacks, or Asian-Pacifics. Advertisers live in constant fear of offending even the slightly prejudiced. Consequently, these ethnic children, no matter how talented, are often discounted from a lot of commercials simply because their faces are mirrors of their nationalities.

Generally, ethnic types are precluded from attending even the first interview for a commercial because the casting director puts out a call for "only all-American types" or "no ethnic kids." But sometimes, if the call isn't made that explicit, one slips through and then the cut comes during the actual casting session.

On one three-day marathon search for a toy commercial, the interviewers were having a hard time because they needed a specific kind of child: a young girl, ten to twelve, who was beautiful, sexy, and strong. For the first two days a parade of beautiful children marched by, some slightly sexy but all exuding docile sweetness rather than strength. Finally, a beautiful twelve-year-old with long, dark hair and a pale, olive complexion strolled in. She was perfect. I marked a star by her name, sure the commercial-makers were relieved to have *finally* found what they needed. But when she left the room, without a comment, the producer flipped her picture onto the "No" pile. I was shocked. "Why don't you want her? She's just what you're looking for."

"She's ethnic," he said matter-of-factly. "And ethnic is too extreme for most kids to be able to relate to."

Do not despair, however, if your child's face reflects his heritage. Commercial-makers are loosening up these days, and there are a growing number of "United Nations calls." And, too, there are some national commercials that can't be done by anyone but an ethnic child. Casting directors for those spots are finding that there just aren't enough ethnic types to meet the demand.

Joan Lynn is a businesslike but warm casting director for Bob Giraldi Productions in New York, the production company that makes all of the Ragu spaghetti sauce commercials. "I have a very difficult time finding authentic Italian kids for Ragu spots," Lynn says. "I have literally run out of Italian actors in New York. Either they've already done a Ragu commercial or they've been used in competitive products; either way, I can't use them. For some reason, there seem to be very few Italian kids in New York who want to act or are signed with the agents I use. So lately I've had to go to Little Italy to cast." In short, Joan Lynn is literally picking her actors off the street.

In addition to major commercials such as the ones for Ragu, ethnic children are used more frequently in commercials to be shown in regions where their particular ethnic group is in a majority. Also, there are a number of local advertisers—television stations, banks, and area businesses—that use ethnic children because they are more representative of the local audience than the all-American kid.

While ethnic and off-beat Character kids are at the bottom of the ladder when it comes to getting work, another group in the Character category is at the top: the all-American, kid-next-door type. These are the children who look like they're straight from the Midwest, the ones who make you think when you see them on TV, "What's so special about him? He looks like every child in my neighborhood." That is true, and it is precisely the reason this type of child is the most successful of all commercial kids: He is considered to be representative of the American child.

Advertisers want people to identify with the actors in their ads. For example, the woman watching a "Mommy-kiss-the-boo-boo" bandage commercial must believe that she could be that comforting mother and her child that crying kid. Such transference is part of what makes the woman buy the advertised brand of bandage when she shops.

In order to get such identification with the largest number of women, the advertiser must take an average of all mothers and all children to come out with the mean mother and child, those who share the greatest number of characteristics with all the others. For children, that is your basic, white bread American kid. He is Middle America in miniature, the silent majority's son, grandson, nephew, and neighbor.

But there is another reason this all-American type is the most often used in commercials: He is the least offensive to the greatest number of people. Remember that advertisers don't want their products associated with anyone who might offend the white, Protestant masses who are the major consumers today. So rather than risk even a slight feeling of distaste or, at worst, an unofficial boycott, most advertisers prefer to go with the child who has no noticeable minority traits.

And, too, the all-American child is often the child of the advertiser. As one ad agency person put it, "A lot of our clients are WASP, and they want children in the ads to look like their own kids."

The people such a policy is most likely to offend are, of course, members of the minorities. And it is their pressure for change that has made the opportunities for minority children—black, Asian-Pacific, and Hispanic—far greater in today's commercial business than ever before.

Unfortunately, that's not really saying much more than that the racial barrier has certainly been breached. Like other breakthroughs in racial discrimination, the extent to which advertisers seek and/or allow minority kids in their ads has depended on the amount of pressure put on them by the individual minority group.

That being the case, it is understandable why black children are cast more often than Hispanic or Asian-Pacifics. They were, in fact, the first to break the color bar, with no small thanks to Rodney Allen Rippy, who proved to advertisers that black could indeed be very beautiful when it came to upping profits. Prior to Rippy, most black kids were seen in commercials aimed only at the black audience. Such ads were generally only shown during black-oriented television programs. Today, however, black children are seen not only in all-black commercials, such as the black versions of the Coca-Cola ads, but in white-oriented spots as well.

Still, considering the fact that it has been estimated blacks spend about $70 billion per year, their visibility in commercials isn't anywhere proportionate to that. "I think it's valid to say that industries selling baby food, and industries selling diapers and other things for children, are remiss in not including enough blacks in their commercials," Carolyn Jones, a black partner in a New York advertising agency, told *Ebony* magazine. "But I don't think it's racial. I think it's just that nobody really thinks about it, and neither are they that interested. They [casting directors] just go ahead and cast for children and adults, without spending a moment deciding whether or not blacks ought to go into a commercial."

That's a major complaint among all the minorities, but it certainly isn't true of all casting directors. Joan Lynn, for example, says, "I try to use as many minorities in commercials as I can. If I'm not allowed to use them as principals, then I'll put them in as extras. In fact, the ad agencies here have a minority quota agreement with SAG, so they always request that we hire minority extras in a commercial that has white principals."

Hispanics are not as prevalent in commercials as blacks, but the same kind of pressure that worked for the latter is beginning to achieve similar results for actors of Spanish origin. *Nosotres,* a national, activist group for Hispanics, is the prime organization behind the pressure. So far, however, they have proved more successful on the East Coast than on the West. Anywhere, though, Hispanics have an advantage over the other two minorities: With their dark hair and eyes, they can often slip into the ethnic category—and therefore more commercials—quite easily.

The real minority in the commercial business today, however, are Asian-Pacifics. According to James White, of the Mary Ellen White agency in New York, "There just aren't that many roles for Orientals. The demographics of the market are such that in ten commercials done per day in which five or more actors are used, there is probably only one black and no Orientals."

That doesn't mean that Asian-Pacific children are totally absent from the commercial scene. In fact, according to Sumi Haru, an Asian-Pacific actress who is national chairperson of SAG's Ethnic Minority Committee, "I'm seeing more and more Asian-Pacific children in commercials. Previously, we were a silent and scared community. We didn't want to do anything to rock the boat. However, now we're learning that the squeaky wheel does get the attention, and we're increasing pressure on advertisers to include Asian-Pacifics in the commercial scene."

An indication of the improving situation for all minorities is the fact that most agents now carry minority children on their books.

It used to be that these kids were signed only by agents who specialized in minorities. Today, however, there is sufficient work for minority kids in commercials to warrant keeping a variety of ages and sexes on every agent's client list. As Jean Walton, head of the children's department for Ann Wright Representatives in New York, put it, "I sign up any kids I feel I can get work for. If they're talented, it doesn't in any way discourage me that they're part of a minority group."

By now you should be able to place your child somewhere in the total picture of the commercial world. Is he commercially talented? Does she have the right temperament? Where does he fit on the age and size scale? And into which type?

Answer those questions and you can determine not only if your child is right for commercials but also, to a certain extent, just what the chances are for a really successful career. And that leads to another question you must answer before beginning: Is the effort of getting your child into commercials going to be worth the reward?

3

All About Agents

They've been called every name in the book, from prostitute to parasite, from analyst to angel. Some of them are good, some bad, some kind, and some ogres. The ones who are loved are "career-makers"; the ones who are hated are "thieves." They can be all of these or none, but one thing is for certain: An agent is the single most important person in your child's career.

To understand why this is so, you must first know what they do and how they work. Basically, an agent is nothing more than a salesperson, and the business of agenting is like any other sales business. Agents have a product they want to sell to a buyer. Their income is based solely on commissions, so their aim, obviously, is to sell as much as possible. To do this, they must know exactly what the buyers want in terms of product and then keep a full range of stock, carrying no dead weight and replenishing when necessary. But having a quality product is only half of the sales business. The other half is persuasion. There is constant competition with other salespeople who carry similar products. The one who makes the sale is the one who is most convincing.

For a kids' commercial agent, the product is, of course, the child actor and the buyer is the commercial-maker. The agent's full range of stock translates to at least one or two children of each age and type on her books. Naturally, the bulk of the product will be the most popular sellers: the all-American type. But a good agent must also carry a range of the off-beat Character and ethnic types as well, even if only to satisfy the odd commercial call for them. If the agent succeeds in selling a child to a commercial-maker, she takes 10 percent of the child's pay as a commission.

Sometimes, particularly with a new child, the agent has to work very hard for that money. With other children, the effort involved may amount to little more than suggesting a name to a casting director. But either way, the competition each agent faces is enormous. In Los Angeles, for example, there are some fifty agencies that are franchised by the Screen Actors Guild as representatives for children acting in commercials. Each of those fifty is out for the same slice of the pie: getting kids on their books into every commercial produced in Los Angeles.

The most successful are those agents with a good eye for the child with commercial potential. They can look at what a layman would see as an absolutely average child and *know* almost immediately that that kid has the talent, temperament, and type commercial-makers are looking for. These agents have built a solid reputation within the industry by having on their books only what are called "good kids."

Finding these good kids is a never-ending process. Children grow and change so fast that gaps are always appearing in the different categories of an agent's roster. Moreover, the attrition rate for children in commercials is relatively high. The pace is so difficult for parents, the kid's interests change, family situations alter, all resulting in the child's dropping out of the commercial business.

And, too, children change agents frequently, often hopping from one to another in hopes of better or more jobs. So even once an agent has signed a good kid, there is the constant worry that the child will leave or another agent will "steal" him.

Consequently, a good portion of an agent's time is spent looking for new children. Most claim that their best kids come from referrals by parents of children already signed with them. "I have come to the conclusion," says Evelyn Schultz, "that mothers of children in this business make the best talent scouts for me, because they seem to know the talent. They're out there, they see the competition, they know what kind of children we're looking for, and, frankly, I get my best recommendations from them."

Contrary to the popular dream, not many agents hunt children in their local supermarkets or other such places. "It's rare that that works," says New York agent Jean Walton. "I have had my daughters, my brother, my aunts, my uncle call and say, 'I saw this most beautiful kid today.' It doesn't work, because looks is not all there is to being in the business. We're looking for much more."

The Mary Ellen White agency, however, has set up what their vice president, James White, considers an innovative network of talent scouts. "We have about twenty talent scouts in all of the New York suburbs and in such outlying places as Hartford and New Haven, Connecticut, Allentown, Pennsylvania, Philadelphia, and even Boston. We guarantee that we will sign the children they find to exclusive contracts if they meet our requirements. These scouts are in the bowels of their communities, and they are finding gems in the raw, children we would never know of otherwise."

There is a third way in which agents find new children: by direct inquiry from the parent. Most agents receive between fifty and one hundred letters or phone calls each week from hopeful parents who want to put their child into commercials. Of that number, perhaps only 1 percent are then asked in for an interview. And then only 1 percent of those are actually offered contracts.

This, most probably, will be the route you will follow, and admittedly the numbers aren't very encouraging. However, you can stack the odds somewhat in your favor by knowing how best to approach the agent and present your child.

Getting an Interview

Step One is to make up a list of children's agents whom you want to approach. This is the point at which most parents unfamiliar with the business run astray. They simply don't know where to go to even find out who the agents in their area are. Many such parents will head for the Yellow Pages or the classified section of their local newspaper and blindly choose the agent with the most enticing—"Your Child Can Make Top $$$!!!"—advertisement. DON'T DO IT THIS WAY.

The rip-off field in agenting is ripe where children are concerned. I can practically guarantee you that any agent who advertises in the newspaper or with a display ad in the phone book is going to take your money and give you nothing.

They will tell you that your child is "perfect, but . . ." Following that "but" is: "First we need photographs taken by our special photographer," or "First we need to put him through our training program," or "First we need to have a videotape made of him."

"Second . . ." you will find yourself paying them anywhere from $200 to $600 or more for these special needs. And the most, the absolute most, that they can do for your child is put him up for work as an extra in commercials. That is something your child can do at no charge to you simply by going through the normal Screen Extras Guild channels. Suffice to say that the minute the agency starts toting up what you must pay *them* for the privilege of representing your child, grab your kid, your wallet, and run.

But you can avoid this heartbreak and expense by following one rule: Contact only those agents franchised by the Screen Actors Guild. In Chapter 8 all the SAG branch offices in the United States are listed by state. Find the one nearest to you, call them and ask for a list of the franchised agents in their area who represent children. Not all of them will handle kids for commercials, so your next step is a brief phone call to each, asking if they are a commercial agency.

You want to end up with a list of about ten agents to write to. By now, particularly if you live in an area outside of the major commercial centers, you should have about that number of possible agents to contact. Now you are ready to begin your presentation.

Consider that you are selling your child to the agent. You have two sales tools: a color photograph of your child and a short cover letter. Of these, the photo is by far the more important. You want this picture to be as natural as possible. Forget about the posed shots with bunny fur backgrounds and hands folded under chin. Neither should you send that cute one where she was the third tulip from the left in the school play (and you snapped the picture from the back of the auditorium).

You want to show your child's face in close-up—what the industry calls a "head shot"—and you want to reveal his natural, most animated expression. The best way to do this is to load your camera with film, dress him in school clothes, and snap away as he does what comes naturally, be it playing in the yard or watching TV. At first your child might be somewhat constrained but if you are willing to follow him around, talking as if nothing unusual were happening, he should soon forget you have a camera in your hands. And then you will get the truest photo of your child.

"We like animated pictures of kids smiling," says Evelyn Schultz. "I hate to get pictures of children nude and in the bath tub or in swimming pools. What can you tell about a sopping wet child? And I hate pictures of kids in costume or where they're mugging for the camera. I automatically go 'Ughh!' when I see those and throw them away. I just want a candid shot that shows what the child looks like."

Once you have such a photo you're ready to compose a brief letter (a few paragraphs only) that details your child's age, height, weight, coloring, and any special skills.

This is the point at which you can separate your child from many others in his type category. Commercials call for kids who can do all kinds of things, from roller-skating to handstands to half-gainer dives. Agents have had calls for children who can blow trick chewing gum bubbles or do complicated magic. Obviously the child with a special skill is going to be far more desirable to an agent than one who does nothing.

So include in your letter everything that your child is truly proficient at. Is he a soccer player? Can she ride a horse? Or a skateboard? Play an instrument? Disco dance? Go through your child's activities and interests; you'll find most of them are special skills in commercials. Don't just confine yourself to those that are physically oriented. A lot of commercials are filmed with animals. If your child has one or is totally at ease with them, put it down. For the young child, reading can be considered a special skill as well. And, of course, any lessons that your child takes should go onto your list.

Your letter should contain only these essentials with no additional explanation. It might read something like this:

Dear Agent (use his or her name):

Enclosed is a current photograph of my six-year-old son, Jason. He has brown hair and blue eyes, and fair skin with a few freckles. Jason is thirty-eight inches tall and weighs forty-two pounds. He is in the first grade and is in the advanced reading group.

Jason is a good skateboarder and plays soccer on a weekly team. He also swims well and can do basic dives. He is not afraid of animals, cares for his own cocker spaniel and has just learned to ride a pony. He also takes piano lessons.

I hope you will consider Jason for representation. My phone number, should you wish to reach me, is 386-5151.

Notice that there is no flowery prose in this letter. Nor are there any quotes from neighbors or family who "think Jason is just perfect for commercials." Comments of this sort have no bearing on an agent's ability to spot yours as a commercial kid. If you put them in, they will probably be ignored—and you run the risk of alienating the agent. One agent, for example, gets so furious with that type of approach, she automatically tosses the letter *and* the photograph in her wastepaper basket. Fortunately, she says, her secretary retrieves the really good pictures to show her at a later date when she has calmed down.

Once you send your letters and photographs off, you have just one more thing to do: wait. Agents don't sit in their offices panting for the morning mail and your letter to arrive. When it does, only some of them will go through that day's photographs right away. Some put them in a file for viewing at a later—perhaps weeks later—slack moment. Others are haphazard, slitting envelopes and glancing at pictures while they're on the phone or eating lunch. Whatever their style, remember two things: Yours is not the only picture in the mail, and rare is the child so startling in Kodachrome that the agent will immediately call him in.

You could wait days, weeks, or a lifetime for the agent to call you. So rather than going through the agony of "Is today the day?" set yourself a time limit. If you don't hear from any of the agents within two weeks, start calling them. There are, in fact, some agents who prefer that the parent always make the follow-up call. Even though they're on the constant watch for new talent, they know that their days are crazy and they just might forget to call the parent of that promising kid.

When you make the follow-up call, keep it brief. Chances are your query will be dealt with by the agent's secretary or assistant. Simply give your name, your child's name, and when you sent the picture. Then just one more sentence is required: Are you interested in my child?

There are only two possible answers. If it's "no," don't beg, argue, or ask for explanations. Merely thank the agent or secretary for her consideration and hang up gently.

There may be several reasons, at this stage, that an agent doesn't want to see your child. Most often it's that in the agent's opinion the child doesn't have commercial potential. He may not have the looks for a career or the personality. It may seem unfair to make such a determination based on a photograph, but the fact is that an agent's ability to judge commercial talent is so well honed that most can tell at a glance which kids are worth seeing and which are not. "Energy is what I look for," explains Janice Borovay. "I don't know how to explain it any more than that. When I look at the photograph, if the picture just jumps off the page, then I call them in."

Your child might be turned down because of a minor facial quirk that you think is cute, or even don't know exists, but that would preclude his appearing in commercials. It could be something as innocuous as a birthmark, a scar, crooked teeth or obvious facial hair.

Yet another reason a particular agent may not be interested in your child is that the agency already has enough children in that type category. Most agents don't like to have type conflicts among the children they represent. If they already have their full quota of six-year-old, red-haired Huck Finn types and that describes your child, many agents wouldn't see him no matter how good he may be.

Unfortunately, you may never know why an agent has refused your child; it is rare that they'll have the time or inclination to tell you. But because their decisions tend to be so subjective, you shouldn't be discouraged if the first few responses are negative. If, however, by the fifth agent, your child still has not been asked in for an interview, you must accept the fact that he is not right for commercials—at least this year.

Next year he may be perfect. It's not uncommon that the six-year-old who froze in front of the camera will beam forth with all his personality at seven. Or the chubby eight-year-old will slim down to a real cutie at nine. So if you see a discernible change in your child after a year or so, then it's worth the effort of going through the whole picture-taking and letter-writing business again. If, however, after this second time around, he is still refused by all the agents, then resign yourself to the fact that you have a charming but noncommercial kid.

More than two times at bat and you're just doing yourself and your child a disservice. "I have kids who have been knocking at my door and sending me pictures year after year," says Sandra Firestone. "In fact, every time we are mentioned in the trade publications, I will get pictures from these kids. They're the same ones I've been getting for years, and that everyone else in New York has been getting. It should be obvious to their parents by now that these kids are just not right for the business and there's no reason to keep putting them up for it."

But what happens if an agent is interested in your child? If the child is under four, then the agent will most likely explain to you the whys and wherefores of the baby file. "Below four, we don't even interview them," says Evelyn Schultz. "Because they change so greatly every three or four months while they're young, it would be useless to see them. So we just keep a card file with their pictures in it. Then when we get a call for a baby of a particular age, we go through the file and look at the pictures to see what children we have who fit the description of what the casting director is looking for. But there are so few of those calls that we don't even bother to sign kids that age to a contract. It's not worth going through all the paperwork. We just ask the parents not to contact another agency if we've agreed to represent their child."

If, however, your child is over four and an agent is interested, a day and time will be set up for you to bring him in for an interview.

Rejoice and Prepare!

The list of do's and don'ts is short but critical. You want your child to have the best possible chance of being accepted by the agent. Follow these orders and he will.

1. *Don't make a big deal of it.* Yes, you're excited and nervous. Yes, this is a big day for you. Yes, you want your child to turn on that sparkling personality and dazzle the agent. But if you communicate any of that, through word or deed, you are practically guaranteed to take a nervous, uptight child, either frustratingly mute or appallingly hyperactive, into the agent's office. Nothing cramps a kid's style more than the desperation of knowing that his parents' dreams depend on him.

2. *Do tell your child where you're going.* Preferably the day before, preferably with as little emotion as possible. The depth into which you go in your description depends on the age of your child and how much he can understand. Since you've already discussed the fact that the child would like to do commercials, you can now just say that you're both going to meet someone who helps children get on TV. Explain that this person only wants to talk to him for a little while. Assure him that nothing special is expected, that he should be natural, say what he feels like saying and do what he feels like doing.

You can do all of that in about three sentences. If you spend too much longer on it, emphasizing that there's nothing to be afraid of, the child will know for sure that there is. Do encourage any questions, but watch how you respond. Never say, "If the agent thinks you're cute enough . . ." or "If they like you . . ." or anything that implies the child is about to go through some sort of a test. You'll be putting the beans of rejection up your kid's nose if you do.

3. *Don't dress your child specially for the interview.* "We tell parents not to dress their children up for the interview," says Evelyn Schultz. "We want them to be comfortable, relaxed, and in as normal an atmosphere as possible. There's something about dressing a child up that puts him on his best behavior, and he sits there like a gentleman. You can't get any idea of what kind of personality he has."

Agents prefer to see a child dressed in normal school clothes, which, since the interview will take place after school, makes it very convenient for you. Don't buy a new outfit or make any special effort. Although the night before should definitely be a bath and hair wash night, forget the rollers. You want your child's hair shiny and clean, not tortured into some elaborate adult style or ribboned and rippled à la the 1950s. Two ponytails are fine; braids are nice, too. If your son has a natural cowlick, leave it alone. Don't bother with the Brylcreem or hair spray.

What you're aiming for in your child's appearance is absolute naturalness. As Iris Burton, a Los Angeles agent who represents some of the top kids on TV, told one mother, "If your little girl is going to do commercials, she's got to be commercial. And that's called giving them what they want, which is your average little kid from Iowa and not Beverly Hills. That means no jewelry, no nail polish, no earrings, no makeup. On weekends she can do whatever she wants and wear whatever she wants. She can march up and down Main Street in a tiara for all I care. But from Monday to Friday, she's got to be plain, simple, and natural. She's got to be a little girl."

This is particularly good advice if your child is near or in the teen years. That's a time when most kids are desperate to look older. I've seen twelve-year-olds clomp into interviews on platform heels three inches high, hair sprayed like Farrah Fawcett's, wearing dresses fashionably slit to midthigh. These kids end up tottering out of the interview, rejected. Boys, too, often fancy themselves studs from *Saturday Night Fever,* wearing tight shirts and tighter pants. If this sounds like your child, you'll have to put your foot down and put out the jeans, hide the electric rollers, and lock up the makeup. If he can't understand and accept the wisdom of what you're doing, then he doesn't belong in the business anyway.

The basic rule of simple and natural applies to you as well. Like it or not, this is your interview too. No one much cares if you dress young or old, but do change from your wash-the-floor clothes into something more public. "I always look at the parents' shoes," says Janice Borovay. "I know that sounds silly, but if they shine their shoes and keep them heeled, it tells me they have some kind of self-respect. The fact is that if the parent doesn't have any class, then the kid won't either."

4. *Be on time for the interview.* Promptness is a must in this business where minutes are translated into dollars. If you're late for this initial interview, the agent will surmise, correctly or not, that you will probably be late for job interviews as well.

The Interview

It would be nice if every agent held the same kind of interview. You could read a description, know exactly what to expect, and thus prepare yourself and your child for the experience. But, unfortunately, no two agents interview in exactly the same way.

Some see children every day of the week; others have one marathon session every week to ten days. Some agents call the kids in in large groups; others talk to each child individually. Some want the parent present; others keep the parent waiting outside. Some agents spend just five minutes with a child; others interview for up to half an hour. Some structure their interviews according to a set procedure; others just wing it, letting the child set the pace.

How an agent interviews is largely a matter of her personality

and particular experience with the process. Iris Burton, for example, sees kids individually on whatever afternoon happens to be
most convenient, interviewing them from her decorator-perfect
home above Sunset Boulevard in Hollywood. Burton has only
been an agent since 1975, but her success has been phenomenal.
She is a former child star herself, a New York kid whose mother
would fake excuses so Iris could leave school early to audition, in
falsies and tap shoes, at the Copa. That background, combined
with her New York street smarts and a cynical attitude toward
parents and the child entertainment industry, has made her, as she
puts it, ". . . controversial. I'm not out to win the Miss Con-
geniality contest though. I'm out to do my job."

Her job this afternoon is interviewing a five-year-old called
Andrea, who has just arrived at Burton's hilltop office with her
mother and older brother. The three of them sit close together on
a chintz sofa in the middle of the long room, listening wide-eyed
as Burton does a mile-a-minute phone hustle for a TV job for one
of her clients. Her hands are flying, a haze of blue smoke from an
ever-present cigarette fills the air, and the finishing, poker-table
touch is her language, which is, to put it mildly, colorful. In perfect contrast, at the other end of the room, is Burton's young English secretary, a dour woman who is as proper as a duchess as she
quietly works her way through a list of phone calls to parents, giving them interview times for their kids' commercial auditions the
next day.

Finally Burton slams down her phone and turns to Andrea.
"C'mon, get up," she orders not unkindly, waving the little girl
to the side of her desk. As Andrea stands, nervously swinging
from side to side, Burton looks her over, from the huge, plaid
bow atop her long, honey-toned hair down to her saddle shoes
and knee socks that match her blue jumper. The scrutiny switches
to Andrea's face. "What's this mark under her eye? You're going
to have to put Erase on that. How tall is she? What's she weigh?"
Her questions are snapped out, no-nonsense, and Andrea's mother,
a young woman trying hard not to be cowed, barely has time to answer. "Let me see your teeth," Burton demands, and Andrea
opens wide, revealing a gap smack in the middle.

Her mother laughs nervously. "You had to ask that. She just lost her front tooth."

"You bet I ask," retorts Burton. "You can't do food commercials without teeth. She'll have to get a flipper. In this business, we start them on false teeth at an early age.

"Okay, Andrea, Mommy's going to leave now." Burton turns to the mother. "Aren't you, Mommy? Just take brother and walk around outside for a while.

"Now, Andrea, I want you to move back until I tell you to stop. Back, back, back, back. Okay, stop there. I want you to talk to me and I don't want you to fidget. Okay? Do you need to have your mother with you?"

"No."

"Why are you wiggling? Do you always wiggle?"

"No."

"Well then, don't wiggle now. Put your hands at your sides. Now, what do you like to do?"

"I like to make little pies in my oven and I like to . . ." For about five minutes, Burton and Andrea chat back and forth. The little girl is verbal, smiling, and, despite anything Burton says, fidgety.

"Okay, I'm going to ask you one more time not to wiggle. You cannot wiggle and jiggle. No more of that and no more twisting around. You have to stand still, and when you talk to me you've got to look at me. All right?" Andrea nods. "Tell me what kind of food you like. Do you like hamburgers?"

"Yes, and french fries."

"Good. Do you like cereal? Kellogg's?"

"Yes. And you know what else I like? Cheerios."

"Do you like pizza? Do you like . . ." Burton's concentration on food is not arbitrary. A large number of the commercials kids do are food spots, and directors are very careful not to cast children who don't like the particular product. The child who is a picky eater is going to be eliminated early on from many of these national spots. Burton's food questions are aimed at determining if Andrea's career would be so limited.

But Andrea is giving all the right answers, and despite her wiggling, Burton knows that she has good potential for the business. "I have a gut feeling about certain kids. About those that will work and those that won't. And I go by my feeling."

At the other end of the spectrum is James White of Mary Ellen White in New York. White is a graduate of Yale, MIT, and the University of Chicago, and he runs MEW like a Wall Street conglomerate. "Other agents talk about signing kids on gut intuition. They say there's something called a 'commercial look' that tells the agent the child will be successful in the business. I say no to that. If you can't quantify the qualities, then it's not a business."

MEW's interview is specifically designed to determine a child's ability in the shortest possible time. As soon as a child is accepted for interviewing, a one-paragraph commercial script is sent out to be memorized. The interview itself is in two parts, takes two minutes, and is recorded on videotape. The first part tests the child's ability to deal with the script. "If they come back with it less than memorized," says White, "then that is one indication that they are not right for the business."

The second part of the interview seems like merely a conversation between the agent and child. Actually, according to White, "We have devised techniques that trigger conversation. For example, the agent will ask, 'Who did you have a fight with today?' That is one question children cannot answer with a yes or no. They must elaborate."

MEW sees kids every day, starting at 3:30 P.M. No decisions are made until much later, when the agents will review all the tapes of children interviewed that afternoon. "Any doubts one of our agents may have about a child are erased then," claims White. "The better children show up very clearly on tape once you compare them all."

Though James White and Iris Burton are equally adamant about whose method is better, both see similar results. Mary Ellen White is a large agency and Burton's is small, but both carry some of the top commercial kids on their books.

The fact is that the difference in interviewing procedures actually counts for little when it comes to an agent's success. What *is* important is the agent's ability to spot the child with commercial potential. Sometimes that's easy; the qualities discussed in Chapter 2 are very obvious in the child. But other times, one or more of them may not be as apparent—or as strong. Then the agent has to juggle, to weigh up whether, say, a child's great imagination will make up for his somewhat less than outgoing personality. Or will her enthusiasm outweigh the fact that she's physically not the best type.

See if you can do it. Five children are sitting, waiting for an interview. Two will walk out with an offer of a contract; three will be told "Thanks, but no thanks." You play agent; which are the two with commercial potential?

See them first in the agent's cubbyhole of a waiting room. Seated, standing, somewhere near their mothers, each has been given the same short script to practice reading.

AMY—She's a miniature beauty, at seven looking a lot closer to four or five. Her hair is deep red, long and shining. Her eyes are blue-green, fringed with curly, dark lashes. Dressed in a matching denim skirt and jacket, she stands swaying in front of her mother, an overweight woman of about thirty with a determined look on her scrubbed-clean face. Amy's total concentration is on her face as over and over again, they read through the script. "Try it this way, Amy . . . Okay, that's better, but do it again . . . No, you forgot the third line . . . Again . . . Okay, again . . . Amy, you're lisping; stop it . . . Again . . . Smile . . . Again . . . Again . . ." Amy follows the orders with never a moment's hesitation. And through it all, she drags a Mason Pearson hairbrush through her thick, glossy hair.

FREDERICK—A husky eight-year-old, already looking like a fullback. He's got a devilish gleam in his brown eyes and a cowlick in his dark hair that rivals Dennis the Menace's. Earlier in the day, he was probably a picture of neatness. His mother, a middle-aged woman with freshly permed gray hair, has dressed him in navy slacks and a clean, white shirt. But the pants are wrinkled now and his shirt front sports the remains of his after-school snack. His script lies crumpled in his mother's lap, a landing strip for the toy plane Frederick is vroom-vrooming through the air. "Don't you want to read your script, honey?" his mother whispers, her tone showing she already knows the answer. And sure enough, Frederick's only response is a double-dive, vroom-vroom crash landing in her hair.

DEBBY—Blond curls in bunches, sparkling blue eyes, a smattering of freckles across her short, pug nose. She's a friendly little girl, starting up conversations with the children on her right and her left when she's not marching around the room, engrossed in reading her script, or studying the mass of composites that totally cover the walls. "Debby, come here," her mother calls out, putting down the copy of *Good Housekeeping* she has been reading. She pulls a comb, hairpins, and a tiny, fold-up lint brush from a huge leather handbag that matches her elegant leather boots. Debby comes and stands and fidgets as her mother twirls her curls into sausage-size ringlets and brushes the last little bit of lint off her daughter's red velvet jumpsuit.

ANDY—A small page boy of six hunched up in the crook of his young mother's arm, his light blue eyes darting around the room, his nail-bitten hands nervously rolling the hems of his green plaid shorts. His mother's wan face mirrors his, and her hands, too, are continually moving, smoothing Andy's silky, blond hair, straightening his red, clip-on bow tie, and tucking in his already taut shirt. The script, neatly folded in half and half again, is in the side pocket of the blue vinyl handbag sitting by her feet.

TONY—Dark hair, dark eyes, a ten-year-old version of Travolta in *Saturday Night Fever*. His beige slacks are tight, his gold flowered shirt open to the fourth button. Around his neck is a thin S-chain, on his wrist a chunky ID bracelet, and the little finger of his left hand sports a red star sapphire ring. This kid has style, confidence, and, it seems, sophistication beyond his years. But his face belies the pose: open, fresh, albeit definitely ethnic, he still looks, from the neck up, very much the child. Still, there's an air of independence or aloneness about Tony, even though he's sitting next to his mother. She is engrossed in a paperback novel, her eyes seeing only the print before her, her hands moving only to turn a page or pat a stray curl in her blue-black pompadour. Tony, too, is a picture of concentration as he studies the script lying flat on a leather portfolio on his lap. It's the type models carry to display their photographs and at the top, in large gold letters, are stamped Tony's initials.

By now, after seeing them in the waiting room, you should have some idea of which ones won't be the lucky two. But you're ahead of the agent here; she hasn't seen any of these kids yet. Still, by the time she calls them into her office, the first major test of her interview is over. Call it the Waiting Game. She keeps them dangling in the outer office at least half an hour after their designated appointments. A report from her secretary will tell her which children have been able to sit relatively still and which ones have wreaked havoc with the office. The latter, no matter how good, have not a chance of being signed.

Test two: The first impression. As the agent smiles and waves the children into her office, she's looking them over, immediately noticing the more apparent presence or absence of commercial talent. She spots Andy's fear, the tear-filled eyes and wobbling chin that started the moment he had to leave his mother. Amy's beauty—that's a positive. But she seems tense; when the agent smiles at her, Amy looks straight ahead, too intimidated to even return the look. Debby, however, bounces in, greeting the agent like she's known her for years. Next Frederick, disheveled still but marching ramrod straight. He's got a good look, she thinks, natural and cute but—she checks his age on the data card his mother has filled out—he certainly is big. End of the line is Tony and the agent's eyes narrow as she takes in his flash outfit. That's definitely a minus. But then he smiles at her, a winning, childlike grin. That's definitely a plus.

At this point, the agent isn't set in her opinions yet. However, there are some who do make their final decision in those first few seconds. Says Janice Borovay, "I can tell within five seconds whether they have it or not. That doesn't sound like much, but it's more than they'll get on an interview for a commercial. There, if the kid doesn't project his personality in the first *two* seconds, the interviewers are going to be turned off."

But our agent has designed her fifteen-minute interview to give each child the greatest chance to prove his or her potential. Her name is Mary Grady. She's one of the top children's agents in Los Angeles. A woman whose years of experience began with her own son Don, one of Fred MacMurray's brood in *My Three Sons*.

"Sit down, children," she says, motioning them onto the overstuffed, fake-fur-covered sofas facing her desk. The room is sunny and cheerful. There are plants all over, some sitting on the gold carpet, others hanging from pastel macramé hangers that end in huge, fluffy pompoms. Knicknacks are scattered here and there, and picture postcards are tacked to a bulletin board. The total effect is warmth, which matches Grady, a shortish woman with streaked hair and half-lens granny glasses hanging on a multicolored beaded chain around her neck.

"I'm Mary Grady," she says. "I hope . . ." Suddenly a pure white poodle with a blue rhinestone collar and matching blue ear bows trots out from behind the desk. "Oh, and this is Tutu Grady. Sit down, Tutu . . ." Tutu plops in a patch of sun on the carpet. "Now, I hope you all know why you're here today and that there's no reason for you to be nervous. We're just going to talk for a little while and play a few games. So sit back and relax. Now, first we're going to have a little contest. We're going to see which one of you can keep talking the longest telling me about yourself."

The results are revealing. Remember that she's looking for the child who is spontaneous, doesn't need drawing out, thinks quickly on his feet, and communicates well with adults. As Grady's competitor Evelyn Schultz puts it, "The children we want are the ones who aren't afraid to talk. You don't have to pull the words out of them. You don't get just a yep or nope answer to your questions. Their eyes don't wander all over the room. They look directly at you and they *talk!*"

"I'm Frederick!" He leaps to his feet, arms board-straight at his sides, shoulders pulled up in a mock Marine stance. "I'm in the third grade. I'm eight and . . . I'm great!" He falls back on the sofa, dissolving into giggles.

"My name is Amy and I'm seven years old and I'm in the second grade and I'm . . . and I'm . . ."

"Do you have any brothers or sisters, Amy?" Grady prompts.

"Yes, I have a baby brother. He's six months old. And I have a cat that I got last week and . . ." Amy is beginning to relax.

"My name is Andy . . ."

"I can't hear you, dear. Can you speak up?"

"My name is Andy . . ."

"How old are you, Andy?" He holds up six fingers. "I want you to tell me, not show me. Remember we're going to see who can keep talking the longest."

"I'm six."

"Do you go to school?" His head bobs up and down. "Remember, Andy, talk."

"First grade . . ." Barely a whisper.

Grady gives up. "Very nice. And you, dear?" She looks at Debby, who has just slid off the sofa, inching toward the dog on the floor. "Please sit back on the sofa and tell us your name."

Debby bounces far back into the cushions, the fur throw cover a crumpled heap under her. "I'm Debby. I'm six going on seven and I'm in the first grade. I have two brothers and a dog and a parakeet. I take ballet, tap, acrobatics, singing, disco, tap—did I say that already?—baton twirling, and I can do ten routines. Want to see a cartwheel?"

Grady stops her in mid-slide off the sofa again. "Not right now, thank you."

Tony stand up, clears his throat and begins. "My name is Tony. I'm ten years old and I'm in the fifth grade. My favorite subject is English, and I've been in two school plays! I'm starting acting classes on Saturdays soon. I play soccer and baseball after school, and I'm learning disco dancing on Wednesdays. I have an older sister who's helping me . . ."

At this point, Grady has already made a final cut: Andy. Although he has potential in terms of size and looks, he is too shy and withdrawn for a career in commercials—at least now. In another year or two, he may have more confidence and be able to launch out on his own; today, however, he's just not ready for the industry.

The other child she is pretty sure about is Debby. She's the best

size, small; the best type, all-American; and she definitely has that
outgoing, confident personality that signifies commercial talent.

About the other three, Grady still isn't sure. Amy has the size
and the looks and now that she is more at ease, she is becoming
outgoing. Frederick is a big "if": He's a good all-American type,
but he is very large for his age. Moreover, Grady can see that he
might be a problem as far as temperament is concerned. Tony has
the personality and the temperament, but his seeming sophistication is against him. Grady knows that the industry wants children, not miniature adults. Also she's not sure whether she needs
an ethnic child in his age category right now.

"Do you all have the scripts that you were given when you
came in? This is a sample of what a commercial script looks like.
You'll see that there are two parts. I'm going to pair you up so everyone has a chance to read at least one of the parts. I'd like you
to try to be as natural as you can. Try not to sound like you're
reading it. Pretend that you're just talking to your best friend."

Not all agents check children for their ability to read. Those
who don't believe that a child's looks and personality are
sufficient to make him successful in the business. That may be
true; however, it is equally true that the child who doesn't read is
going to be limited in the number of commercials he can be sent
out for. If the script has only one or two lines and the child can
be spoon-fed it for memorizing before the interview, then there's
no problem. But there are a number of commercials that have
complicated scripts, and for those, only kids who read well will
do.

Naturally agents want to sign kids with the minimum number of
limitations on their opportunities for casting. Consequently, given
two children with equal talent, looks, and temperament, the agent
will almost always take the reader over the nonreader.

Obviously, no one expects a preschooler to be able to read.
Those agents who normally give older children scripts generally
play "a little game" with the younger ones. It's called an *improv*,
short for improvisation, and is a common theatrical training technique for actors of all ages. A dramatic situation is set up around
which the actors create a playlet, giving full rein to their emo-

tional involvement and imagination. For children, it's a game of "let's pretend." Let's pretend we're two cowboys arguing over who gets to ride the best horse. The child who can really get into this game shows a good ability to concentrate, lack of inhibition, and, above all, imagination.

Mary Grady uses a more structured kind of improv. Instead of letting the child make up the situation as it develops, using whatever words come naturally, she not only sets out a fully developed plot but gives the children lines to speak as well. Basically, she is exploring their ability to remember as well as their potential for taking direction.

"Pretend I'm your mother and you come in from school and ask me, 'What are we having for dinner tonight?' I tell you spaghetti. But you just had it for lunch at school. So you say, 'Oh, Mom, do we have to have spaghetti tonight?' " Grady's voice is pure kid's whine here. " 'Can't we go to McDonald's?' "

Amy is the hands down winner of this improv game. She mimics Grady perfectly on the "Oh, Mom . . ." and her eyes just shine at the thought of McDonald's. In fact, all the children do better at this than with the script-reading. Perhaps it's that, with the exception of Tony, they're all at the earliest stages of their schooling. Tony, with his experience in "two school plays!" not only reads well but even, one could say, acts. That's a plus for him in Grady's eyes: even though he will be limited for commercials because he is an ethnic type, he can be sent out immediately for "theatricals," i.e., television and film.

Grady's final question seems most innocuous: "I'd like each of you to tell me why you wanted to come here today."

"To be a star!" Frederick shouts out.

"A star? Why would you want to be a star?"

"So I could make bushels of money. I want to be in commercials so I can be rich and buy myself lots of things and everyone will think I'm great. I'll be the Greatest like Ali, I'll be . . ."

"That's enough, Frederick. Please sit down." Frederick is doing a little jig. "Frederick, did you hear me? I said sit down." He sits. "You know, you're acting a little bratty, Frederick, and I want to tell you what that says to me about you. It tells me that if I sent you out on an interview, you would act bratty there too. And that's bad. No one likes bratty children who don't listen when they're spoken to and who act smart. So if you can't behave yourself, you have no business being here.

"And another thing. You shouldn't want to be in commercials because you want to make money. None of you should even be thinking about money. Leave that to your parents and me to worry about. You should just be having fun and enjoying yourself. That's the reason for being in commercials, the only reason.

"Now, Andy, can you tell us why you're here today?" He shakes his head no. "Didn't your mommy tell you?"

"No."

"Well, you're here to see if you'd like to be in commercials. You watch TV, don't you? Do you think you'd like to be one of the kids in commercials on TV?" Andy shrugs his shoulders. "Tell me, Andy, what do you think you'd like to be when you grow up?"

"A policeman! My daddy's a policeman." Andy's eyes light up with the first sign of animation from him yet.

"That's very good. A policeman is a good thing to be. And, Debby, why are you here today?"

"I want to be in commercials. I think it would be lots of fun. I watch them all the time at home and sometimes I even pretend that I'm the kid in them. And I'd like to be in a series too."

"Don't you think it would bother you not to go to your own school any more? You'd miss all your friends, you know."

"Yes, but I'd make lots of new ones. And anyway, I want to be an actress when I grow up and this is a good start."

"That's very true," says Grady. "Most of the kids in series started off doing commercials. How about you, Amy. What do you want to be when you grow up, an actress?"

"Ummm, no. A nurse."

"That's a good profession, Amy. Your parents must be very proud of you."

"Yes, but . . . well, they'd like me to be a movie star. But I don't know . . ."

"Are you here today because your parents want you to be a movie star?"

"I guess so. It makes my mom real happy."

Grady just nods. "Tony, how about you?"

Ever poised, Tony reels off his speech like he has memorized it. "I was a model when I was little, but I stopped when I started school. My mom said I really enjoyed it so I asked if I could start again. I want to be an actor. I really like acting and I've been told that I'm pretty good at it."

"Tell me, Tony. If I sent you out on an interview, would you be willing to wear jeans and take off your jewelry?"

Tony looks bewildered. "Well, sure. I guess so."

"Good—and your hair. Did you just have it cut?"

"No, I just had it washed and styled." His expression has now switched to pride. "I go every week to have that done."

"Every week???" Grady is shocked.

"Oh, yes, but don't worry," Tony reassures her, completely misunderstanding Grady's surprise. "We get a discount on it."

Grady's interview has finished and as the children file back into the waiting room, she has already made her decisions. Have you?

We know for a start that Andy is out because he's too shy and withdrawn. Perhaps if his mother had talked to him first and told him at least where she was taking him and why, he might not have been so intimidated. However, it's too late for that now; neither Grady nor any commercial-maker is going to spend the time to reassure and draw out such a child.

Debby, on the other hand, needs no coaxing to speak. If anything, she is a little too aggressive. But Grady isn't really worried about that; the few times she had to quiet the little girl, Debby listened immediately. Such occasional need for rebuking is, Grady knows, small penalty to pay for Debby's natural enthusiasm.

It isn't difficult to figure out that Frederick will not be accepted. The fact that he is a good all-American type and has the personality associated with commercial talent is far outweighed by his size and his temperament. He is, as Grady told him, a potential behavior hazard on the set, one no agent or commercial-maker would willingly deal with.

Now we're left with two children—Tony and Amy—whose futures are yet undecided. Which one will get the contract? If you guess Amy, you're wrong. And probably surprised. After all, Amy has the looks, the size, the temperament, and, once she relaxed, the talent of a true commercial kid. What's more, her script-reading wasn't so bad and her improv was terrific. So what's missing? Desire. Amy doesn't want to be in commercials; she's doing it to please her parents.

Agents view parents who put children in commercials when they're not eager to do it as little less than child abusers. The nightmare memories of Stage Mothers and the havoc their ambition wrought with their childrens' lives still haunt Hollywood. And while in previous times such unfortunate children were at the mercy of their parents' drive, today they have a protector in every agent in the business. They simply will not take on a child, no matter how good, unless they are sure the child wants the career.

"I will not be a party to having a child miss out on a lot of life and have to do something that he doesn't want to do because of his parents," says agent Jean Walton. "I've sat and interviewed kids and asked them, 'Why do you want to do this?' And they say, 'Oh, my mother or my father wants me to.' I don't want any part of that. Let those parents take their child elsewhere."

However, there are few elsewheres. Every reputable agent is on the lookout for the coerced kid. They all ask the important question—"Do you want to be in commercials?"—in one way or another. Some even use elaborate ploys to ensure that they're getting the truth.

"My technique for pulling the truth out of these kids," says Janice Borovay, "is to lead them through a little drama. Say it's a boy. I ask him, 'What's your favorite thing in the whole, wide world to do?' Nine times out of ten, he'll name a sport, say, baseball. So then I say, 'What does it feel like when you're up there pitching a game and the score is close. There are two outs and the batter's up. Strike one, strike two, strike three—you've struck him out and won the game. Tell me how you feel then.'

"His eyes will light up and you can see his excitement and energy as he describes it. Then I say, 'Okay, you know that feeling.

Is that how you feel when you think about doing commercials?' If he says no, then that's it. I know it's something he doesn't want to do and I won't sign him."

With Amy turned down, Tony is obviously our second winner. However, he is not, in Grady's mind, a sure bet. For one thing, he is an ethnic type, a definite limit to his commercial potential. And while he does have an outgoing personality, he is not particularly childlike. But Grady is banking on the fact that stripped of his sophisticated clothing, his slick hairstyle (which she'll insist he leave natural), and aided by his dramatic ability, Tony will come across sufficiently to make him worth her while as a client.

After the children leave, Grady calls their parents in to make her decision known. The depth to which any agent goes in explaining to a parent why she doesn't want to represent the child varies. Some agents might tell Andy's mother that he is too shy to do well in commercials. Some agents might tell Frederick's mother that he is too undisciplined to do well in commercials. Some agents might tell Amy's mother that she is too disinterested to do well in commercials. And some agents might just say to all three parents, "I don't feel like I could do the best job for your child."

That statement is ambiguous and often has the effect of sending the parent off to another agent, particularly since it is often followed by, "But don't take my word for it. See what some of the other agents in town have to say."

If that's the response you get, feel free to follow their advice. You may find the next agent welcomes you with open arms. But by no means should you start dragging your child around to every agent in town. If you get five or more refusals, take the hint. And look long and hard at your child again. What weak points are you missing that these agents are picking up on? If you can discover what it is that is causing them to reject him, you have a chance to do something about it.

If you honestly cannot find any reason these agents are saying no to your child, then look to yourself. One of the most common reasons for an agent to turn down an otherwise good commercial kid is because the agent doesn't want to work with the parent.

Sandra Firestone speaks for the majority of agents when she says, "I'm very careful about the parent. I'm as careful about them as I am about the children I take on. I have turned down very good kids because they had a pushy parent."

Pushy Parent, Stage Mother, Hollywood Father—they all describe the parent who is determined that the child have a career no matter what. These parents are in high gear when they approach an agent, sure that they know better than anyone how to achieve their goals.

"I had a mother come in with her two kids one time," remembers Janice Borovay, "and she brought me a portfolio of pictures from when she was an actress. 'I just want you to know that I know all about the business,' she says to me as she's showing me these photographs from 1950. I'm trying not to get annoyed, but when she drags out a picture of her with the Motion Picture Academy and says, 'What do you think about this?' all I could say was, 'It would look better on your wall.'

"I didn't sign her kids just because of her. I don't deal with the children, you know. I have to deal with the mothers. And if I meet one who is going to be a pain, I just refuse to work with her."

Borovay's example is a particularly good one, because agents find that most of the "pushy parents" are working out a dream from their own youth of becoming a "star." They are using their children to attain the fame, or even just the career, that they never had. These are the parents whose ambition is single-minded, who ignore their child's welfare, happiness, and well-being anytime it stands in the way of their success. And in the agent's self-appointed role of guardian angel, refusing to accept the child of such a parent is the protective measure.

If any of this sounds like you, my only advice is: Cool it. If you're pushing Johnny on the stage because you want to be there yourself, keep him home and find a neighborhood theater group for your talents. If you're barrelling into agents' offices with a barrage of demands and questions, ease up. Let them lead the interview; they're the experts.

That isn't to say that you should be self-effacing or mute. Just don't tell the agent how to do business or solicit promises of the stardom you *know* your child deserves.

"When a parent says to me, 'What are you going to do for my child?' or 'Is it going to be worthwhile for my child to go with you?'" says Evelyn Schultz, "I tell them, 'If I'm taking your child that shows you that I'm interested. I don't take children just to have their names on my books. I'll do the best I can to get your child out on an interview. But it's up to him to get the job.'"

Your Turn to Choose

No one says that you have to sign with the first agent who offers your child a contract. You can—and it might be the best non-decision you ever made. Or you might find that three, six, or nine months down the road, you not only hate this person you're dealing with every day, but she's just not doing much of anything for your child.

The simple fact you must remember is that like any other professional, there are good agents and bad agents, agents you'll love and agents you'll hate. As with choosing, say, a lawyer, you can, with some careful assessment, avoid hooking up with an agent you dislike. But while the Bar Association can give you some background information for determining the worth of an attorney, only experience will tell you whether your child's agent is good or bad.

If there were such an advisory organization for referrals on agents, it would undoubtedly be made up of casting directors. For the simple fact is, an agent is good when a casting director says she is. Into that general stamp of approval go a number of specifics that casting directors cite most often as being intrinsic to a good agent.

A good agent has taste and signs only talented commercial kids with the agency. An agent is only as good as the children she represents. Without the "eye" for discerning talent, temperament, and type, an agent will fill her books with kids who never quite make it in the business. And if the children she submits are rarely chosen for jobs, casting directors will soon stop wasting their time calling her.

Inherent in the ability to choose talented kids is the fact that *a good agent understands what the business calls for, this year, this month, this commercial.* Agents must understand the psychology of commercial-making, that it's a business of trends and images. They must be up-to-date on the "in" types and ensure that they have the appropriate kids on their books. Too, they must be clear on the vagaries of specific advertisers. The agent, for example, who doesn't know that General Foods almost exclusively casts WASP kids and therefore doesn't maintain a wide selection of that type on her books will never be prepared for those major, money-making calls.

The good agent understands what casting directors are asking for. This may sound elementary, but when you consider the short-hand casting directors sometimes use, it isn't. If a call goes out for a ten-year-old Tatum O'Neal type, the agent must send out gutsy, short-haired tomboys. When a casting director asks for an eight-year-old intellectual boy, the agent immediately translates that to "slightly thin, serious, dark-haired, and put glasses on the kid when he goes in for the interview." A good agent would never send a pug-nosed blond with broad shoulders, even if in reality he was an intellectual with an IQ to rival Einstein's.

The good agent caters to the individual casting director's tastes. Joan Lynn, who casts for Bob Giraldi Productions in New York, prefers real-looking, down-to-earth Character types. Her favorite agents know that and would never send, unasked for, an ethereal Beautiful child to one of her interviews.

And there's a casting director in Los Angeles who swears at one agent every time the call goes out for a six-year-old blonde. This agent has a child of that description on her books who also happens to be the daughter of the casting director's close friend. Yet the agent never submits the little girl for the particular casting director's jobs. "I have to call her every time and remind her to send Sally to me," says the casting director. "That's the sign of a bad agent. You'd think it would be obvious that if I wanted to see anyone, it would be Sally. And the ironic thing is, every time I have to remind her to send me Sally, the kid gets the job."

The good agent has a wide variety of commercial types. Think of it as one-stop shopping: In a business where time wasted is money lost, no casting director wants to make more phone calls to agents than necessary. But the casting person *does* want a variety of children within the specified range to submit to the commercial-makers. Consequently, the agent who has a broad selection of types and ages on the books is at an advantage over the agent who carries, as some do, only Irish kids or only Beautiful types.

The good agent has integrity. "Some agents are a real pain in the ass," says one top commercial producer. "They don't play by the rules. They do whatever they have to to get you to see the kid without considering if the child is right for the job."

Such agents don't hesitate to send a red-haired, freckled ten-year-old on a call for a Beautiful six-year-old. The result is an unnecessary rejection for the child, a very annoyed casting director, and a commercial-maker whose lasting memory of the kid is that "something was wrong with him."

The agent whose business is based on these six points is, for the casting director, a good agent. For "good," read "trusted," and a trusted agent is one given the greatest opportunities in the business. Casting directors are very selective in the agents they call on when seeking actors for a particular commercial. They simply have neither the time nor the inclination to give every agent in town the opportunity to submit for the job. So they develop a working relationship with a small band of agents whom they trust. "It's usual for a casting director to work with only a few agents," says Joan Lynn. "I deal most of the time with what I consider to be the four top kids' agents. My number one is Regina at Joe Jordan Talent Agency. She's the only one I trust to send me kids I've never seen and the only one I'll accept casting suggestions from. Regina knows my taste and she knows what we're looking for here. But more than that, she's the most honest agent in the business. She has never steered me wrong.

"The other three I call regularly are William Schuller, Mary

Ellen White and Bonnie Kid. I don't bother with any of the other agents unless I'm having a hard time casting a commercial."

This is the point at which a casting director's good agent becomes a child's good agent. For if the most basic definition of a good agent from a casting director's point of view is the one who is trusted, then a good agent, from a child's point of view, is the one who gets him out on the most interviews.

A child's success in commercials ultimately is a function of the number of interviews he goes on. James White has figured that the ratio of interviews to jobs won is twenty to one for the newcomer and four to one for the experienced child. It may sound as if those numbers wouldn't be difficult to realize: After all, the agent only has to get twenty commercial calls, send the child out and—voilà! —he gets a job. However, it doesn't work that way. No one child, even the best, will be right for every, or even most, of the calls his agent gets. If, say, the kid is in the ballpark for one out of every four commercials, then to fulfill that twenty-interview requirement, the agent must be getting a minimum of eighty job calls.

It's all a question of numbers. The more jobs the agent is called for, the more one of her kids will be right for. The more the child is right for, the more interviews he goes on. The more interviews he goes on, the better his chances of getting the job. All of which boils down to one thing: You want your child with the agent who gets the most calls.

But here's the rub: Sitting in the agent's office with the unsigned contract before you, you have no way of knowing how good, trustworthy, and active that particular agent is. Only after you've been in the business awhile, sat in waiting rooms, talked to other parents, and watched kids from certain agents parade by you time after time, will you know who the good agents in your town are.

There are, however, a couple of questions you can ask that may give you a hint as to the agent's worth. Like, "Which of your children have I seen lately in commercials?" The agent probably won't reel off a long list, but listen carefully for brand names. If, for example, Kellogg's, Mattel, and McDonald's are mentioned, then chances are this agent meets the criteria for a good agent. Not only are kids from the agency successful, but this agent is obviously trusted enough to be called to submit for the major national commercials.

You can also ask how many children the agent has signed to exclusive contracts. Good agents tend to be very selective. Even if they're big agencies, they will rarely have more than three hundred kids on their books. The agent that has many more than that *may* be one who is indiscriminate in the choice of clients. And that is a sign of a bad agent.

One choice you are equipped to make now is whether you want to go with a large agency or a small one. There are pros and cons to both. The advantage of a large agency is that they have generally been in the business a long time and have built up their reputations with the top casting directors. That, along with the fact that they have a wide selection of types on their books, usually means that they are getting a lot of the commercial calls.

The disadvantage is that your child can get lost in the shuffle. An agent will work hardest for the child she remembers well. In a large agency, with hundreds of kids floating on the books, there is always the chance that your child will be forgotten.

A small agency generally carries fifty to one hundred kids on their books. Here your child will probably get more personal attention than with a large agency. Smaller agencies—who boast of being "boutique houses"—often function less as clearing houses for commercial calls and negotiators than as career managers for the children they represent. However, the disadvantage to the small agency is that they are sometimes the newer ones, and that may mean they haven't established themselves with the casting directors yet.

Now stop a moment and notice how many qualifiers are in these last paragraphs. All those "cans," "mays," "generallys" and "usuallys" are there because there are no absolutes concerning the question of large versus small agency. There are large agencies that have been in the business for years who have absolutely awful reputations with casting directors and only get the rare call for commercial kids (They may be tops with adults or for theatricals). Likewise, there are many small agencies that have been established for only a few years who have the best reputations in town.

So what you're left with now is the fact that at this stage, what you're making is a very personal decision. The only sure advice that will last is: If you like the agent, sign with her. "This is a personality business," says Jean Walton. "You come in, sit down with an agent, find out if you can work with one another, the kinds of things your child will be sent on, how understanding she's likely to be. Then you make the decision: 'I like or I don't like what this person has to say.' "

The Aftermath

Okay, you've made your decision and signed on the dotted line. Now what? At this point, your new agent will give you what has become her standard spiel about the business. Some agents have got it down so pat that they hand it out on a mimeographed sheet usually entitled "Tips to Help Your Agent" or "What You Need to Know."

"All clients will need to obtain a Social Security number and a work permit and join the union." The Social Security card you can apply for immediately; the work permit isn't necessary until your child's first job is imminent; and joining the union doesn't happen until after he has worked. We'll go into the specifics of all three in a later chapter.

"Times for interviews are after school. Calls for interviews are given either the day before or, usually, the morning of the interview so clients must be available on momentary notice. I need all phone numbers of all clients so I can reach you during the day. THIS IS IMPORTANT!" It is so important that many agents ask you to get a telephone answering service of some sort. Even if you are generally around the house all day, you can't afford to miss your agent's call because you slipped out for a loaf of bread or to chat with the neighbor down the street. You must have *one* phone number at which you can be reached or where a message can be

left *at all times.* As one agent told a mother, "I don't want to go 'dialing for dollars' trying to find you."

"All clients must be prompt for their interviews." Your intentions on this one may be the best, but they can go awry if you don't know where you're going. Now is the time to buy a map of your city and familiarize yourself with the areas where commercial interviews are generally held. If you have to rely on public transportation, get the bus schedules so you can plan departure times well in advance.

"All clients must have professional photographs taken and reproduced for distribution." Your agent will probably give you the names of one or two photographers who specialize in pictures of commercial kids. Call them both, ask for a price, choose the cheaper, and set up an appointment for a session.

These pictures are in black and white and will either be a head shot—to which a mimeographed résumé sheet will be stapled—or a composite. A typical résumé sheet is shown on the next page. A composite, in its simplest and most frequent form, is a two-sided lithograph. On the front is a head shot of your child with his most appealing expression, accompanied by his name and vital statistics and the name, address, and phone number of the agent. On the back are two, three, four, or five smaller photographs showing the child in a variety of poses and moods. He may be a picture of dejection on the front stoop, of grim determination at bat, of exuberance on a skateboard, or of ecstasy eating a hot fudge sundae. Some agents also put a blurb on this back page, something on the order of "Billy is a delightful blend of athlete and scholar. He reads three years above his grade level and is captain of his Little League and soccer teams. . . ."

Whether you go for the head shot/résumé or composite depends totally on your agent. If the agent prefers composites, ask the photographer in advance if you should bring any special clothing or equipment to the session. In any event, it is always a good idea to bring along several changes of clothing to provide a variety of looks for the photographer to choose from.

Once you get to the studio, hand over your child and take a back seat. What the photographer needs from you he will ask for.

TOMMY OKON.

UNIONS: AFTRA #130243   AGENT:
                SAG NY084656
                                       PERSONAL MANAGEMENT: STUDIO V.

AGE RANGE: 9 - 11

HEIGHT: 54 inches

SIZE: 12

HAIR: Medium Brown

EYES: Brown

S.S.#:   057-58-9207

TELEVISION COMMERCIALS

    Coca-Cola - "Mean Joe Greene", as "The Kid"
    T.W.A. - "Happy Birthday, Tommy"
    Hershey Whatchamacallit

    Other current conflicts upon request

VOICE OVERS

    T.V.
    Radio
    Slide Films

FEATURE FILMS

    Joe Brooks' Production of "If Ever I See You Again", as Kevin

SPORTS

Archery	Roller Skating
Baseball	Skate Board
Basketball	Skiing
Bicycling	Soccer
Football	Street Hockey
Horseback	Tennis
Ping-Pong	

What he will never need from you is advice. Accept the fact that *he* is the expert here. He knows how to relax your child, how to select the best poses, and how many pictures to take. If you are hovering, making suggestions and fiddling with your child, you stand a good chance of alienating the photographer, upsetting your child, and absolutely ruining the shooting session.

Before you leave the photographer's, get a firm date for when the proof sheets will be ready. Stage Two of the picture-taking process is to take these printed but not enlarged pictures of every frame shot at the session to your agent. From them she will choose those to be enlarged. These enlargements are not the final choice, so expect to pay for more pictures than will ultimately be used.

When you have the enlargements, the agent will choose the picture for the head shot and those for the second side, if you're going with a composite, and arrange their layout. Here too, your advice is neither needed nor wanted. As one agent puts it, "If a mother picks the pictures, she's going to take the ones that will look best on the mantel. *I'm* going to choose the ones that the casting people will like."

The final stage of the process is to have the final choice reprinted for duplication. Usually this is done as a lithograph, and your agent will probably give you the name of a good printer. The first runoff should be about five hundred, half of which you give to the agent and half you keep to hand out on interviews.

"If you have a problem or question, feel free to call me. However, phone calls to check on whether I have an interview for your child waste your time and mine." Rest assured that the moment your agent has something to tell you, she will call. You may feel like a wallflower waiting for an invitation to the prom, but get used to it. Sooner or later that phone will ring, probably when you least expect it, and the voice at the other end will say, "I've got an interview for Johnny tomorrow at four. Got a pencil? . . ."

4

The Interview: Getting the Job

It's late in the afternoon of a perfectly normal day. The kids are out playing, the potatoes are peeled and Dinah's on the television singing the blues. The phone rings and you pick it up, your mind still on the meatloaf. The voice at the other end takes a moment to register. When it does—*Oh, my gosh, I can't believe it!*—panic buttons depress at once. "I have Josh's first interview set up for tomorrow at five."

Suddenly your just-another-day turns upside down. You're happy, you're nervous, you're excited, you're petrified. There are a million things to think of, to ask, to do, all racing through your mind at once. *How should I dress him, what shall I tell him, why did they finally pick him, what will they do with him, what's his competition, how can I help him, what will the other parents be like, will I have to do anything . . . and on and on . . . ?*

On and on your questions go, but the two-minute phone conversation with your agent barely satisfies them. She tells you where to go, what time to be there, and not to dress him in anything special. Nothing more—and certainly not enough to quell your churning stomach. This is trial by fire.

Rest assured that six months from now you'll look back at this

afternoon and smile at your worries. All those things which loom
so large today will be second nature by then. But that's no conso-
lation for what you feel now. So going on the principle that this
book is experience by proxy, let's take your questions one at a
time.

Why Did My Child Get Chosen for This Interview?

The answer is simple: Because he finally matched the character
and type breakdown for a commercial his agent was called for.

But to start at the beginning: This day, so very important to
you, is just one in a string of others for the people who make the
commercial. It begins in an ad agency, where a creative director,
an art director, and a copywriter combine their talents to create a
commercial.

They start with an idea, a concept, and work their way up until
they have before them the words and pictures that, put together
on film, are the commercial. At this point, however, it exists only
on paper, on storyboards, to be exact. A storyboard is a color car-
toon that, frame by frame, breaks down the action of the commercial.

Once the storyboards are completed and approved by the advertiser, the active work of producing the commercial begins.
First a production company is hired. Their responsibility is to find
and coalesce all the different components that will go into making
the paper storyboards a film commercial. Most production companies are headed by a director. He either works with just a small
staff of production aides and contracts out for the necessary technical crew or he maintains a large staff comprising all the personnel needed for producing a commercial.

Either way, at this stage, the next most important person is the
casting director. Whether she is an independent hired for that one
commercial, a staff member of the production company, or on the
staff of the advertising agency, the casting director's job is to put
together a roster of actors for each role in the commercial, all of
whom are potentially right for their characters.

Charlie Aiken, the Perfect Commercial Child.

With her blond hair and blue eyes, Danielle Helmer is a Beautiful type *(above, left)*. Darrin Gardiner is the most popular type, an all-American Character child *(above, right)*.

Paula Hoffman's red hair and freckles are just what commercial-makers want *(below, left)*. Chad Kraus's smiling photo jumps off the page at you—a perfect example of a head shot *(below, right)*.

A smattering of freckles, blond hair—Gary Lee Cooper has the "white bread look" of a true Character child. This is a good example of a typical L.A. composite.

Shelby Balik

BIRTHDATE: January 16, 1971
HEIGHT: 49"
WEIGHT: 50 lbs.
HAIR: Light Brown
EYES: Brown

Shelby is an enthusiastic and outgoing young performer! Her film credits are numerous and include roles on the CBS Movie of the Week "Son-Rise", the NBC Special "I Love You", "The Redd Foxx Special", T.A.T.'s "The Little Rascals", MGM's "Dog Soldiers" and Universal's "Storyteller". In addition, she has earned numerous television commercial credits, both on-camera and voice-over and has done many photographic assignments.

She loves to read, and enjoys being and talking with people. A lover of ballet, she has studied acting with Lois Auer. Shelby enjoys all little girl pursuits, particularly her favorites .... swimming and roller skatting.

As beautiful as she is, Shelby Balik is still considered a Character child because her features aren't perfect and her hair is dark.

Armed with a breakdown describing each character, the casting director puts out a call to agents, detailing the specifics of what the actors must look like and do. The agents then submit lists of clients who, in their opinion, best fit the descriptions. From those lists, the casting director chooses those few actors who she feels are right and assigns them times for interviews. This is known as prepping the commercial.

But let's be more specific. Remember the Shout commercial with Shelby Balik? Actually Shelby was just one of four children hired for that spot. Each was featured in a separate vignette: Shelby washed the dog, a small boy greased his skateboard, a second boy played soccer, and another little girl ate an ice cream cone.

The production company was Swanson Productions, Inc., headed by Glen Swanson. The casting director, contracted just for that job, was Sheila Manning.

Manning is a short, chubby woman with a whiplash sense of humor, a hearty laugh, and an all-encompassing warmth that makes her a favorite of most who know her. But it is her phenomenal memory and her ability to assess exactly what commercial-makers are looking for and then slot the perfect actor into the role that has made her one of the top casting directors in Los Angeles.

"Hi, Dorothy, it's Sheila. I've got a Shout commercial interviewing day after tomorrow. Two girls, two boys, eight-to-tens. Not too pretty and not too Character. They'll have some dialogue, and any laundry product will be a conflict. Can you call me back with names?"

Dorothy Day Otis, one of about eight agents Manning will call, is a tall woman, model thin, with a Dutch boy bob and a wide, warm smile. She turns to her files and starts pulling out kids in the eight-to-ten age range. "Actually, we do a span on ages," she explains. "We'll also take our really sharp seven year olds and even go to our small elevens. All that matters is that they *look* within that specified age range.

"But the problem here is defining what is actually 'not too pretty and not too Character.' So much of beauty is in the eye of the beholder. And as for Character, well, does Sheila mean that the client doesn't want freckles? Or doesn't want a child with shaggy hair? In cases like this, when the casting person isn't more specific, it's left to us to determine what she actually means.

"Okay, now I have a working list of kids who are in the age span and who I think fit the type. Then I look to see which ones can't handle dialogue and eliminate them. Once I've done that, I'm left with my short list. But there is one more consideration—the conflict. We keep a file card box that alphabetically lists all of our clients who have a commercial running. Now all I have to do is check the kids on my list to see if they have a laundry product commercial that is still current. Those who do can't be sent up for this one."

The more detailed the breakdown, the more elimination points there are for the agent in making up the list of submissions and the fewer possible kids there are for the spot. "Normally we submit very few names," says Otis. "We never go to the casting director with a whole slew of submissions. We're very selective and pick only those kids we think are absolutely right for the commercial. But even though casting directors know that, it doesn't mean we always get them to take all our kids. Let's say we submit five names. Sometimes the casting director will take all five and sometimes she'll take only one. If that happens and we think the other four are really great, we'll quickly, because her time is precious, explain why we feel so strongly about the other four. Generally, she'll listen to our reasons and, if she can, give us a couple more appointments. But sometimes she will say, 'Sorry, but I only have the one time slot available and I want to go with your best.'"

Back at Sheila Manning Casting, Manning and her assistant, Jody, look like they're playing a fast game of Hot Potato with the three telephones. "Don? I've got a breakdown on the Shout commercial . . . Sheila Manning Casting. Okay, you've got the names for me? . . . Iris? Sheila wants you . . . Sheila Manning Casting. Hold the line . . . I've got the breakdown . . . You've got names? . . . Hold the line . . ."

Jody's fingers are flying from hold button to talk button to dial buttons, a phone cradled on each shoulder, writing furiously name

after name on a yellow legal-size tablet. When Manning takes the
calls from agents with names, she makes her choices then and
there. If they come to Jody, the long lists are handed over for
Manning's scratch and scrawl culling of those she won't see.

Basically her decision is based on her memory of the kids submitted and her subjective opinion. She may think this child is too
pretty, that one is too Character. She may remember one as a kid
who freezes on dialogue, another as a child who is over-dramatic.
If the child submitted is one whom she has never seen before, there
is the decision whether to take a chance and possibly waste everyone's time with a kid who may be awful. Like so much of the entertainment business, there's a Catch 22 about seeing new people.
"We're always looking for new faces," says Manning. "But it
takes a good sales job and my trusting the agent to actually get me
to see a new kid."

Finally, the end of Manning's day arrives—somewhere about
7:30 P.M. Jody's last job is to type up the final list of kids who
will be interviewed for the Shout commercial. Each child has been
slotted into a specific interview time, five minutes apart, starting at
3:30 P.M.

Prepping is over. What's to come is two days of interviews, an
afternoon of callbacks, and, finally, the actual casting decisions.

How Should I Dress My Child?

All of the directives about dressing for an interview with an agent
are equally true about dressing for a commercial audition. Your
child should look clean, neat, and, above all, childlike. There are
kids, of course, who appear at interviews in tattered shorts and T-
shirts. And there are kids who flounce in dressed in their Sunday
best. And both these kinds of kids do sometimes walk out of an
interview with the job. However, with all that competition out
there, you would be well-advised to exercise some care in what
impression your child makes. And the best way to ensure that it's
a favorable one is to dress him the way commercial-makers prefer
to see kids dressed. So let's spell it out one more time: School

clothes or play clothes, well-fitting and flattering, are far and away the best choice.

There are times when your agent will suggest a special outfit. If the commercial is for a Little Lord Fauntleroy type, for example, she may ask that you put him in a suit. Or if he's out for the part of a baseball player, your agent might advise that he wear his Little League outfit. Her reasons are twofold: The child who is dressed for the part has a positive effect on the commercial-makers' ability to envision him in the role. And, too, the special clothing influences the child's behavior so that he not only looks but *acts* the part. What happens is that, for example, the child in the suit immediately strikes the commercial-maker as physically right for the role. And the prim and proper attitude that wearing a suit brings out in the child suddenly makes him emotionally right for the role.

There are also agents who are so specific about what their kids wear on interviews that it almost becomes a uniform. Iris Burton's girls, for instance, are easily identifiable at auditions because they're always the ones wearing jean overalls with their hair in pigtails. Obviously, this is Burton's attempt to ensure that her kids look like little girls no matter how old they are. However, it is a policy that can backfire. On one interview, after the fifth eleven-year-old had walked in with pigtails, the executive producer, Reed Springer, said, "I wish they'd stop sending all these kids in with their hair in braids. It's really getting boring. And a lot of these kids look just awful with their hair pulled back. I know the agents tell the mother to put the kid's hair in pigtails, but the mother should ignore them if she knows her daughter doesn't have the ears or face for it."

Don't misunderstand Springer. It isn't so much that he is anti-braids as he is pro the parent emphasizing his or her own child's individuality. After all, who knows better than you what flatters your child? But the agents' argument is: Who knows better than they what commercial-makers like to see? In the end, it's a narrow road you must tread between your opinion and the agent's, always keeping in mind that love can make you blind *but* agents aren't omniscient.

Perhaps even more important than what clothing your child actually wears or what hair style is his general grooming. I don't have to tell you to bathe and wash his hair the night before the interview; that should be a matter of course. But remember that you're going to this interview *after* school. That means after a day of getting hot and sweaty and rumpled and stained. So run a last minute muster before you set off for the interview. Wash his face, comb his hair, change his shirt, and pull up his socks. *And* check his hands. This may sound silly, but according to Springer, "Ninety-nine percent of these commercials show the kids' hands. It's inexcusable for a child to come to an interview with chewed, dirty nails!"

What Should I Tell My Child About the Interview?

Your approach to this should be no different from your preparation for interviews with agents. You're going to be walking the same tightrope between telling him enough to ensure his imagination doesn't go into high panic gear and not saying so much that you create pressure to perform or succeed.

How much detail you go into depends on your child's age and ability to comprehend. Certainly you want to tell him that he is going for a commercial interview, that there will be adults there, and that they will be asking him some questions and perhaps playing a game with him. You don't want to overload a preschooler's mind with talk of videotape equipment and picture-taking. But the older child should certainly be forewarned about that as well as any dialogue he may be expected to read.

The most important thing you can do after your basic explanation is to ask your child, "How does it sound to you?" Chances are the answer will be "Great!" But if there are any qualms, they'll surface now in questions. Answer them honestly, but don't overdo it. Compare the interview session to your home-movie-making, stress the short time he'll be talking to the adults, and *don't* tell him not to be nervous. If he isn't already, you'll tip him off to the fact that he should be. And if he is scared, you certainly won't forestall his fears by telling him he shouldn't have them. Reassure him that nobody expects anything other than that he just be himself and, most important, that there is no way he can do anything wrong.

Now is probably the best time to begin nipping the rejection bud before it even blooms by explaining to your child just why commercial-makers choose the kids they do. Myra Unger remembers that the photographer who took pictures for her kids' composites did the job for her. "He told Abe and Judy, 'When you go on an interview, there are times you will be chosen just because you look like another actor's brother or sister or child. That means that you were the right type for the job. And when you're not chosen, it's because you weren't the right type for that particular part. The producer may love you and think you could do a terrific job, but you're too small or not the age they want or your hair isn't the right color.'

"Abe and Judy kept that in the back of their minds and soon realized themselves that whether they got a job or not had nothing to do with how good they were and that it was something beyond their control."

No matter how far you choose to go in your explanations, remember that the worst thing you can do is make your child feel this interview is important to you. Whatever your feelings—hope, fear, elation, or determination—hide them. If you communicate any of that to your child, through word or action, you will, at the least, sow seeds of desperation to succeed that will only undermine his chances. Remember that how well your child does in these interviews depends almost totally on how calm and secure he feels. Your job, then, is to build a cocoon of confidence around him from which he can go out, strut his stuff to strangers, and return, feeling good about himself and what he has done.

What Happens Once We Get to the Interview?

First things first: You've arrived on time, without friends, family, or doting grandparents trailing along for the show. Expect to walk into a mini-madhouse. Most interviews have twenty or thirty children, spaced to arrive at five-minute intervals. Many of them also have adult actors interviewing at the same time. So add the kids plus their parents plus the adults, put them all in a small waiting room, and you have a real crowd.

Don't expect the casting director to be hanging around. He or she may pop in and out of the waiting room or have an assistant sitting there, or you may be on your own. The first thing to do is find the sign-in sheet.

These forms—on which you fill in appropriate blanks for your child's name, agent, Social Security number, time of interview, time you arrived, and whether this is the first, second, or third interview for this job—are required by the Screen Actors Guild. Union regulations dictate that an actor can only be interviewed for a commercial twice without being paid; the third interview requires a specified fee. The union also protects against commercial-makers keeping actors waiting around for hours, as has often happened in the past, by setting a time limit for the interviews. If an actor is kept waiting longer than an hour for any one interview, he must be paid.

These rules apply to all actors, no matter their age or even if they are not union members. The sign-in sheets are SAG's way of determining when the rules have been broken and what payment is due.

Obviously these sign-in sheets are of the utmost importance to you. If you don't see one sitting on a table, ask where it is. Or look for the group of parents and kids hovering in one spot, waiting for the pen.

Near the sign-in sheet you may also see a stack of fill-in-the-blank index cards. These are "size cards," appropriately named because they are for recording your child's height, weight, and clothing sizes (including shoe and hat). Size cards aren't required for every commercial interview; however, you should always be up-to-date on these vital statistics just in case.

If there is dialogue in the commercial, you'll see a scattered pile of duplicated scripts nearby. If you don't see them, don't assume there's no dialogue. Ask the casting director. Otherwise your child may be in for an embarrassing moment during the interview. "Honey, it's your responsibility to find out if there's a script as soon as you get to an interview," one annoyed director told a young girl. "If you're going to be a professional in this business, you'd better learn now that there are certain things expected of you. And getting a script and learning it *before* you come in here is one of them."

Actually it is a good idea to start training your child to find the sign-in sheet, size card, and script alone. As one casting director put it, "These are small things that may seem easier for the parent to do. But it's very important that the child learn they're his responsibility. After all, it is *his* interview. Besides, going through the whole procedure himself is a good way for him to gain confidence."

Paperwork dealt with, you're now faced with anywhere from a five-minute to an hour wait before your child is called in for his interview. How you spend that time is up to you. For some parents, it's an invaluable period of closeness and communication with their child. "I always bring a book we can read together or a game to play," says one mother. "I find that spending the time quietly with me helps keep my daughter relaxed and gives her a sense of security that carries through to the interview. And, too, our lives are so busy these days that it's often the only way we can spend time together alone."

Other parents let their children fend for themselves and use the wait for their own personal enjoyment. For busy parents with not a moment to call their own, that interview becomes a gift of time. They walk in, aim their child at the sign-in sheet, and immediately become immersed in a novel or crossword puzzle.

Then there are the parents who see the interview strictly as their social time. They're veterans of the commercial business, they meet each other time and time again on interviews, and lasting friendships have formed.

For the kids, the waiting time can be anything from a study hall to a play group. It's a great time to finish homework, color a picture, do a little daydreaming. Or as one little boy said when asked how he felt about interviews, "I love them. I get to see all my friends then and we play games and stuff like that."

Of course, on interviews where there is dialogue, the waiting room scene takes on a different tenor. There are lines to practice, and while some children prefer to study the script by themselves, many have their parent help them out—at least with the "big" words.

How Much Help Should I Give My Child With the Script?

As much as he wants. If he's an unsure reader, by all means go over it so that he is familiar with the words. But don't try to drum it in or play director and coach line readings. New York manager Sandra Firestone advises, "The parents should pace themselves with the children. If the child starts getting restless because you've been going over lines so much, just stop then and there. You've reached the point of diminishing returns.

"I learned that with my son. I found that after we'd gone over it two, three, four times, that was all he could take. He'd get worse and worse on it each time after that. It just doesn't help to drill the lines into a child. He's going to be totally unnatural when he goes into the interview."

There are some times when the casting director will specifically ask that you not help your child at all. Listen to the request; there is a good reason for it. On the Shout commercial, for example, the director wanted the children to say "Shout it out!" in as unrestrained and enthusiastic a manner as possible. So Sheila Manning told each parent, "Don't rehearse your child. We want her totally natural." But there were some parents who couldn't resist "helping."

Ten-year-old Tammy, her blond ponytail a perfect mass of curls, stood in front of the camera carefully listening to Manning's instructions. "Tammy, we're going to do a little improv. What's your favorite kind of ice cream?"

"Um, chocolate."

"Okay, you've just gotten a great big double-scoop chocolate ice cream cone. Boy, is it ever good! You start eating it. Yum, each lick is really terrific! You just love it! All of a sudden—wham! The ice cream falls off the cone and straight down the front of your dress. Right then, I'm going to go, 'Oh, no, what's your mom going to say?' And you answer?"

"Shout it out."

"That's right. Now, let's try it."

Tammy is perfect on the improv. Her concentration is total and you can almost see the ice cream. Her pink tongue flicks out, lick, lick, a real big lick—whoops! Her face falls as the ice cream plops off, plunging down, leaving an imaginary chocolate trail down her blouse.

"Oh, no, what's your mom going to say?"

Instantly the woebegone expression on Tammy's face is replaced by a cheesecake smile. She opens her eyes unnaturally wide, arching her eyebrows. *"Shout* it out!" You almost expect a tapdance to follow, but she holds her position, arms flung in the air, smile set, until Manning speaks.

From a little girl eating an ice cream cone, Tammy becomes a miniature actress giving a dramatic line reading. This is exactly what Manning didn't want to happen and there is no way she can get Tammy to relax on the line. Her mother's well-meaning rehearsal has set those inflections in Tammy's mind forever.

Needless to say, Tammy didn't even get a callback for the Shout commercial. Sad to say, it was her mother who sabotaged her chances. Unfortunately this happens fairly frequently. A parent's natural tendency is to want to "do it all" for the child. But you *must* remember: Commercial-makers are looking for the inherent ability in kids they cast; they'll never see it if the child is a mere puppet, manipulated by a parent.

Is There Anything I Can Do or Tell My Child to Help Him Get the Job?

Your child will win the part because he looks right, acts right, and is right for the role. If you start coaching him, you could tip the balance against his chances. Don't tell him what to do, what to say, or how to act. Don't pinch his cheeks for color, comb his hair even one last time, remind him to smile, shake hands, or stand straight.

Listen to Abe Unger and remember his words when you are tempted. "I think it's really bad for the kids when their mothers or fathers tell them what to do and how to do it. My mom used to fuss over me that way. But she stopped after my father took me on an interview and let me do everything the way *I* wanted to. He just said, 'Here's the comb. Fix your hair, read the lines, and let's go home.' He didn't even bother to check my clothes, and so I went into the interview with my shirt out, my dungarees messed, and my sneakers untied. *And* I got the job. After that, my mom left me alone."

Abe's mother left him alone, she says, because she suddenly realized that he knew better than she what to do when he got to the interview. You must trust your child. After all, knowing what to do in the interview is part of being commercially talented. Coached kids tend not to get the part; they lose their biggest asset: their naturalness.

Moreover, certain kinds of coaching will annoy, if not alienate, commercial-makers. During interviews for a doll commercial, there was a run of little girls who would slouch into the room with no expression on their faces and stand somber while the producer gave them instructions. But as soon as the camera started rolling, they would snap to attention, slap a kewpie doll smile on their faces, and bubble, *"Hi!* I'm Susie . . ."

After a time, the director sighed and said, "You know, every one of these kids has been told to say 'Hi!' in that really big, fakey way. They think it makes them stand out from the crowd. But if just one of them said something different, that's the one you'd remember."

What Happens When They Call My Child In?

This is it. Give him a kiss, a hug, and tell him to have a good time. *Now* you can give vent to your nerves, chew your nails, swallow the antacid. And wonder what's going on inside that inner sanctum, who is there—and why.

Almost always present is the director of the commercial. The director's job is to determine which kids have both the looks and talent to give a performance that goes along with his interpretation of the ad. Many directors are associated with or head their own production companies, and usually they are the ones who run the interview sessions.

Also part of the production company is the director's assistant, known as the producer. The producer's job is to oversee all aspects of production—casting, location, crew, and so forth—with a mind to the allocated budget for the commercial and the time schedule.

If the interviews are being videotaped, and most are, there will be a videotape operator standing amidst a tangle of wires, one eye to the camera, a finger on the Start button of the recorder. The videotape operator is either an employee of the casting director or the production company.

Those three people are almost always present at interviews. Sometimes there, in varying numbers, are the advertising agency personnel. Generally they include the art director and the copywriter, the creative team who designed and wrote the commercial in the first place. Their job is to ensure that the director's interpretation of their work and the performers chosen—along with the location, wardrobe, and all—truly represent the commercial they created.

Then there is the ad agency producer, whose responsibilities are similar to those of the production company's producer except, of course, they're from the agency's viewpoint. Another agency person who might be present is the account executive, the liaison between the people who make the product being advertised, the client, and the commercial-makers. The account executive is there to ensure that the casting conforms to the needs, prejudices, and preferences of the client.

At some interviews, the client sits in on the interviews as well. That doesn't mean the president of General Foods or chairman of Lever Brothers; rather, the client is the employee of the company who is responsible for the advertising of the particular product.

Since any or all of these people may be taking part in the interview process, the group greeting your child can number from one to eight or even more. However, whatever their number, the first thing they will ask for, after they say "hello, how are you?" is the child's composite. It is the single most important tool in casting. In the average interview session, where upward of twenty kids will be seen, the composite is the commercial-makers' memory. Even when the interviews are videotaped, the composites are still essential. Commercial-makers don't usually run these tapes when making their initial choices unless there is some question about the child's performance. They choose their short lists from the composites.

Yet it is amazing the number of children who will walk into an interview with no pictures, just excuses. "I forgot them." "My pictures were taken two years ago and I don't look the same, so I didn't bother to bring them." "My agent said you didn't need composites on this interview."

"I can't believe it," said one producer, tired of hearing these excuses repeated over and over. "I mean, where do these kids think they are? Those pictures are a kid's calling card *and* his advertisement. Without them—well, my rule is 'no composite, no remember.' A child would have to be incredible for me to even consider calling him back if he hasn't brought his composite."

Let that be a lesson. There were some talented children who never got noticed that day, simply because they hadn't had their pitcures with them.

What happens next, after your child hands over the composite, depends on what kind of commercial it is and whether the child is to be window dressing, star, or somewhere in between.

For some commercials, the director just wants, at least for the first interview, to take a brief look at all the children put up for it and then whittle down the list to those few who are right for the job. First interviews for Polaroid spots, for example, just consist of the casting director taking a snapshot of each child. The Polaroid people go through the photos and then choose those children whom they want to read for the commercial. If your child is on one of these look/see interviews, he'll be in and out before you even have time for a really deep breath.

In other commercials, particularly those with no dialogue, the director is looking for a certain personality type, a specific, often undefinable, quality. "This is a bite and smile commercial," said Glen Swanson as he interviewed kids to be in a Milk Board spot. "There's no dialogue, just reactions. It's a commercial that is supposed to make the viewer feel good, so what we're looking for is smiles."

Swanson's way of finding those smiles was to talk to the kids, loosen them up with a couple of jokes, then have them drink a cup of water. You see, it wasn't just a simple smile he wanted but one that really came across at the same time the child was drinking. That's no easy feat: A grin through a glass can look a lot like a leer.

The Milk Board auditions were also a good example of another type of interview. Call it the Put-Your-Money-Where-Your-Mouth-Is audition. When a commercial requires some sort of specialized ability from a child, be it athletic or other, the director will rarely take the agent's, parent's, or kid's word that the kid can pull off the stunt. If at all possible, the director will put the kid to the test.

One vignette Swanson was casting required a teenage boy and girl to roller-skate. The casting director had specified "roller skaters only—and they've got to be very good at it." She rented a dozen or so pairs of skates, and the hallway outside the interview room became a skating rink. As the kids appeared for their auditions, they were told to lace up and take a couple of practice runs. The results were telling. There were some kids who hadn't seen skates in years, others whose experience was the odd day out at the beach, and a couple, like one handsome fifteen-year-old called Peter, who had never had on skates until he heard about the interview. Then he went out, bought a new pair of skates, and spent the entire evening practicing,

How did it happen that these kids, who had sworn up and down they were veteran skaters, spent most of their interview splayed out on the floor? The sad but true fact is that agents, parents, and even the kids will lie about anything if it means a chance at a job. And sometimes with very sorry results.

Brian Crouch, another director who specializes in children's commercials, tells of the ten-year-old boy he cast in a commercial that took place in the snow. "I asked him if he had ever been on a toboggan before. 'Oh, sure,' he told me. 'I'm an all-around athlete and I've been in the snow lots of times.'

"When we got on location and that kid saw the hill and the sled, well, he panicked. I could see it happening, and I knew if I gave him even one time down the hill to try it out, I'd lose him. So I shot the scene without a rehearsal. But when we looked at the film that night, the fear in his eyes was so obvious we had to do an emergency casting session and get another kid."

It may be hard to believe any parent would place a child in jeopardy, but every director has at least one story like Crouch's. Some are even worse. And though they're sometimes told as cocktail party jokes, no one thinks they're funny. And everyone remembers who the kid is and who the parent is and who the agent is. So don't be tempted to join these "Tell-The-Man-You-Can-Do-Everything" parents—it's a very short way to cancel your child's career.

Another type of commercial interview is the one where the commercial-makers are looking for a certain interaction between a number of actors. The child has no dialogue—it's either a voice-over or he's the silent child of actor-parents with speaking roles—but he must look and act like a member of the family.

If you live in Portland, Oregon, or Cleveland, Ohio, you may remember a commercial for a window cleaning product that featured a brassy, ballsy maid called Sunny. That spot, a regional test market commercial, is a good example of a family-oriented ad where the child is more or less window dressing.

Associates & Toback was the production company, and it was in their Hollywood offices that the actors, male and female, old and young, gathered for the interview. There were four characters in the spot: a husband and wife, thirtyish, attractive; an older character actress to play Sunny, the maid; and a little boy, the son, aged six to eight.

In groups of four, the "family" matched by coloring, the actors disappear into the dark office where Norm Toback, the director, and three ad agency people are slouched around a table. The room is a jumbled mass of cushy Naugahyde chairs and videotape paraphernalia. The rough wood-paneled walls are hung with award plaques, family photos, posters, and all manner of memorabilia that Toback has collected in his award-winning career.

He's not that large a man, but he gives the impression of being bearlike, with his shaggy hair and pepper-and-salt beard. Probably there's the actor somewhere in his background. He colors his conversation with a wide variety of theatrical accents, accompanied by appropriate gestures and expressions. The effect is funny and, especially for the actors, comforting. You can see their nervousness seep away as Toback explains the set-up.

He takes particular time with each of the little boys. "You're sitting with your mom and dad at the breakfast table when there's a knock at the door. You open it—just pretend there's a door there—and in bursts this really weird woman. She'll give her line and ruffle your hair, and you look at her like she's really, really crazy. Then move to the side. Wait a couple seconds and then walk around to behind your father. I want the two of you to look at each other like 'Who's this crackpot woman?' I don't want you to say anything, just react to her and to whatever she's saying."

Each family has a chance to rehearse the scene several times. Toback coaches them, guiding them toward the interpretations he wants. When he decides that they're as ready as they can be, he says "Okay, that's good. Let's get it on tape now."

The start of every taped interview, no matter what the commercial, is the "slate." This is where the actor, looking straight into the camera, gives his name, his agent's name, and, with kids, his age. The slate is used purely for identification during the casting. Out of a long afternoon of videotaping, it's the only way of knowing who is who when the time comes to review.

This is not a particularly difficult scene for a child to do, particularly with Toback there giving all the help he can. "C'mon, Billy, let's have more of a reaction when Sunny comes through the door. This lady is nuts! And you're just standing there like she's nothing special." "Look at your dad, Sam, not at the camera. Make believe you're really at the breakfast table. How do you act with your own mom and dad—kind of warm and loving? That's how you should be now. . . ."

It seems as if there are two kinds of kids trying out for this job. Either they're stolid, standing without any discernible emotion on their faces, or they're wild, darting in and out of the scene, doing everything short of waving the proverbial hankie in front of the adults.

One little boy—Gene the Great, he proclaims during the slate —has flaming red curly hair and an obnoxious manner unrivaled by any of the others. He tweaks his nose, he waves his hands, he bellows lines he's not even supposed to be saying, and he pulls rubberband faces at the camera. Talk about scene-stealers! But unbeknownst to him the cameraman slides his focus just short of Gene's face. Later, when the tape is reviewed for casting, Gene the Great is only a waving finger, occasionally floating into frame.

This parade of parents and kids has been going on for about two hours when a cute kid, pleasant and calm, with a smattering of freckles and unruly blond hair, walks in. It isn't so much his looks that make him stand out as his quiet air of—well, of professionalism. Somehow he instinctively slots himself into the scene the adults are playing: a typical family at the breakfast table. When Sunny knocks at the door, a look of curious surprise comes over his face. As she bounds in, the boy's eyes say "Who's this crackpot?" to his father. And when the cleaning product does, albeit in pantomime, a good job, you couldn't imagine a child more pleased with the results.

The boy's name? Gary Lee Cooper. "It isn't only that Gary was far and away the best of the kids we saw today," Toback later says. "But also that I've worked with him before, and I know that whatever I ask him to do when we're shooting the job, he'll do."

The casting director isn't surprised when she's told to book Gary for the shoot. "I knew he'd get it," she says. "He was the only kid I sent in there from my A list of children. The rest were all B's. They're adequate for the part but not excellent."

The most difficult of commercial interviews is the one where children are principals, with lines and action. To give a better idea of what is involved for a child in such a commercial, let's follow an actual commercial through casting and shooting. The name of the toy company and details about the doll have been changed, but the specifics of producing the commercial are real. One Christmas the Dollie Toy Company brought out two new dolls. The Spy Sisters they were called: Dawnlight and Blackstar. They had masses of hair and statuesque—in scale, of course— bodies. They came dressed in tight-fitting patent leather army fatigue tops and shorts and their bodies held a secret mechanism: when their legs were pushed up and out into a deep knee bend, their arms sprang up into a fierce karate pose.

The Spy Sisters were designed for an older girl, one whose role models were strong, liberated women. So the commercial was written to appeal to that type of child, with the two girls appearing in it mirroring the dolls as much as possible. Physically this meant that the child activating Blackstar had to have long, black hair like the doll's; the one handling Dawnlight was to be a red-head. And not only did they have to be that very specific type and have that very specific coloring, they also had to be good actresses: There were lines in this commercial, difficult ones, and action.

Normally Dollie casts very beautiful, innocent six- to eight-year-olds for their doll commercials. But the call that was put out for this one was for "eight- to ten-year-olds, long hair, one brunette, one redhead—you can send blondes but make sure they'll put a rinse on their hair. No sweet types; we want gutsy nymphets. In fact, think Barbarella as a preteen. And I only want kids who can handle dialogue; they've got to be good readers!"

The casting director knew it wouldn't be an easy commercial to cast. By the time she was finished, she had contacted almost every agent with children in Los Angeles. It took three days in all, and over seventy girls were seen.

The initial interviews were a winnowing out process in which the producer, Reed Springer, was looking for four things: Did the child have the right look? Was she animated? How well did she move the doll? Could she take direction?

Because there were so many kids to see, many of whom would not be at all right for the role, Springer decided not to bother with the dialogue until callbacks, where only those girls with the greatest potential would appear and more time could be spent with each. For these first interviews, the kids were brought in in pairs—one dark, one fair—and only five minutes was allotted to each set.

In order to determine in such a short time which kids had the four qualities he was looking for, Springer devised an improv for them. "We're going to pretend we're having a fashion show," he says, handing a doll to one of the girls. "I want you to use your imagination and move her around just like you think a real model would move. And you're going to be the photographer," he gives a toy camera to the other child. "You're going to walk all around taking pictures of the doll. But I don't want you to just snap away. Be like a real photographer and direct her. Tell her where you want her to go and how you want her to move. Okay? Everyone understand? We'll do it first this way and then we'll switch roles."

There's a brief rehearsal before the girls slate and the taping begins. After a short time, it becomes obvious that Springer's improv is the perfect test—and not too many girls are passing it. "Jennifer has an okay look but she's too somber. She's not animated at all." "Ann's too roundfaced and heavy for this. We don't want any angelic types." "Karen's a real klutz with the doll. All she did was bounce it around." "I like Candi, but we need someone more aggressive and energetic." "Lynn moves the doll well, but there's something funny about her neck." "Susan's got the right look and she's animated enough, but I think she's too mature. We don't want to go too old." "Andi's cute but she's too young." "Beth is too ladylike." "Barbie's too sweet."

On and on it goes. Two piles of composites are growing on the table in front of Springer. The smallest stack is of those kids Springer wants to see again; the larger one is of those he doesn't. But even those girls in the select callback pile are not perfect. "But," says Springer, "my rule of thumb is, if they have even a bit of what I want physically, they're worth a callback. Maybe they're

not animated because they're intimidated by the other kid. You
know, it's hard for a real tall child to be with a tiny one. And a
talker can really cow a kid who's a little shy. So if I think maybe
that's what has happened, I'll see them again. Then I'll put them
with someone else in the callbacks and hope the new chemistry
will produce better results."

Callbacks

Even so, there are only twenty of the seventy girls asked back for
another audition. And it is in these callbacks that the real work
begins. There are now six people crowded into the interview
room: Springer, his assistant producer, the ad agency's creative
director, the production company's producer, the director, and the
tape operator. The videotape machine has been set up for both
color and sound. The scripts, all-important now, have been duplicated and are stacked out in the waiting room next to the sign-in
sheet.

By 3:15, the girls are beginning to arrive. As soon as they sign
in, the casting director hands them their scripts and, because the
lines are tricky, specifically asks the parents to help all they can.

The day is hot and sunny, the waiting room small, and the
walkway outside the casting offices seems the coolest place to
work. Through the open windows wafts a many-voiced mumble as
the kids practice their dialogue: *"En garde!* Defend, Dawnlight
. . . Make ready to greet our foe! . . . Position! Advance, Blackstar . . . The enemy is near!" Perhaps these lines don't seem
that difficult, but they are meant to have a strong but dreamy
interpretation. When you combine that with the physical activity
involved in activating the doll's leg mechanism—well, you have
something akin to the old rub-your-stomach, pat-your-head trick.

Springer and the rest are oblivious to the noise; they're running
through their game plan. The ten sets of girls have been scheduled
for fifteen-minute interviews. This will, hopefully, be enough time
not only to assess their looks and energy but, more important, to

allow the director, Jordan Bernstein, to work with each girl in an effort to draw some sort of performance from her.

No one in the room thinks the job ahead will be easy. So far they have only seen two girls who are physically right for the roles. Unfortunately, both had been sticklike and mute in the first interviews. "If you can goose them up, we may be able to go with them," Springer tells Bernstein. "If not . . ." If not, they'll have to lower the physical standards and cast on talent.

It's 3:30. Time to begin. One last word to the tape operator. "We don't want to waste time or tape with kids that we can see right away aren't going to work. So watch my hands. If I give you the thumbs down, don't bother to tape that kid. We'll just let her run through it and she'll never know the difference."

The first two girls are shown in. Smiles all around. "Hi, Mary. Hi, Hannah. We're glad you could come today." The procedure that will be followed all afternoon is set: greet the girls, explain the scene, rehearse, slate, tape, and thank you. But for Mary and Hannah, it's abbreviated: Bernstein's thumb is pointing down. "Mary wasn't bad," he says in the postinterview critique. "She was kind of blah, but I suppose I could have gotten her energy up —a little."

The next two are Lynn and Diane. Both are experienced commercial kids; both are good actresses. But Lynn's a tomboy, togged out in tennis whites, and Diane is dressed straight out of Vogue, with a slit skirt and sky-high heels. Their look may not be right but their talent is, and Bernstein works hard with them.

He's a rotund man with wispy hair and a large, creased face, dressed in gray slacks and a matching gray sweater. He chuckles a lot, mostly at his own jokes, flip one-liners that bespeak a caustic wit. But the kids don't hear that; they see him as a jolly man who calls them "Picklepuss," teases, and makes them giggle.

It's all part of his work technique, relaxing them, "goosing" them up, giving line readings in a squeaky falsetto. Lynn and Diane swing right along with Bernstein's mood, and when they finally leave, after their full fifteen minutes, Springer says, "I think Lynn is my second choice. We'll have to do something with her

hair; it's too much of a curly mop. And we'll work around her
teeth—they're crooked—but she does have that quality we're
looking for."

"Both of them are strong theatrically," says Bernstein. "And
they're intelligent and seem like nice kids. But don't you think
Lynn is a little ethnic-looking?"

"No, I think she can pass. How about Diane?"

"She's a really good actress. Did you hear how she picked up
on that 'enemy' line?"

"Okay," says Springer. "Let's put them both in for second
choice." Their composites make the first in the Yes pile.

Next up: Beth and Liz. Bernstein's eyes roll up and his thumb
goes down as Beth starts her slate. Not that she isn't a pleasant little girl, but her pug nose and freckled face are far too Character
for this commercial.

Liz, on the other hand, is a California surfer type: tall, blond,
slim, and sexy. Bernstein sees some hope there. "Okay, picklepuss, let's try and give it all you have."

Liz whips around and narrows her eyes. "I am *not* a picklepuss,"
she hisses.

"Boy, if she wasn't so nasty, she'd be good," Springer says in
the critique.

"Aw, that doesn't really bother me," laughs Bernstein. "But
don't you think she's a little too chubby in the face?"

"You can probably censure that by going in tight in the close-
up," answers Springer. "But I hate her hair, the way it falls in her
face. And she's lazy and doesn't stand up straight. Still, she is
striking and she does have that older face that we're looking for.
But she sure is one spoiled little girl, and I question whether we
can take four hours of her. But . . ." He tosses her composite
into the Yes pile.

As the next two girls walk in, Springer whispers to Bernstein,
"These are the two I told you about, Jordy. Neither of them can
act but they really have the best look we've seen."

Erin has thick black hair; Joy's is deep, rich red. Both of them
are nothing short of gorgeous. And, with the script, nothing short
of awful. In fact, Erin is hopeless, a beautiful lump of a child.

"C'mon, look alive," Bernstein pleads playfully. "We'll bite your leg if you don't get it right. Okay, we won't bite your leg, but just don't sound like you're dead."

Nothing works. It's not that Erin doesn't try; she cranks the lines out in her harsh, grating voice, never altering her expression —what there is of it—despite Bernstein's line readings.

He moves on to Joy, who, by comparison, offers some hope. Bernstein moves in. "Do the line like it's a miracle what happens to the doll."

A miracle. Joy's eyes bug out, her voice leaps up a register. This, someone has obviously told her, is how you show surprise..

"My God," says Bernstein, enthusiastically. "You have improved."

"Well, she *did* get better," says Springer afterward. "She improved 100 percent."

"Sure," snaps back Bernstein. "And that puts her up to a minus three. If we had an easy shooting schedule, I'd say okay. But we don't and I wouldn't want to take a chance with her. Too bad, though; she has a nice look."

"Well, let's throw them in the hopper for third choice anyway," says Springer.

"How about fifth instead? Look, Reed, we have our second choices, Lynn and Diane. And we have Liz. Frankly, I'd rather work with Liz than Erin or Joy. So she's a smart aleck. At least, that gives me something to work with. Let's make her fourth, hold third place open and, if we must, put Erin and Joy fifth."

It's 4:30 now and there's some quiet nail-chewing going on among the commercial-makers: Not one kid has been that great yet, and what if none are? Bernstein's high energy level is on the wane. As the next girls walk in, there is nothing outstanding about them to give anyone a boost. "Okay, Blondie, you go first," Bernstein says to the smaller child, Sherry. He sinks lower in his chair and points his thumb at the floor.

When it's Mona's turn, Bernstein barely looks at the pretty little girl with soft, dark eyes and long, brown hair. Until she begins to read. Then everyone sits up straighter. Her "The enemy is near" has a mysterious air to it, her voice is deep, her face dreamy.

Bernstein tapes her twice without a word. And when she leaves, "Not bad, aye? Mona for Blackstar."

"She sure softens the Barbarella and chains," Springer agrees.

"The other one, Sherry, she's a mercy killing, but Mona—wow! Now maybe with Lynn we have a number one choice."

Everyone is breathing easier now and even when the next two girls are immediate thumbs down, no one makes a comment. But with the seventh set comes Shanee, blond, pretty, and enthusiastic. "She's a good little actress," says Springer. "And she really comes across on camera. Let's put her with Mona for first choice."

The next two girls, Nancy and Chris, become the second-choice group. "We're starting to get some nice problems now," says Bernstein. "Do you like Nancy better than Mona for first?"

"No, I don't think she has Mona's charm. Let's keep our order the way it is until we make the final decisions."

Only four more girls to see and out of the next two comes one hopeful, Judy. She's another blond, California-pretty kid, and she has an intriguing, husky voice. "She was an honest 'fair,'" laughs Bernstein. "Her scene partner was an honest 'forget it!' Seriously, Reed, what would you give Judy. Out of one to ten, a four, maybe?"

"No, she was worth more than that, Jordy."

"Okay, a four and three quarters."

Finally, the last two girls: Kara and Ann. No one pays much attention to Ann; she's a definite thumbs down. But Kara! She is so bright, so enthusiastic, so good with the lines that Bernstein doesn't have to say a word. Except when she's gone. "That's it. That's our other number one."

The Final Decision

What happens next is called by some the "dog and pony show." Springer pins the composites of the eleven kids in his Yes pile onto the cork wall. Even though they've spent time already discussing the possible choices and their order, no final decisions have been made.

So now it's mix and match time: "Try Shanee with Nancy for the second choice. No, that won't work; Nancy's too small for Shanee . . . How about Nancy and Chris for second, like we said before? . . . Yeah, but Shanee has to work with someone. . . . Okay, we've got one too many, then. Who can we drop? . . . How about Lynn. Isn't she the one that's too much out of the realm looks-wise? . . . No, but why don't we do this: Put Shanee and Judy as third. And dump Liz. I'm bored with her. She really *is* a picklepuss—as well as a real pain in the ass . . . Okay, how does that look to you now?"

Ultimately, the choices come out exactly as they did in the callbacks. Mona and Kara are the first choice, Nancy and Chris are second, Lynn and Diane are third, with Erin and Joy fourth. And Shanee becomes the backup girl.

On commercials with kids in principal parts, a backup child is almost always hired. The backup serves two functions: He or she is present on the set just in case something goes wrong with one of the children actually doing the commercial. Kids do get sick, ornery, or overtired. And, unlike adults, you can't force a recalcitrant child to work. Without a backup child to step into the star's shoes, an entire shooting day could be lost. Not that it happens very often, but it's cheap insurance—just a session fee to the backup kid—that most commercial-makers think well worth it.

In California, where the number of hours a child can work is strictly determined by law, the backup child is often used as the hand model. The director will save those scenes that show only the child's hands for last. That way, if he has used up his time with the principal child before he has finished shooting, the backup child can be brought in and no one will be the wiser.

Although these choices are final in the minds of Springer and his production team, the ultimate decision is always the client's. At some dog and pony shows, the client is right there, arguing for his favorites along with the rest of the team. When the client is in a different city and no representative is present at the interviews, tapes of the final choices are sent to the client's home office for his decision.

Dollie Toys prefer to make their decision at a preproduction meeting held at the advertising agency. The first half of the prepro is strictly agency personnel. Springer tacks composites of the four sets of girls to a bulletin board. "Originally, we went looking for girls who had the right look and hair color," he explains. "But we only found two. And they just couldn't hack the copy. Jordan tried to pull a miracle with them, but neither had the energy level that we needed. So rather than going with nymphets, we went with two very pretty girls with lots of hair. They're both excellent actresses. They articulate well, and they follow directions. They're exactly the same height—which we were looking for—and both have good teeth and hands."

The Dollie people hear none of this; the connotations are too negative for the ad agency people, who want to go in with a "Look at these great kids we've found!" attitude. When the two Dollie representatives are welcomed into the meeting, they are met with a united front.

Springer switches off the lights and punches on the videotape machine. The tape has been edited so that Mona's and Kara's interviews, although nowhere near each other in reality, follow one after the other, with the remaining seven girls trailing in succession.

The few objections from the Dollie people are quickly answered. "That Kara looked too serious," said one.

"She isn't, though," said Springer. "It was just the direction we gave her."

"I'm worried about her teeth."

"Her teeth are fine. There's a shadow on the tape that makes them look prominent. They're not, but you'll just have to take my word for it."

"I like that Nancy. She has really great eye expression."

"Yes, but we feel she's too young. Remember we're going for the older child."

"Their hair isn't really like we thought it would be; are you going to do anything about that?"

"We'll have a hairdresser on the set. Besides, you really can't tell from her composite, but Kara is like a little Farrah Fawcett. And we'll play that up."

"Wel-l-l, can we run through the tape once more?"

"Sure."

"Okay, we'll go with your choice: Kara and Mona."

Kara and Mona won't know they've gotten the job until the next day. There is a specific pecking order for giving the booking. The producer or director tells the production company, who tells the casting agent, who tells the agent, who tells the child.

Don't try to second guess what will happen by prompting your child for every word the interviewers said. If he wants to tell you what went on inside the room, he will. Sometimes he won't even know. One little boy, for example, tells his mother after every audition, "Gee, they were really nice to me. I'm sure I got that job." He's been wrong every time.

The kindest, most helpful thing you can do now is smile at your child, take him by the hand, and lead him off for a special treat just with you. The interview you have no control over, but afterward your support and love can make all the difference.

If you go light on the interview and strong on the love, you will ensure that your child is never spooked by auditions and that he never feels he's failed or disappointed you. And after all, this is just another day, remember? The interview is just another interview, remember? And if the phone never rings, it doesn't matter, remember?

When it does ring, now or in the future, and it's your agent with good news, that's the time to sit back and applaud: Congratulations! Your child is now a real commercial kid.

5
The Shoot: Doing the Job

The second phone call: It may come a day, a week, a month after that first call. It might follow your child's third, thirteenth, or thirtieth interview. You may know it's coming, because your agent has a "feeling," or it might be out of the blue. Whatever the circumstances, that first booking call is bound to make you feel proud and excited, and determined to do everything you can to help your child succeed.

Those first two emotions are fine reactions—indulge yourself. But the last, that strong-jawed resolve that you will do everything possible to ensure that your child gives a master performance and is so charming, so adorable on the set that he'll be hired again and again and again—that you can just forget.

You might as well know right now that you neither can nor should have any part in the shooting day that is to come. In fact, if you so much as roll your eyes or clear your throat, you are liable to incur the wrath of the commercial-makers. They don't want you coaching your child on his lines; they'll do it. They don't want you fixing his hair; they'll do it. They don't even want you pulling up his pants or straightening his tie. If any of that needs to be done, they'll do it.

You're on that set either because the law says you have to be or because your child is too young to be left alone. If you step out of line, which means into the commercial-makers' territory, you may well be asked to leave. It's not unheard of, and it's happened more than once because a mother won't stop brushing her child's hair or pinching his cheeks for color or any other seemingly innocuous act. Accept this fact: To the commercial-makers, you are a necessary evil. And accept another: Your only role from now on is simply that of chauffeur.

Your first bit of running will be, if your state is one which requires a work permit for kids acting in commercials, to gather all the necessary data—birth certificate, doctor's examination, school reports—and apply for the permit. Your agent will fill you in on all that is needed.

The agent also will tell you where and when to go for the wardrobe call, and what to bring. For some commercials, the kids are kitted out in costumes specially bought or created. In others, the child's costume is straight out of his own closet. And sometimes it's a combination of the two.

That was the case with the Spy Sisters commercial. To play up the sexy, strong image as well as echo the dolls' outfits, it was decided early on that Kara and Mona would wear leotards in the same colors as the dolls' clothes. It seemed a relatively easy task to find one gold and one midnight-blue leotard. After all, disco dancing was at its height, and every store seemed to have some portion of their stock devoted to shiny Spandex leotards in all manner of styles. However, when Doris Lynn, the producer of the spot, went on her shopping trip, she discovered that shiny, sexy body tops are not made in sizes to fit ten-year-old girls. Most manufacturers hadn't gotten past the rough knit, loose-fitting leotards in pale pink, pale blue, and pale yellow for kids that age.

When Mona and Kara arrived for their wardrobe fitting at 5:00 P.M. the day before the shoot, Doris Lynn greeted them with her compromise purchase: The leotards *were* shiny Spandex, but the blue was more baby than midnight and the gold was a less than bright yellow. However, they fit tightly and Lynn was soon satisfied with them and with the neutral slacks the girls had brought with them.

One of the benefits of having your child wear his own clothes in a commercial is that he gets paid for it. Not a princely sum, but enough to cover cleaning, wear, and tear. For that reason, many parents of commercial kids build a separate wardrobe for their children to wear at work. Slacks in basic colors, sports shirts and blouses, jeans, T-shirts, party wear, and swim suit should cover most calls. And shoes. It is rare that commercial-makers will provide footwear, so it is wise to ensure that your child has casual shoes, sneakers, and dress shoes, all in good repair, to wear on the job.

Although your agent will tell you where the commercial is being shot, you should check on specific directions at the wardrobe call. In fact, since many commercials are filmed at private homes, leased specially for the day, the production company often draws up maps to ensure that no one gets lost.

The Spy Sisters commercial was shot in the backyard of a home high in the Hollywood Hills. By the time the girls and their mothers arrived at 8:00 A.M., the crew had already been there for an hour, setting up their lights, cameras, and all the other technical paraphernalia the film business is never without.

However, just because the crew started setting up ahead of time doesn't mean they were ready to start shooting at eight on the dot. It's always the intention of film-makers to keep to their shooting schedule, but it rarely works out. It's not that crews are slow or lazy. It's just that somehow cameras have a way of needing new parts, cables twist and fray, sets sit too precariously, and lights break in transit.

The first order of any day on a commercial set is, for the actors, paperwork. There are contracts to be signed and W-4 income tax forms to be filled out. For these three California kids, there is also the work permit to be handed over. The teacher/welfare worker, Alice, is already waiting for them in a small bedroom in the house that has been designated the "schoolroom." California law also requires that three hours of the girls' eight hours on the set be devoted to schooling. Each has brought a day's worth of work from her own school—this, too, is state-mandated—which Alice collects along with their permits.

Between the three hours of school, one hour of play, and four hours devoted to the business of making the commercial, the day ahead is well mapped out for Mona, Kara, and Shanee. Right now they're off to wardrobe, another room in the house where they'll change into their "costumes" and have their hair fixed and any necessary makeup applied.

For their mothers, however, this is just the beginning of an aimless eight hours. They find a quiet spot to sit, under a tree, close enough to the action to be able to watch, far enough from it to be out of the way. It's easy to tell which mother belongs to which child. Dark-haired Mona's mom is a short, chunky woman with a homey face creased in smiles. Shanee's mother is the thin one with the same blond hair and fine, fair complexion as her daughter. And Kara's mom is an intelligent-looking, attractive woman who has passed onto her daughter her firm jaw and athletic build.

Since Mona and Shanee go to Saturday acting classes together, their mothers know each other well. The two of them sit close, chatting about interviews and agents, jobs done and jobs lost. Kara's mother has placed her folding chair a bit to the side. Occasionally, she joins in the conversation but for much of the day she is engrossed in a novel she is reading.

Now see the scene: The backyard has a glorious, panoramic view of the San Fernando Valley, today untainted by smog. The yard is lush green, grassy with almost tropical borders of palm trees and succulent plants. Smack in the middle of the grass is a gray wooden platform, walled in half by a swath of white gauzy cloth.

On one side, the smaller of the two, the camera has been set up on a dolly, a structure resembling an Erector Set, which can crane the camera up and down. There is a seat on the dolly and on it sits Jordan Bernstein, peering through the camera's viewfinder, analyzing the setup of the sandbox where the commercial's action will take place. Bernstein is not only director for this shoot; he is also the cameraman. Sitting next to him is the production assistant, PA in commercial lingo, whose most prominent prop is a large stopwatch hanging from a cord around her neck. A commercial is written for a specific period of time; this one is thirty seconds. Each segment of the spot, each separate action, is allotted a definite amount of time within the whole. One of the PA's jobs is to time each take so the director can tell whether he has to speed that action up or slow it down.

The other two principals of the production team, Reed Springer and Doris Lynn, are standing nearby. Springer is now the creative coach as part of his overall effort to ensure that the final commercial does, in fact, represent as exactly as possible what the creators of the commercial intended. Doris Lynn, who is contracted for this commercial by Seven West, the production company, is acting as the general caretaker of all the technical aspects of the shoot. She's the smoother of tempers, the facilitator of lighting changes, set alterations, and so forth.

While the serious work of commercial-making will take place on the small side of the platform, the larger side is devoted to eating. Film sets of any sort are notorious for the huge amounts of food that are constantly available, and this one is no exception. A long table has been set up, bearing massive canisters of coffee, boxes of doughnuts and sweetrolls, bagels, cream cheese and lox. By nine o'clock, however, the table looks like the tail end of a Jewish wedding: The full complement of ad agency personnel plus the Dollie representatives plus the crew, the kids, and various other onlookers have had their fill.

Suddenly from the working side of the platform comes Jordan Bernstein's voice. "Okay, we're ready to begin," he tells Doris Lynn. "Let's bring out the dolls and the girls."

The first sequence to be filmed, frames one through four, is an establishing shot of the two girls playing with the dolls. This shot is called a legal shot. It is necessary, because the commercial will show the dolls in a desert setting. The legal shot lasts two and a half seconds, which will establish that the dolls aren't really in a desert, just in the hands of two average little girls playing in an average backyard sandbox.

Legal considerations are probably more important in filming

commercials to be shown to kids than any other type. And it is
these considerations that make this Dollie shoot so difficult. For
instance, the child and the doll can never be shot looking directly
into the camera. That would connote a hard sell, forbidden in
children's commercials. Rather the commercial must be shot so
that it is clear to all the kids watching that they are just looking in
on a scene of the two children playing.

The action begins with the two girls holding their dolls aloft,
and then wafting them downward as if they were floating from a
helicopter. The dolls will come into the shot together, landing
in the sandbox, each on one precise spot, called a mark. The final
frame of this segment will be a close-up of the dolls, the "beauty
shot," showing, obviously, how beautiful the dolls are.

In the final print of the commercial, when it's actually shown
on TV, there will be music at the opening and a single female
voice chanting, "Enter the Spy Sisters . . . Dawnlight . . .
Blackstar . . ." with an off-camera announcer stating, "Each sold
separately." But these sound elements will be put in later in
postproduction. Right now it's "Quiet on the set. Girls in position.
Okay, mark it . . ."

"Marking" is an unfamiliar term for a very familiar action.
Think back to all the movies you've seen where there's a scene
showing an old-time film being shot. When the director would
bellow "Action!" through his megaphone, a small blackboard
with white chalk writing on it would be shoved in front of the
camera. Then two disembodied hands would bang the hinged
clapper stick on top down against the blackboard. The name for
that board is, appropriately, a clapstick board, and it is still used
today for marking, or slating (because the early boards were
made of slate), the shot. The chalk writing is pertinent information used for identification purposes during editing, such as the
name of the commercial, the director and/or cameraman, the film
roll number, the number of the scene or sequence, and the take.

The take number is the one that was always being erased by
that disembodied hand so the next higher number could be
chalked in. "Take" in film-making is really another name for
"try"; every time one specific piece of action is filmed, it's called a

take. Because it usually requires many takes before a director is satisfied—when he calls out "cut and print"—there has to be some means of identifying which take is which in the many feet of film shot for each sequence. So for every take, there's a mark, a visual cue on the film that corresponds to a running written record the PA keeps of the timings and the director's comments for each take. That way when the film has been printed and is being edited, the editors can go through the PA's notes and see, for instance, that the only takes that came in on time in that particular sequence were, say, numbers five, twelve, and twenty-four. And of those three, twelve was the one where Kara stumbled on her line and twenty-four was the one Jordan Bernstein liked best. They then can quickly run through the film and look only at take twenty-four.

When sound is involved in filming, as with this commercial, the mark has another purpose, which is where the clapstick on top comes in. The film is shot and the sound is recorded on two different machines. When it comes to editing them, the film strip and the sound tape must be synchronized so that when the actors' lips move, the correct sounds come out. In order to synchronize the film and tape they must be edited together, so that they both begin at precisely the same moment; if they're off by even a single frame of film, it will be obvious. When marking the shot, the moment when the clapsticks come together is recorded on both the film and the sound tape. When the editor sees the clap in a single frame of film and hears it on the tape, he knows he has his sync point.

After "Camera, mark it" come just two more directions: "Standby" and that old familiar "Roll 'em." When sound is included on that particular shot, there's an additional cue, which comes from the sound man: "Speed," he says, meaning that the tape recorder is going at full speed, ready to record.

But that will come later in the shoot; this sequence is silent. Right now it's "roll 'em." There is, it turns out, only one real difficulty with this sequence. The girls tend to dive-bomb rather than float when dropping the dolls down. The problem seems insurmountable—how do you teach kids grace in such a short time?—until Reed Springer hits on a solution. "Moon River," that dreamy song from *Breakfast at Tiffany's,* has just the right tempo and is of just the right mood to get the girls to glide the dolls down. So frames one through four are easily shot with Springer crooning ". . . wider than a mile . . ." from the sidelines.

The second sequence, frames four through eight, are much more difficult, because they involve the activation of the doll. Not only is this a tricky manipulation for ten-year-old hands to handle, but it must be done "just so." The fingers have to be in a special position. "When you hold the doll on camera," Springer tells the girls, "don't grab it around the waist. Take hold of it really far down on the legs with just your two fingers. And remember, these dolls are supposed to be people. They have to be held in an upright position all the time."

There's yet another consideration to this sequence: the legal one. To satisfy Federal Communications Commission requirements that the commercial show exactly how the doll is activated, the camera must clearly pick up the child pushing the doll's legs up and out. But there is a question of taste here. Activating the doll is not the most delicate procedure to display. The problem is solved by shooting the activation from behind. That way the legal requirements will be met without the shot appearing so . . . well, so unladylike.

While Jordan Bernstein changes his camera angles for this new sequence and the gaffer alters the lighting, Mona and Kara go back to their schoolroom to do their lessons. At the end of the day, Alice, the teacher/welfare worker, will hand in written reports on their work to the School Board. These reports, which are not so much grades as assessments of their attitude toward the day's lessons, go into the girls' files. After a certain number of bad ones, their work permits would be revoked.

California is very serious about ensuring that nothing gets in the way of its children's schooling. If your state is laxer, it will be up to you to make your own rules. Missing a day of school here and there won't harm a kid. On the other hand, bringing schoolwork to the set is one sure way of keeping a child busy through all the waiting periods when he's not actually before the camera.

"Okay, we're ready to begin," shouts Bernstein. "Let's bring out our little blond lady."

The word goes back to the schoolroom and Kara appears, trailed by the hairdresser who is brandishing a brush in one hand and hair spray in the other. Kara's long, blond hair has been curled off her face and teased for a fuller look. Up close, the beads of lacquer coating each curl are visible. But through the viewfinder and in the final print, Kara's hair will be a smooth, shiny replica of Farrah Fawcett's mane.

Kara is the star of this sequence. The first shot, actually frame five, will take up where the previous sequence left off: Kara and her doll in close-up in the sandbox. The voice will continue chanting, "They're your make-believe warrior women." Kara, in frame six, will activate her doll at the same time she gives the line *"En garde!* Defend, Dawnlight." The doll's arms will shoot up into the karate position and the next frame will be another close-up of Kara with the doll now in what the Dollie people call the "heroic pose," giving the rest of her line, "Make ready to greet our foe."

This sequence turns out to be the most difficult of the day. It has little to do with Kara's interpretation of the line or even her skill at activating the doll. She does both well—but slowly. At the end of each take, the PA announces, "two seconds over," "three seconds over."

"C'mon, baby girl, I know you're trying to do a good job, but feel free to do a fast one," flips Bernstein. "Okay, let's try it again. Happy days, sweetheart, let's see a smile."

With take after take coming in over time, the tension starts rising and Bernstein's good mood begins to slip. "Do me a favor," he snaps at the PA, who is playing the announcer for this sequence. "Can you read the lines like you speak English? You sound a little bit like the Wax Museum, and it's hurting the actor."

"I'm just trying to reduce the time," she replies.

"Okay, okay," and turning to Kara, "C'mon, blondie, let's speed it up."

Another take. When Bernstein yells "Cut!" Kara asks "Is that fast enough?"

"A little faster and you'll have it just perfect," the PA reassures her.

Kara's smile has become set and there's worry in her eyes. Bernstein sees it. "You're doing a good job, baby. Don't worry, just try again. C'mon now—smiley, smiley, smiley. Okay, one-two-three, action . . . Cut! That looks good this time."

"How long did it take?" Kara asks.

The PA checks her stopwatch. "Perfect, exactly on time."

And a good thing too. Kara's willingness to do the scene over and over until it's perfect is unquestioned, but it's a tiring process and the adults know they've been playing a Beat the Clock of sorts: How many takes could they do before Kara got too tired?

This is always a problem when working with kids. No matter how earnest a child is, there comes a point where fatigue sets in. When that happens, no amount of will on the kid's part or chivvying from the director will stop the scene from sliding downhill.

Some directors are insensitive to that point, and wonder why they don't get good performances from their young talent. In the commercial business, directors specialize in one or another type of commercial. Some are food directors; their forte is making old, cold pizza or lukewarm, soggy cereal look luscious. Others are animal directors, experts in making the cat meow on cue. And still others are children's directors, artists at getting peak performances from kids.

It helps if a children's director likes kids and likes working with them, but it isn't necessary as long as he understands something of child psychology. Award-winning director Bob Giraldi says, "I don't really like working with kids. In fact, they're my least favorite—right next to animals. That's because you can't really direct children. You have to con them, herd them, frighten them, or love them into getting what you want from them. You can't really talk straight to kids like you can to adults. For a grown man, it seems to me the silliest thing in the world to be involved in."

The younger the child, the truer Giraldi's statement. Rodney Allen Rippy, some say, didn't chortle about Jack in the Box hamburgers because he loved them so much but because the director had his assistant under the table tickling little Rodney's feet.

Often the skill in being a children's director is in taking advantage of the particular child's quirks or personality. There are a number of commercials that were so successful because a director stayed with the child's delicious way of mispronouncing a word or mishandling the action. "I had one commercial that was absolutely *made* by a funny bit the little girl we used just did naturally," remembers Brian Crouch. "She was playing a real rich kid in a pizza commercial. All we wanted her to do was pick up a piece of pizza from a silver tray and eat it. But this child, Arlene, was a real little lady, and after she had picked up the pizza, she refused to take a bite until she had licked all of her fingers clean. It wasn't in the script; it was just something she *had* to do. And it was perfect for the spot."

That sort of thing is a bonus in the commercial business, and a director has to be quick to spot it and flexible to stay with it. If he insists on sticking to the storyboards, he'll direct out that choice moment that could make his commercial a gem.

The end of Kara's sequence coincides with lunch. The catering firm has set up a trestle table on the lawn, bearing trays of hot food. Companies that cater commercial lunches never give the standard breaded patty and macaroni salad that is typical large crowd fare. These firms are most often run by just one or two people who are gourmet cooks. One woman specializes in soul food, down-home spareribs and yam pie. Another does Greek cooking, moussaka and baklava. Today it's Italian: hot, cheesy lasagne, green salad, and strawberry shortcake.

Sitting on the grass under a tree is the art director of the commercial. "You know," he says, "this is the first time I've worked on a spot with kids. There's a whole different atmosphere on this shoot. It's more jovial, looser." He plops a cream-covered strawberry in his mouth. "But I guess you have to be that way with kids."

That's true, and the good kids' directors know it. If you brow-beat children, you'll get a browbeaten performance. Tension shows easily in the eyes, and few youngsters have the poker face to hide their fright or unhappiness. But not every director working with children is a kids' director—or is good.

"I was on a set once with six kids and a director who just didn't know how to work with them," remembers New York manager Sandra Firestone. "During the course of shooting the scene, the kids went through all the stages a child can, from enthusiasm to being dragged out at the repetition to a very silly stage. The direc-tor got real mad during the silly stage and stopped shooting. I thought to myself, 'You idiot, this is when you *should* be shooting because the kids are really alive!'"

If that was the worst a director ever got with children, it would be fine. But there are horror stories floating around about the lengths some directors go to in getting kids to do what they want. There are tales of kids getting pinched when the director wants them to cry or tickled to the point of misery when he wants them to laugh. However, these undocumented stories are, for our pur-poses, just rumors, to be treated as such.

What is fact, though, is the way some directors are totally una-ware that they are working with children who are sensitive to crit-icism and vulnerable when it comes to adult behavior. This is where, if there's no welfare worker on the set, you must watch out for your child.

Is he getting past the point of tiredness and moving quickly to exhaustion? Is the director, or anyone else on the set, being cruel —or crude? Are they asking for something beyond his ability? Have they stopped considering his needs because getting the com-mercial done is their prime concern? You know your child best; it is up to you to protect him. Make sure you're not being supersen-sitive or overprotective first; if you're sure you're not, go talk to the director.

After all the advice about keeping quiet on the set, not getting in anyone's way, and letting the experts do their jobs, you will probably find it difficult to act. And, too, your desire to see your child succeed may make it hard for you to rock the boat. Most mothers feel that way. On a soft drink commercial shot in the middle of California's rainy season, with a script that depicted high summer, the commercial-makers wanted the children to run through a sprinkler set up on a lawn. It was fifty degrees out and drizzling. The welfare worker on the set went up to the director and said, "I really don't think these kids should do this scene today. It's too cold and wet. Can we put it off till tomorrow?"

"Oh, don't worry, we're all ready for that," the director answered. "We've heated the water in the sprinkler and we'll have people waiting with towels to wrap around the kids as soon as the shot is finished."

The welfare worker wasn't satisfied; she knew how many takes they'd have to do before "the shot is finished." And while she did have the power to just send the kids home despite the director, she decided to leave the decision up to the parents. She gathered them into the camper that served as the classroom and told them the situation.

The parents all looked at each other. They were obviously concerned, but none were willing to actually say the word that would pull their child off the shoot. Finally the welfare worker said, "Well, I don't know about you, but if it were my child, I certainly wouldn't let him run around dripping wet in a bathing suit in this weather."

That was all the parents needed. One by one, they said, "No, I won't permit my child to do that." And the scene was postponed until the next day.

There are no such problems on the Dollie set. Jordan Bernstein is a kids' director and a good one. He not only gets the performance he wants from them, he makes them feel good in the trying. Kara, back in the schoolroom with only her lessons to do for the rest of the afternoon, says, "Jordy is *real* nice. He makes a game out of what we're doing. And he's always saying funny things to make you laugh. When he saw how bad I was feeling this morning, all he did was say 'C'mon, smiley,' and it made me feel like a new person."

Now it's Mona's turn to find that out. Her sequences work almost in reverse of Kara's. Mona has to push the doll's arms back down while saying her line. It doesn't require any fewer takes to get the sequence right, but somehow, perhaps because Mona hasn't Kara's serious concern with perfection, the tension never gets to the point it did in the morning.

By four o'clock, the kids are finished. Mona's mother stuffs the huge tapestry she has been needlepointing into a bag. Kara's mother slips a marker into her book before tucking it into her purse. And Shanee's mom just gives her somewhat disappointed child a hug. "Still," Shanee says as the six of them trudge up the hill to their cars, "I liked this shoot better than any other."

"You did?" Kara is astonished. "You like being the backup kid?"

Shanee looks resigned. "Well, no. I guess not. I'd rather be the main person. But still," her face brightens, "this is good experience."

The kids are gone, but Bernstein and his crew still have work to do. There are several more shots in which the girls don't appear that have not been filmed yet. And then there's postproduction: The film must be edited and music and voiceovers recorded and dubbed before the final print goes to the toy company for approval. The work of producing the commercial officially began several weeks before, on June 13. It wouldn't finish until July 16, when the 16mm print of the spot would be shipped to TV stations all over the country. And it wouldn't be aired until sometime in October.

But for Kara, Mona, and Shanee—and for your child—the end of the shoot is the end of the job. And the only reminders of it will be when you see it on TV—and when the money starts rolling, or dribbling, in.

6

The Nitty Gritty:
The Law, Unions, Money

Once upon a time children were a very precious commodity to their parents. It had nothing to do with love or respect; rather, children were property, owned by their parents the same as a house or a mule. And just as the mule could be hired out and the house leased, so too could and were children sent to work—in the mines, in the quarries, in the factories, day and night for twelve-, fourteen-, sixteen-hour shifts. Their age made little difference; the youngest of children could bring in money to feed, clothe, and house the family. And the youngest of children could be crippled or killed in backbreaking, dangerous jobs.

The fancy term for that is economic exploitation, and it took two hundred years and the destruction of innumerable children before our government finally passed a body of law that protects kids by regulating their employment.

Child Labor Laws

The child labor laws are many and varied; not only does the federal government have a set, but each of our fifty states plus the

District of Columbia and Puerto Rico have their own individual child labor laws. Basically these laws are designed to protect the health and safety of children. They set minimum ages for
employment, restrict the kinds of jobs children can do, and limit
the number of hours and days kids of different ages can work. In
some states, where the law is also concerned with the child's
educational welfare with respect to employment, there are further
restrictions that deal specifically with schooling.

Because these child labor laws differ from state to state, it is
difficult to generalize about them. However, one thing is certain:
Before your child can be employed, he must have that slip of
paper called a work permit, an employment certificate, or some
variation on those words.

Most states call for the child to apply for the permit in person.
In some states these permits are granted by the state employment
office, in some by the Department of Labor, and in others by the
Board of Education. All states require the child to bring written
permission to work from a parent or guardian. Some states also
want a signed statement from a doctor attesting to the child's
physical fitness to work. And others insist on permission from the
child's school principal and set a minimum grade level.

Although it is your responsibility to ensure that your child has a
work permit, your agent will give you all the information you
need. It is her responsibility to be thoroughly up-to-date on how,
when, where, and how often you must apply.

Social Security Cards

Every employed person, regardless of age, must hold a Social Security card. These are easily obtained by applying at your nearest
Social Security office. Although your child won't need one until he
actually works on a commercial, most agents suggest you get his
card as soon as he is signed by them. The Social Security number
is one of those pieces of information asked for at every commercial interview.

Don't forget that a Social Security number is not just a means of identification; a certain percentage of your child's earnings will be deducted for Sòcial Security payments.

Taxes

Even for kids, taxes are one of life's certainties. And commercial kids especially have cause to gripe about them. The problem is not the mere fact of taxation but that the government doesn't acknowledge the financial eccentricities of the commercial acting business.

The amount of state and federal income tax to be deducted from a paycheck is determined by how much a person earns per day. That's fine for people who work every day. They earn, say, $40 a day, five days a week, fifty-two weeks a year. Basing their tax deductions on $40 a day ensures that they pay exactly the right amount of tax for someone in their yearly income bracket. However, commercial actors don't work every day. They may work one day a month and earn $275 for that day. But they are taxed as if they earn $275 a day every day. A little simple math says that their tax deductions are based on an annual income of $71,500. An actor in that tax bracket, who actually earns much, much less, is losing most of each paycheck to the IRS.

Of course, the government doesn't actually keep the money. At the end of the year, when the commercial actor totals up his earnings, he only pays taxes on what he actually made. And if there's been an overpayment, as is commonly the case, the government gives the money back. But that's a whole year that the money has been in the IRS's pocket and not in the actor's.

To get around that, many actors claim eight or nine dependents when they fill out their W-4's. Their taxes are still based on the day rate, but with all those exemptions not too much money is taken from their paycheck. However, come April 15, if they have worked a lot, they can end up with a nasty surprise in the form of a tax bill.

There is another way around the problem. The Internal Revenue Service has a specific regulation stating that a person who only works for one employer in a particular week can have their taxes withheld on a weekly rather than a daily schedule. You must apply for this change when filling out the W-4 for your child. There are mimeographed forms available at your local SAG office that you can just hand in with the W-4 on every job your child does. This form is a Declaration Regarding Income Tax Withholding. On it, you "swear under the penalty of perjury:

1. That ————————— is the only employer for whom I am working during the calendar week commencing on ———————— 198—.

2. That should I hereafter secure additional employment for wages during said calendar week, I will notify the above-named employer of said fact within ten (10) days after the beginning of said employment.

3. That it is my desire to have my state and federal income taxes withheld on a weekly rather than daily schedule pursuant to Internal Revenue Service Tax Regulation Section 31.3402 (b)-(1) (d) (2)."

When tax time rolls around, you will start receiving W-2 forms from every company for which your child has worked. If your child has done more than one commercial for one company, they will total the earnings on one W-2. Sometimes, however, you'll get a W-2 that lumps several jobs done by different companies together. This is because those companies use a talent payment operation, a firm that specializes in payroll for commercials. You should check each of the W-2's to make sure that the earnings and deductions listed on them are the same as those given on the wage and earnings statements that accompanied your child's paychecks. If you find any discrepancies, talk to your agent; she generally keeps financial records for each client.

Once you have all the W-2s in front of you, add up your child's earnings. If his total annual income is below the minimum set by the IRS for filing a tax return (you'll find these figures on the tax tables in the front of the 1040 books), all the withheld tax money will be returned to your child. However, you still have to file a return in order to get the refund.

Always file a separate return for your child. It ensures he will get any refund due and also establishes the child as a professional. It does not mean that you can't claim him as a dependent on your own return. Regardless of earnings, any child who is a full-time student is still a dependent on his parents in the eyes of the IRS. It is very important, therefore, that you list his occupation on his tax forms as "Student/Actor."

You will also need to figure what deductions your child can claim. All "ordinary and necessary" expenses incurred by actors are deductible. It would be impossible here to list every expense that qualifies; there are just too many. Suffice to say, most of the money you spend that relates strictly to your child's career is deductible, including agent's commissions, union dues, photographs, résumés, postage, telephone answering service, and travel, to name but a few. To claim these deductions, you need to fill out Schedule C of Form 1040.

A word of warning: Don't think the IRS will just take your word that you've actually had all these expenses. You *must* keep receipts to document your deductions. Start a good bookkeeping system now by buying a date book in which you will list every interview and job your child has. Keep a record of your mileage when toting him to and fro. Write down every career-related expense, every bill you pay. Keep all of your receipts and file them. Pay by check as much as possible; checks are accepted as proof of the expense. Don't treat any of the above lightly, figuring the IRS will never check up on a kid. Many a commercial child has been audited, some in their first year in the business.

Although it is possible to make out your child's tax return yourself—all the information you need is available from your local IRS office—you may, at least the first time, find it too confusing. So you can do what many actors do: Save yourself time and aggravation by hiring a tax accountant. But make sure you find one who is familiar with theatrical tax deductions; otherwise you'll still end up doing most of the work yourself. Don't view a tax ac-

countant as an unnecessary expense: The money he can save you
will be more than repaid. Besides, his fee is tax deductible.

Worker's Compensation

Yes, if your child is put out of commission by a falling boom
mike or short circuiting cables, he can claim Worker's Comp.
Don't laugh: Such accidents do happen.

Should your child be hurt at all on a set, you must immediately
report the accident, no matter how minor, to the director or
producer. It is then their responsibility to file the Worker's
Compensation Report. Yours is to make the claim.

You may or may not receive benefits in the form of weekly cash
payments compensating for time lost on the job. However, you
will always be refunded for medical care.

Unemployment Compensation

Los Angeles agent Iris Burton tells the story of one family she
knows of who have seven commercial kids. Each of them works
often enough to qualify for unemployment and each of them
collects during the weeks without commercial jobs. Sometimes
their local unemployment office sees all seven lined up for the
weekly handout. At just over $100 each, that's an enviable family
income.

The requirements for qualifying for unemployment vary from
state to state. There are some, for instance, which disqualify all
kids under the age of fourteen. Those who do pay out to children
generally apply the same rules to them as to adults. The working
year is divided into cycles, and a child must have worked a minimum number of days within a cycle in order to qualify. The
weekly benefits are, as with adults, based on the child's total earnings in the qualifying cycle.

If your child works enough to qualify for unemployment and you decide to apply, check your state's regulations at your local unemployment office. It's usually a division of the State Department of Labor or Employment.

Contracts

In most cases, the law does not hold contracts signed by children to be binding. Therefore, a parent's signature is usually required to make the contract a legal one. However, in some states special rulings have been passed allowing that contracts signed by children in the entertainment industry are binding. In the majority of cases, the parent is still the one to sign the commercial contract, not the child.

There are only two contracts you will be faced with: the agent's and the individual contract for each job your child works. Both are pretty much standard throughout the industry. The latter will be given to you when you arrive on the set for the day's shooting. If anything about it seems amiss to you, don't sign—call your agent. That way the question of breaking it need never arise.

Your contract with the agent is another question. In the rare case that you only have an oral agreement, all you need to do to break it is write the agent a letter terminating your agreement as of that day. Be short, succinct, and pleasant. You don't have to give any reasons; if you choose to, make sure they're polite (i.e., not libelous). Make two copies of the letter, one to keep yourself and one to send to your child's union.

If, on the other hand, you have a signed contract with your agent and you wish to break it before the expiration date, you have two choices. The first is built in for you by the income clause, which is standard on all contracts of SAG-franchised agents. This clause states that if the agent has not gotten your child fifteen days of work within a ninety-one day period, the contract can be declared null and void without any further ado. If that is the case, you should point this out in a registered letter to

the agent (again sending a copy to the union) terminating your
contract as of the day of the letter.

The commercial business being as haphazard as it is, only a
rare agent can fulfill the income clause. However, if your agent
has fulfilled it and you still want to break the contract, get a lawyer. A good one, who preferably is experienced in entertainment
law. Lawyers, like doctors, specialize. And just as you wouldn't
go to an obstetrician for a broken arm, you shouldn't go to a divorce lawyer when breaking a show business contract.

Unions

When you hear talk of "the union did this and the union says
that" being bandied about the offices and sets of commercial-
makers, that union is usually the Screen Actors Guild. Mostly
what you'll come away with is how SAG stops talented actors
from getting jobs or how SAG is squeezing the industry dry with
its insatiable demands for more money.

Don't believe it. SAG exists solely to protect actors against
film-makers who willingly or not have often exploited their talent.

SAG is one of five performers' unions, all chartered by the
American Federation of Labor/Congress of Industrial Organi-
zations (AFL/CIO). Though they are independent guilds, each
existing for a different branch of the performing arts, the five—
SAG, American Federation of Television and Radio Artists
(AFTRA), Equity, Screen Extras Guild (SEG), and American
Guild of Variety Artists (AGVA)—are grouped together under
the aegis of the Associated Actors and Artists of America (the
Four A's).

Before the guilds of the Four A's were formed, life for a performer was, as an AFTRA pamphlet describes it, "something
from Act I of *Cinderella*. Your fees weren't even worth mention-
ing—and often the employer didn't!

"Whether or not you got a job and what you were paid (*if* you
were) depended on:

1. How fast you could talk.
2. How desperate you were for work.
3. How closely related you were.
4. How much cheaper you'd work than the next fellow.

"Then, outraged by such conditions—sick of being at the mercy of the employers . . . performers from all across our land banded together to better their conditions. . . ."

It's the story of the unionization of any industry. Money, job security, working conditions, benefits—the Guilds have laid down strict rules about these. They have contracts with employers— studios, theaters, TV and radio stations, production companies— that dictate these rules. A Guild member may not work for any employer who doesn't sign the contract. And if a signator-employer violates that contract in any way, the Guilds can wield the same ultimate weapon as other unions, the strike.

SAG is the union of commercial actors because most commercials are made on film. If a commercial is shot on videotape, the actors must belong to AFTRA.

Eligibility Qualifying for membership in the Guild sounds easy. SAG asks that only one of three conditions be met for an actor to be eligible.

1. If he's been a member of one of the other Four A's for more than a year, he can join SAG immediately; if his membership is less than a year, he can join SAG when he has a definite commitment for a job.

2. If he's never been a member of the Four A's, he must present a letter from the employer stating they want to use him for a principal role or speaking part.

3. If he has already completed a film job and can prove it by showing a contract, pay stub, or verifying letter, SAG will allow him to join.

Notice one thing: All three conditions, for the new actor, demand employment before SAG will admit him. And that leads to one of the biggest stumbling blocks of becoming a commercial actor.

Here's a true story that happens more often than not in the business. An eight-year-old girl was making the rounds of commercial interviews. The agent who had signed her knew she would be terrific for TV. She was a tiny child with straight brown hair and brown button eyes. Not only was she cute, in your average, next-door-neighbor way, but she was bright *and* bouncy *and* about as outgoing as you'd want. She was a tomboy type and going along with that look was the most marvelous husky voice graveling out of a tiny kid that you'd ever heard.

She hadn't been on many interviews when a director fell in love with her. She had everything he needed, except for one thing: a union card. And though he wanted to hire her, he couldn't, because there were other kids up for the job who were just as right for the role as she, and they were SAG members. "She's a great kid," the director told the little girl's mother. "That voice is adorable and I'd really like to use her. But the union says I can only hire a nonunion child if she's the only one who can do the job. Don't worry, though. She's so good that someday soon someone will be able to justify hiring her."

That little girl's name was Kristy McNichol, and that "someday soon" came when Kristy's brother, Jimmy, already a SAG member, was hired for a job where they needed a little girl to play his sister. *Then* the director had an acceptable reason for giving Kristy the job.

The law that establishes when a nonunion member can be hired is referred to as the Taft-Hartley waiver. It is actually part of the Labor Management Relations Act of 1947, which outlawed the closed shop practice of hiring only union members.

The Taft-Hartley waiver is the one way around the "which came first, the chicken or the egg?" problem of getting started in commercials. You can't get a job without a union card and you can't get a union card without a job—unless the commercial-maker has just cause to invoke the Taft-Hartley waiver.

That just cause doesn't have to be as rare as in Kristy's case. On a Milk Board commercial, for example, one segment called for several teenagers to be roller-skating just before they were shown in close-up drinking big glasses of milk. None of the three kids who were hired was a union member. The casting director's reason for hiring them, as stated on her Taft-Hartley waiver application, was: "We required young teenage roller-skaters with perfect teeth and bodies for this commercial. As Skye had all of these attributes and also the perfect skin (hard to find in young teens), and as we saw many other kids, and as she intends to pursue a career as an actress, we request she be allowed to work under the Taft-Hartley provision."

Casting people handle Taft-Hartley requests often enough that they are seldom of concern. Nor should you think much about it. It may seem a bother, but look at it this way: If the union wasn't so strict about whom they let in, the business would be glutted and competition would be greater than it already is. By restricting membership and therefore work to those who have talent and are serious in their career intentions, the union is providing job protection for its members.

Joining the Union Once your child has worked under the Taft-Hartley waiver, he has thirty days in which to join the union. He can work as many jobs as he wants in those thirty days without even having to join SAG at the end of that time. But if the child intends to keep on working after that, you must make application and fork over the money.

The joining fee for SAG depends on whether an actor belongs to one of the other Four A guilds. If not, then there is a flat initial fee of, at this writing, $525. $500 of that is the SAG initiation fee, and the remaining $25 is the first installment of the semiannual dues.

If, however, your child is already a member of one of the other guilds, the SAG initiation fee is determined at the time of application for membership and is based on the amount of the initiation fee paid to the other Guild.

Because performers tend to work in a variety of media, membership in more than one guild is not unusual. The first guild joined is then known as the "parent" guild and is the one which gets the full initiation fee.

Dues are paid twice yearly to SAG and are based on a sliding scale, depending on how much your child earns.

MEMBERSHIP CLASSIFICATION BASED ON ANNUAL EARNINGS IN THE GUILD'S JURISDICTION	SEMI-ANNUAL DUES	SEMIANNUAL DUES FOR MEMBERS WITH OTHER FOUR A UNION PARENT
Class 9 up to $2,500	$ 25.00	$ 15.00
Class 8 over $2,500 to $5,000	$ 30.00	$ 15.00
Class 7 over $5,000 to $10,000	$ 41.00	$ 20.50
Class 6 over $10,000 to $15,000	$ 56.00	$ 28.00
Class 5 over $15,000 to $25,000	$ 78.50	$ 39.25
Class 4 over $25,000 to $35,000	$105.00	$105.00
Class 3 over $35,000 to $50,000	$157.50	$157.50
Class 2 over $50,000 to $100,000	$217.50	$217.50
Class 1 over $100,000	$287.50	$287.50

AFTRA's initiation fee is currently $300.00. Their dues, too, are based on a sliding scale according to the actor's gross income of the previous year. They are, however, slightly lower than SAG's for some classifications and higher for others.

GROSS INCOME IN AFTRA'S JURISDICTION	SEMIANNUAL DUES
$0 to $2,000	$ 22.00
$2 to $5,000	$ 34.00
$5 to $10,000	$ 50.00
$10 to $15,000	$ 65.00
$15 to $20,000	$ 72.50
$20 to $25,000	$ 87.50
$25 to $37,500	$112.50
$37,500 to $50,000	$150.00
over $50,000	$200.00

As with SAG, the initiation fee and dues are less if the actor is a paid-up member of another Four A guild, unless the member has a combined gross income of more than $25,000 a year.

SAG and AFTRA both offer a variety of benefits to their members. They have pension and welfare funds, provide low-cost life insurance, group hospitalization, and major medical insurance, and member-owned credit union. All but the credit union are free to members of the guilds. The credit union, which is a combined SAG-AFTRA effort, charges a one-time membership fee of $1 and charges $5 for each share bought.

For all this, what, besides their dues, do the guild members give in return? Total loyalty. Members *must not* sign with an agent who is not franchised by their guild. They *must not* accept employment for less than the guild minimums. They *must not* work for a producer who has not signed the guilds' contracts. They *must not* work with an employer who is on one of the guilds' Unfair Producers lists.

All these "must nots" are the basis of the strength-in-numbers power of the guilds. SAG and AFTRA, like other unions, can offer no protection if their members don't give them that power. In the winter of 1978, SAG and AFTRA were negotiating for a new contract for commercial actors when they hit an impasse with management (the Association of National Advertisers and the American Association of Advertising Agencies). It was over a clause in the contract that dealt with payment for alternate scenes or lines.

Sometimes actors are asked to reshoot parts of a commercial because the spot must be altered as a result of legal requirements or because it is unacceptable to the networks. And sometimes actors are asked to reshoot the spot because the commercial-makers want to change it for creative or marketing reasons. In the past, such changes were made for free. But now the unions were arguing that the reshot commercial constituted a new commercial, and unless the changes were for legal or network requirements, the actors should be paid another session fee. Management argued that even creative and marketing reasons were just cause for reshoot-ing the commercial with no payment to the actor. Or, they said, they would pay, but only if and when the reshot commercial was actually aired.

The unions refused to agree to that, and just before Christmas, 1978, SAG and AFTRA called more than 70,000 members out on strike. All television and radio commercials made with union members stopped. Commercial-makers were forced to use nonunion talent or make commercials that didn't use actors. The results were obvious, and after forty-eight days management gave in.

During those forty-eight days of strike, a lot of actors lost a lot of money. Commercials are the bread and butter of many in the business. However, if they hadn't stuck together and backed the guilds, these actors would have lost even more money in the future.

Money

Probably the most difficult part of having a child in commercials is figuring out how much he is earning from any one spot. The unions have set up a complicated system of payment based on where, when, and how often a particular commercial is shown. As one actress put it, "It's so weird that you don't know what you're going to get paid until you actually get paid."

First there is the session fee. That is a flat $275 for an eight-hour day. However, if more than one commercial is made in that eight-hour period, your child will get another $275 for each additional spot. At the end of the session, you will be told how many commercials were made. If shooting the commercial goes over the eight-hour period, your child will be paid overtime at the rate of time and a half for the ninth and tenth hours and double time after that. In this and other cases where a payment is based on an hourly rate, that amount is one eighth of the day rate, or $34.38.

There is a one-hour minimum payment for each wardrobe and/or fitting call. If your child is there longer than an hour, he will be paid for the additional time in fifteen-minute units. Even if children use their own clothes for a commercial and the wardrobe call is just to check on their appropriateness, they will still be paid the same amount. There is also a small payment called a wardrobe allowance when an actor provides his own clothes. The fee is $15 per costume change for "evening wear"; for regular clothing, it's $7.50 per change of outfit.

Within each city where there is commercial activity, an area has been designated the studio zone. In Los Angeles, for instance, the studio zone is that area within a radius of thirty miles of the intersection of Beverly and La Cienega boulevards. In New York, it is the area within an eight-mile radius of Columbus Circle. If your child ever has to travel twenty-five miles beyond the center of his studio zone, he will be paid for travel time, depending on what day and what time of day the journey is made. If the child is working and traveling on the same day, travel time is included in the work day; however, if the traveling causes overtime, the child will be paid straight time in hourly units for the trip to the set and in quarter-hour units for the trip home. If the commercial is being shot at a location so far away that your child has to make the journey the day before, he will be paid a full day's pay if it's necessary to leave before noon. Between noon and 6:00 P.M., he will be paid for actual travel time with a four-hour minimum payment due. After 6:00 P.M., payment is by the hour for the actual time spent in travel. The rate for the return journey, however, no matter how long it takes or what time the child leaves, is one full day's pay. If, for some reason, the traveling to and from the location is done on a weekend or holiday, payment is at time and a half. In Los Angeles there is also a twenty-cents-per-mile payment for traveling from the producer's studio to another location even though both are within the studio zone.

Once your child does a commercial for a specific product, he cannot do another for a competitive product while the first one is still running. For instance, a child who has a Dr. Pepper commercial still being shown cannot do a Kool-Aid commercial. This is called exclusivity. For most commercials, exclusivity has nothing to do with who manufactured the product. Your child would be violating the exclusivity clause by doing a commercial for Fanta soft drink and then one for Coca-Cola, even though both are manufactured by the same company. However, exclusivity would not be violated if the child did a commercial for Gainesburgers and another for Jello, even though both are products of General Foods.

Sometimes an advertiser will ask for more extended exclusivity, in which case an additional 50 percent of the session fee is added to the actor's pay. Rarely will complete exclusivity be asked for, but when it is, a long-term agreement is made guaranteeing the actor continuing employment and/or payment. Complete exclusivity can only be granted with the consent of SAG.

Any child who makes an American commercial that will also be shown outside the United States, Canada, or Mexico will qualify for a foreign use payment. If the commercial is to be shown in the United Kingdom, the session fee is tripled; for use anywhere else the session fee is doubled.

All these extra payments can be peanuts when it comes to the money to be made from residuals. Residuals are, in essence, payments made for each time the commercial is shown, and it is from residuals that those huge sums of money are earned by commercial kids.

The amount of the residual payments depends on which category a particular commercial falls into. The most lucrative is the Class A Program commercial. That is a network spot shown across the country at the same time on every station belonging to that particular network. Class A program commercials pay a specific amount for each use. What that amount is depends on how many times the commercial is shown. There are also Class B and C Program commercials, but they are much rarer and pay significantly less.

PROGRAM COMMERCIALS

Program Use	*Payment for On-Camera Principals*
CLASS A	
1st Use	$ 275.00
2nd Use	110.41
3rd Use	87.60

4th–13th Use	87.60 each
13-time Use Guarantee	1,146.71
14th Use	42.01
14th–18th Use	82.47 each
CLASS B	
13-time Use Guarantee, including New York	617.60
13-time Use Guarantee, excluding New York	503.75
CLASS C	300.19

Dealer commercials are those that are shown nationally but have a tag end promoting a local store. The advertiser offers them to the individual dealers carrying their products. The dealer then puts his "Come buy at Smertz Hardware" or whatever at the end of the spot. Dealer commercials come in either the Class A or B variety, and payment is based on thirteen uses.

DEALER COMMERCIALS

Program Use	Payment for On-Camera Principals
CLASS A - including New York	$1,224.96
excluding New York	1,083.34
CLASS B - including New York	1,883.48
excluding New York	1,625.03

Wild Spots are the most common class of commercial—and the most complicated to compute. Wild Spots are commercials shown in different markets across the country at different times. Each market (jargon for "city") is worth a certain number of units, depending on its population. One million people are worth one unit. Therefore, Atlanta, Baltimore, Houston, Indianapolis, Miami, Minneapolis/St. Paul, Seattle/Tacoma, Mexico City, Montreal, Tampa, and Toronto are all two-unit cities. Cleveland, Dallas/Fort Worth, Pittsburgh, and Washington, D.C., are three-unit cities. Detroit is worth four units, Boston and San Francisco are each five, and Philadelphia is a six-unit city. All other cities are worth one unit each with the exception of New York, Los Angeles, and Chicago. These are the three major markets and are treated separately.

The formula for determining payment of a Wild Spot commercial is: the number of times the commercial is shown multiplied by the set fee for each unit.

WILD SPOTS

Number of Uses per 13 weeks	Payment per Unit for On-Camera Principals
1	$275.00
2–25	10.45 each
New York alone	599.80
each additional unit	3.85
Chicago or Los Angeles alone	522.50
each additional unit	3.85
Any two: New York, Chicago, Los Angeles	825.00
each additional unit	3.85
All three: New York, Chicago, and Los Angeles	968.00
each additional unit	3.85

Notice that in both the Program and Wild Spot payment charts, the first use of the commercial is worth $275. Actually, the actor gets no money for that first use; the $275 session fee is considered the payment. It is also considered payment for the first holding fee. A holding fee is defined by SAG as a guaranteed payment due to performers for each thirteen-week period (called a fixed cycle) in which the employer wishes to retain the rights to use the commercial but is not actually showing it. As long as the holding fee has been paid, the exclusivity clause is in effect and the performer cannot take a commercial job for a competitive product. After that first fixed cycle, if the advertiser wants to retain exclusivity even though he has still not aired the commercial, he must pay additional holding fees to the actor.

Each commercial has a maximum period of use, 21 months from the date of the beginning of the first fixed cycle. If payment is up-to-date and if no performer objects, a commercial may be automatically renewed for subsequent periods of use. If a performer wishes to object, i.e., wants to be released from exclusivity or to negotiate a higher rate of pay, then he must notify the employer in writing. This must be done no earlier than 120 days nor later than 60 days before the end of the maximum period of use.

The various payments—session fees, holding fees, residuals— do not come in one lump sum. But SAG has set up a definite schedule of when each must be paid. The session fee is due twelve working days after the session. The holding fee is due twelve working days after the beginning of the fixed cycle. Residuals for Wild Spots are paid fifteen working days after the beginning of each cycle in which they are used. Class A Program commercial residuals are calculated by the week and are due within fifteen working days after each week of use.

If payment for any of these is not made on time, a late fee is attached. If payment is up to twenty-five days late, there is a three-dollar late fee for each working day missed. After twenty-five days, if you still haven't received any money, you must notify your child's agent or SAG. If the full payment plus penalties isn't then paid within twelve working days, there is an additional penalty payment of seventy-five dollars plus ten dollars per working day.

All of this material will seem very confusing to you now. When your child's checks start coming in, however, they will be accompanied by vouchers that must identify the commercial, the sponsor, the date of the session, the use, fixed cycle dates, and the type and number of uses. Once you have gone through several vouchers to check that payment is correct, all of these unfamiliar terms, definitions, and payments will seem quite clear.

Spending the Money On his twenty-first birthday, a young

man who had spent his childhood as a commercial kid went to his mother and asked her for the money he'd earned.

"What money?" she asked. "There isn't any."

"What do you mean there isn't any? I know I earned thousands of dollars over the years. What happened to it?"

"Remember that Cadillac I drove around in?" his mother smiled. "And the mink coats I wore? And the jewelry I bought? And the vacations I went on?"

That story is told as a joke, but it is neither funny nor untrue. There are unknown numbers of parents who are living high off the hog on their commercial kids' earnings. And there's no law that says they can't. In fact, the law specifically says that parents may take their child's wages and spend them in any manner they wish. (The Coogan law, which is strictly a California statute and provides that 50 percent of a child's earnings from the entertainment industry be set aside for safekeeping, does not apply, at this writing, to money earned from commercials.)

The majority of parents, however, use their child's earnings much more wisely—and fairly. Exactly what they do with the money depends, to a great extent, on the family's financial situation. There are those who but for their commercial kid would be on the welfare rolls. The situation was never that dire for the Kraus family, but their six-year-old son, Chad, has certainly helped to put the food in his mouth.

"We didn't put Chad in commercials because we needed the money," says his mother, Marla. "But it did come at a good time. We were hurting financially when he did his first commercial, and we used the money he got to pay some bills. But we intend to pay it all back to him when we get in a better financial position."

For parents whose budgets cover the basics but don't stretch to the extras, a child's earnings from commercials can go a long way toward enriching his childhood. These are the children who would never go to summer camp, take piano lessons, ride new bikes, play tennis with their own rackets or ball with their own mitts if they didn't earn the money to pay for all those things themselves. And in New York, where private schools are often better than public, many a commercial kid has paid the price for a fine rather than an inferior education.

In other families, the parents choose to spend their children's money on luxuries everyone can enjoy, rather than just limiting it to the wage earner. Overheard in a Chicago casting office: "My dad just bought a twenty-two-foot motor home from the money I made last year." "Oh, yeah? Well, we're going to Europe as soon as my cereal spot starts paying."

Some onlookers might frown at the implications there, but kids today are much more savvy about the rising cost of living—and much more demanding that their life-styles go with it.

Probably the most common choice parents make is to put their child's money straight into a savings account earmarked for college. "I'm just going to be an actress until I'm sixteen," says Kara Olsen, the little girl in the Spy Sisters commercial. "I want to be a doctor and I want to go to UCLA. But it costs a ton of money to go there so I'm working now to earn enough to put me through college and medical school."

Just sticking your child's money in the average savings account may not be the best idea, however. Tami Lynn, the West Coast manager, advises her parents to invest their money in something with a high return, like real estate. "I think it's wrong for parents just to put their kids' money in the bank unless they can get a really high rate of interest on it," she says. "With the way land prices are going today, I think parents should put the money in that or in some other kind of investment."

Lynn is quick to point out that she doesn't include stocks and bonds as good investments. "They are just too risky to be a good recommendation. I would never suggest that." What she does suggest, however, is that interested parents seek the advice of an investment counselor or business manager. These people are expert at making your money work for you and the fees they charge are, for many commercial kids' parents, well worth the financial advice they give.

Ultimately, how you spend your child's money is up to you.

Whether you use it to feather your nest, finance his future, or any of the choices in between is up to you—and your conscience. No one need ever know what you've done with it. Except your child, who, years from now, just may ask you for an accounting.

7

The Big Apple
and the Big Orange

New York and Los Angeles are the Big Two when it comes to the
business of commercial-making. The first television commercial
was made in New York, and it is still first as far as the numbers
go. However, the percentages change according to the hometown
of the person you're talking to: New Yorkers claim 80 percent of
all commercials are made in the Big Apple; Angelenos insist that
60 percent are made in the Big Orange. Which is correct, and the
reasons why don't really concern us. What does count are the
different methods of operation for commercial kids in the two
cities, and how they will affect you and your child.

Agents, Managers, and Free-lancing

In California the law is very specific. A child cannot work in
the entertainment industry without an agent, one agent with whom
he is signed exclusively. Because there are a finite number of
agents and a seemingly infinite number of children, this law, at its
best, results in a natural selection of sorts. Agents, in order to
avoid overloading their books, are extremely selective about

which kids they sign. As a result the children who are not supremely commercial get weeded out at a very early stage.

Also weeded out, unfortunately, are those children who fall into
the gray area between supremely commercial and not commercial
at all. California agents just cannot afford to take a chance on a
child they are not absolutely certain will work. This is particularly
true of minority kids and ultra-Character types, both of whom are
appropriate for only a limited number of commercial calls.

And, too, California agents are very wary of type conflicts
within their agency. "We try to have one child of every type
within every age category," explains Dorothy Day Otis. "And if
we already have a red-haired, freckle-faced eight-year-old boy, we
wouldn't take on another child of that age and type, no matter
how good he is. That does result in our turning down some good
people, but we don't want our children to compete among themselves. And anyway, how many freckle-faced, red-haired eight-
year-olds can you send out on one interview?"

However, the situation is not quite as discouraging as it sounds.
After all, a type conflict that exists at one agency does not exist at
other agencies. Moreover, an agent's books are constantly chang-
ing: Kids leave, grow up, get fat, lose weight, and so forth. Consequently, Otis and her colleagues always recommend that if your
child is turned down by an agency because of a type conflict, you
immediately knock on the doors of the other agents in town.

New York parents don't have any of these problems, because
New York has no laws to regulate the agent-child relationship. In
fact, an exclusive contract with an agent is the exception there.
The majority of commercial kids in New York free-lance, working
with a number of agents, any of whom can send them out on a
commercial casting call.

This free-lancing system got its start about fifteen years ago,
when personal managers came into being. As James White, vice
president of the Mary Ellen White agency, explains it, "At that
time, New York agents were losing kids at the rate of about 30
percent a year, and they were making no effort to find replace-
ments. They let that aspect of their jobs, the talent scouting,
atrophy. Soon some smart people came along and realized that if

they took over and found kids for the agents, a lot of money could be made from it."

These people, mostly mothers of kids in the business, called themselves managers. Each manager originally had an exclusive relationship with an agent. The manager would scout out the talented kids, sign them to a contract, and then hand them over to the agent, whose only task would be to send them on interviews. And every time these kids worked, the manager would take a percentage of their pay as her fee, just like the agent did.

"Then the managers realized that since every agent didn't get every casting call, the more agents they had a particular child working with, the more calls the kid would be sent on," White continues. "And the more calls the child went on, the better his chances of getting work, and the more money the manager could make. It was simple then to convince the parents who formerly went for exclusive contracts with one agent, in the traditional manner, to sign exclusively with the manager instead. All they had to say was, 'We can get more money for you because we can go to *all* the agents and you can only go to one.'"

Today it isn't mandatory for a child to be signed with a manager in order to free-lance, but it is the common practice. And for a good reason. Agents give preference to seeing free-lancers who are sent by a manager over those who work on their own. This is because agents and the managers they work with have built up a relationship over the years that is based on mutual trust and need. As Jean Walton, head of the children's department at Ann Wright Representatives, says, "My job is made easier because of the managers. They screen the children for looks, temperament, talent, and the desire to be in the business." By the time Walton sees a child sent to her by a manager, it is already a fact that that kid is commercial. All she has to do is decide if she wants to work with the child.

But the manager is not just a talent scout. She is, after all, working for the child, not the agent. The manager is, in fact, the middleman between the agent and the child. Agents do not deal at all with the kids—or their parents—who are signed with managers. And all parties prefer it that way. It frees the agent for the tremendous volume of work involved in casting and it gives the child a personal, available-at-all-times "second" in his corner.

Sandra Firestone, head of Studio V Management, is acknowledged as one of the top managers in New York. She has a small clientele because, as she puts it, "I want to work very, very closely with my people. Kids' managers don't get into career training and planning to the same degree that adults' managers do. So what I try to be is a friend to my people. I answer all their questions and deal with all their problems, both personal and professional. I give them coaching with their lines, advise them on anything from what to wear to a particular interview to where to find a good dentist. Their checks come to me, and I make sure that all those complicated payments are correct. Come April 15, I give them help with their taxes. If I get any feedback from their interviews— and when I do it's generally negative—I'll call them in and work with them on it. I think you'd have to say that what I do is to become very much involved with my clients on a personal level, doing all those things that agents don't have time for."

But more than that, Firestone is directly involved in the casting process. She gets the commercial breakdowns daily from agents who call her either to request a specific child or to ask for casting suggestions. Sometimes it's a simple matter to remind an agent about a child who is perfect for the job. Or convince an agent to send out a child who is new to the business. Sometimes, however, it is only Firestone's ability that can save a casting call for an agent.

"I got a call the other day from one of the agents I deal with regularly and she was laughing hysterically. 'You're not going to believe this,' she said to me. 'But I need somebody who is under five feet, four inches, preferably Puerto Rican, with black as a second choice, over sixteen years old, and a superior gymnast!'

"Well, I just happened to remember this kid I saw coming out of another office in this building. He got on the elevator with me, and judging by his muscle structure I guessed he was a gymnast. He was short, he was Puerto Rican, and he was obviously over sixteen. I knew that he was just what they were looking for, so I got his name and phone number right there in the elevator. No matter how off the wall a call is, there is somebody around who can do it."

Firestone wouldn't sign someone like the Puerto Rican gymnast to a contract; there just wouldn't be enough work for him. In fact, she doesn't sign minority children to exclusive contracts unless "I feel that they are absolutely sensational. There is less work for them and I like to leave them free to pick up whatever jobs they can from all the outlets. Nor will I sign kids who I think *may* be able to work in the business but I'm not absolutely sure. I'll put them on my books and just see what happens. The same is true of kids under five."

The interview process for a manager does not differ much from an agent's. The first step is the introductory photograph. "In almost every instance, I will ask for a picture before I agree to see a child," says Firestone. "It's a lot easier, and in the few cases where I haven't, I've run into problems. Those kids will turn out to be the ones who have braces or acne or something like that. I have a hard time turning people down, and if I get pictures first, then I can weed out those I couldn't possibly work for.

"Sometimes, of course, you can't tell there's a problem from the picture. For example, I won't take a child with a New York accent, and there's no way of knowing he has one unless you talk to him."

Firestone isn't alone in refusing kids with accents. Parents beware! Nothing will kill your child's chances for *any* kind of commercial career faster than a New York accent. What's so bad about the New York accent? If you're a New Yorker, nothing. But if you live in Oshkosh or Canton, there is no way you can identify with a little kid who says "dese, dem, dose, toidy-toid" or even milder versions of the same.

Out in Sandra Firestone's waiting room, there's a twelve-year-old boy sitting with his mother. They're in Studio V's West Side offices on the recommendation of a friend of a friend. Steve, his name is, and not a bad-looking kid, average-sized for his age with a clear complexion and sandy brown hair. His mother is wearing the regulation outfit for chic Manhattan housewives: tweed blazer, turtleneck, designer jeans, and boots.

That outfit is not an uncommon sight in the offices of New York children's agents and managers, who generally agree that the majority of children acting in commercials there come from middle- or upper-middle-class families. It isn't that there is any kind of discrimination against children of poorer families. James White believes that up until recently lower-income families never even thought about the possibility of putting their kids in commercials. "Now, however, a lot of the artwork in magazines like *People* does get the lower-level population going on the commercial child track. But there is one primary problem with kids from the lower-income homes—the speech problem." That old New York accent again.

Steve has just the mildest touch of an accent. Seated in Firestone's office with the late afternoon sun filtering in through the windows, Steve is reading commercial copy out loud, accompanied by the plonk-plonk of his foot beating a nervous tattoo against the metal desk.

TEEN BOY OR GIRL

I USED TO BE UNORGANIZED.
BUT NOW I'VE GOT ORGANIZER BY WESTAB. IT'S A THREE-FOLD NOTEBOOK WITH CLIPBOARD AND PAPER ON ONE SIDE FOR NOTES, AND SIX COMPARTMENTS ON THE OTHER SIDE TO FILE THEM.
THE ORGANIZER ALSO HAS EXCLUSIVE PLASTIC RINGS SO YOU CAN'T PINCH YOUR FINGERS. THERE'S A WHOLE LINE TO CHOOSE FROM. ALL STURDY ENOUGH TO LAST A LOT OF SCHOOL TERMS. IF YOU CAN USE SOME ORGANIZING, YOU CAN USE THE ORGANIZER.

Hear that in your mind read without the slightest bit of inflection, dolefully even, and you will have some idea of Steve's reading.

Firestone is gentle. "In your age range, Steve, copy is almost always happy. It's bigger than life. The only time a teenager is unhappy in a TV commercial is if he has zits."

"Try again, but this time try not to sound like you're reading a composition in class. Think about what you're reading; it's important that you understand it. And don't be nervous. This isn't a contest; you don't have to win."

Steve tries again.

"Well, that's better," Firestone smiles. "A little too fast, but you did have some expression. You know, if you were on an interview, you'd have to stand up while you read. So let's try it that way."

Steve stands, clears his throat, and reads again.

"Maybe it's just not a very good piece of copy," Firestone is charitable, to say the least. "But I do think you need to practice reading before I can make a commitment. What I'd like you to do is find a commercial on TV that has a kid your age in it. Get a tape recorder and tape the commercial. But make sure you get a long enough tape so that there's lots of space left after you've taped the commercial. I want you to use that extra tape to record yourself saying the lines the teen in the commercial says. Do it lots of times, until you run out of tape. And try to sound exactly like the kid on TV does. Reading copy well is just a matter of timing and emphasis, Steve, and you'll be able to learn it by imitating the experts. Then when you think you're ready, call me again and we'll have you come in and read some more."

Why all the emphasis on reading? First, because really only young children can get away with not being able to read copy. They are often a silent member of the family, so even if they can't read, they can still have a fairly active commercial career. But older children—well, as one casting director put it, "Once they're over ten or eleven and have lost their spontaneity, they have to be able to act."

The second reason is that we're talking about New York. It's a theater town, *the* theater town, and that has probably been a big factor in agents and managers insisting that the kids they take be able to read copy. In Los Angeles, personality is much more important than reading ability.

Another carryover from New York's theatrical tradition is the style of photographs used. California commercial casting is always done with composites—those two-sided lithographs with a head shot on the front, four or five different poses on the back, and only the child's vital statistics and union affiliations for copy. Photographs for commercial casting in New York, however, are just the same as for theatrical casting: a head shot with a résumé stapled to the back. Occasionally, when it's for a younger child, the single eight-by-ten-inch head shot will be replaced by four smaller pictures showing different facial expressions.

If Sandra Firestone had decided she wanted to sign Steve, she would have turned the interview to his mother, encouraging her to ask any questions she might have. "Then, if there seems to be mutual interest, I will describe what a commercial interview is like, how to deal with rejection, what kind of money the child can expect to make, the union situation—things like that. I tell them I am interested in signing their child but that I would like them to go home, think and talk about it, and then call me in the next day or so with their decision."

Once both sides have agreed and the contracts have been signed, Firestone begins the process that will eventually result in a commercial career. Photographs must be taken, résumés drawn up, and introductions to the agents Firestone thinks will handle the child must be made. Eventually a breakdown will come in that sounds right for the child and Firestone will suggest him to an agent.

For all she does, Firestone takes 15 percent of her clients' earnings. "The money varies from manager to manager, but 15 percent is pretty much the average. Some managers work on a sliding scale, though, going from 10 percent to 25 percent of the child's earnings. There's one manager I know of who takes 25 percent once a child earns over $25,000 a year. That's a pretty big hunk of money, because with the agent's commission included, the child ends up giving away 35 percent of his income.

"There are some managers who write their contracts at a straight 25 percent, claiming that they will pay the agent's 10 percent out of that. But there are some jobs where the agent doesn't get 10 percent. And on AFTRA jobs, the fee includes the agent's 10 percent, so it is the employer who actually pays it. And with

Oliver Dembling is a typical Ethnic type *(above, left)*. Abe Unger is a good example of the off-beat Character type *(above, right)*.

Mexican-American Lila Meraz is a Minority type who works in both commercials and print *(below, left)*. Seven-year-old Nina Chan already has a long list of commercial and print credits *(below, right)*.

Sayer Sean

BIRTHDATE:	August 21, 1972
HEIGHT:	46''
WEIGHT:	46½ lbs.
HAIR:	Black
EYES:	Brown

Sayer has already earned commercial and photographic credits. He is an effervescent youngster with a vibrant personality.

A typical little boy, Sayer enjoys swimming, skateboarding and riding his bike.

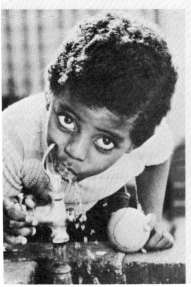

Notice the variety of expressions on Sayer Sean's composite. That's the way it should be done.

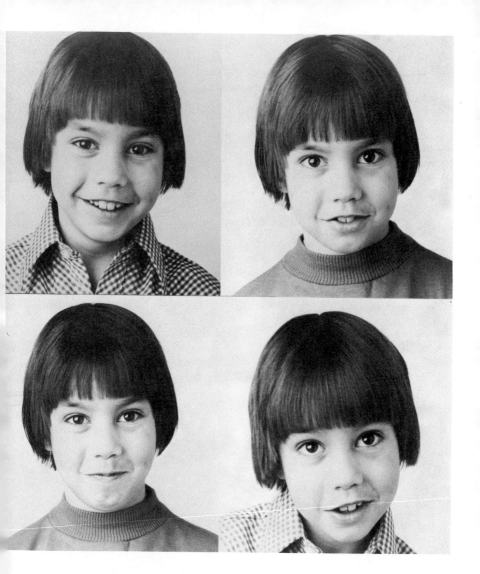

Tommy Okun was the wide-eyed boy in the Mean Joe Green commercial. His pictures are the New York version of a composite.

Nicole Fort, seven and a half, is a perfect model child who has appeared in the major magazines and catalogues.

extra jobs the agent isn't even entitled to 10 percent. When my clients do those jobs, they don't pay the 10 percent and I don't keep it. But the managers who take that straight 25 percent do. And though it may not amount to that much money, to me, keeping that 10 percent is dishonest.

"In fact, I think charging more than 15 percent is self-defeating for managers. And after all, 15 percent is *a lot* of money; anything more than that is just too darn much."

Managers can charge anything they like, because they are not licensed by the state. And because they are not licensed, anyone can set himself up as a manager. All of which has lent fuel to the fire that burns steadily between some managers and agents.

James White calls managers "unlicensed, unregulated freebooters." Bonnie Schulman of the Bonnie Kid agency says, "I think the whole manager/agent situation is a farce." The crux of the controversy seems to be: If managers do the same thing as agents, why bother to have a manager?

"There are only two or three top children's agents in New York," Schulman continues. "So if a child is good and is registered with those agents, that child is going to get in on the calls whether he or she has a manager or not. The agents who are pro-manager don't have an awfully large children's clientele, so they *have* to draw on the managers' lists."

Despite their statements, both Schulman and White work with managers. Schulman says 50 percent of the children she represents are signed exclusively with her. That means that the other 50 percent free-lance, and most will be with managers. White claims he only uses managers when he needs minority children, but he also claims that Mary Ellen White has a reserve of close to a thousand children, three hundred of whom are signed exclusively. That means the other seven hundred free-lance, and, again, most will be with managers.

So it would seem that your choice of placing your child with a manager or going it alone should be based on your personal preference. If you have neither the time nor the inclination to manage your child's career yourself, hire the expert. Jean Walton says that "parents who have little or no knowledge of the business need someone to guide them. And if their child is going to free-lance, that 'someone' has to be a manager. The right manager can make a lot of difference to a child's career.

"But it must be the 'right manager,' and not all of them are. Many don't know enough about the business themselves to be of any benefit. There are mothers who will go out, audition with their kids, and say, 'Gee, why can't I be a manager too?' It's not that simple. Managers must know all about the business, about the different types of commercials, how things are done, what different people are looking for, and so on. And they should know people in the business, the casting directors, the agents. It's not enough to just *want* to manage kids' careers."

But let's back up a step. The decision of whether to go with a manager, and which manager that should be, comes *after* the decision whether your child should sign an exclusive contract with an agent or free-lance. Implicit in that is the fact that an agent has offered your child a contract. After all, if none does, you have no decision: If your child is going to work in commercials, he must free-lance.

But let's say your child has been offered that contract, and now you have to decide whether to take it. What's the advantage of free-lancing? "We all have different eyes in this business," explains Jean Walton. "When I get a casting call, I send out the kids *I* think are right for it. There will be some children who I don't think are right for the job, but who another agent thinks are perfect. If those children are free-lancing with both of us, they'll get the crack at the job that they wouldn't get if they were signed exclusively with me."

Nor would those kids get an interview for that job if the casting director didn't call Walton, and that's another advantage to free-lancing.

There is a disadvantage, however. The agents claim that they work harder and give more opportunities to those children who are signed to exclusive contracts with them. "The kids I sign are more prevalent in my mind when I'm putting children up for a commercial," says Walton. "Why else would I sign them if I

didn't think they were more special than the kids I have as free-
lancers?"

Bonnie Schulman goes one step further. "Even when my kids
are on a par with the free-lancers, I always prefer to send the
ones who are signed exclusively with me."

In California, where a child *must* be signed with an agent, none
of these issues exist. There are managers there, a few, but they are
the icing on the cake rather than, as in New York, the cake itself.
Tami Lynn is the best-known kids' manager in Los Angeles; in
fact, up until a few years ago she was the only one. A major part
of her job is finding new children for Los Angeles agents to sign.
"I find kids I have faith in, who are outstanding, and then when
an agent is looking for a specific type, she will call me. I'm the
source, you might say. Sometimes, though, a mother will already
have her kid with an agent, but will still come to me to manage
the child's career.

"I give them what I call the personal touch. Agents have hundreds of clients, so they can't give that personal touch to each and
every one of them. I'm here when the kids need me, and I'm constantly guiding their careers, telling them what to do and what not
to do. I go over their pictures, test them on interviews. Every
week I hold sessions for my clients where we talk, go over script
reading, interview procedures. I just form them as completely as I
can. I even do public relations for them. For my straight 15 percent, I think I make quite a bit of difference to the child's career."

Lynn is getting more and more involved in the casting process.
She gets the breakdowns every day and sends pictures and
résumés of her kids to casting directors. "Sometimes the casting
directors will call me directly about a child, but most of the casting calls come from agents. We have to be very careful, because
personal managers are not legally qualified to book work in the
state of California. We're trying to promote all kinds of new laws
that will give us some leeway there, but right now we cannot book
completely. We cannot go out looking for work for our kids."

Tami Lynn gets her clients in several ways. "Mostly the parents
approach me. They either know someone whose child is a client

of mine or they've heard about me through the grapevine. I'm always on the lookout for good kids. I don't care where I am—at dinner, shopping—whenever a child walks in, I look at him immediately.

"Once I was in the post office mailing something and I saw an adorable little girl. I just couldn't let her get away, so I handed her mother my card and said, 'If you're ever interested in putting your child in commercials, give me a call.' Well, it wasn't more than three days later when she called me. I brought the child in for an interview, signed her, and she's had an incredible career ever since."

Child Labor Laws

Here's another difference between the two coasts: California has a comprehensive set of child labor laws that have been written specifically for the entertainment industry and that are strictly enforced. New York has almost no child labor laws for commercial kids, and the few that exist are rarely enforced.

The first order of the California laws are the number of hours commercial children can work at different ages. Newborns from fifteen days to six months old are permitted to be on a set for two hours but may only work twenty minutes of that time. From six months to two years old, their total time on the set is four hours, with only two hours of actual working time. From two years to five years old, a child is permitted to work for three hours with a total of six hours on the set. From age six to eighteen, the maximum time on the set is eight hours and four hours is the maximum work time.

No child is permitted to work on a set without a parent or guardian accompanying him. And no set where children work is without a teacher/welfare worker, known in the business as a studio teacher. These studio teachers have complete responsibility for their charges' emotional, physical, and moral well-being. They carry with them their "blue books," which contain all of the regulations covering children in the entertainment industry, and it is their job to ensure that each and every one of them is obeyed.

When a child is not actually working, he is under the supervision of the teacher/welfare worker. During the school year, children over six must spend three of their four nonworking hours doing schoolwork. One of the state's rules is that the child is responsible for bringing classwork from school to do while on the set. At the end of the day, the studio teacher fills in a report on the child's work and attitude; if enough of these reports are unfavorable, the child's work permit can be revoked.

Playtime, too, for the nonworking, nonschool hours of all commercial kids is supervised by the teacher/welfare worker. A trailer or special room must be provided by the producers where teacher and kids will generally be found when the latter are not actually before the camera.

The teacher/welfare workers have enormous power on the set. In fact, they have the ultimate power: One word from them and the children are sent home whether their work is finished or not. Consequently, many commercial-makers resent the studio teachers. You should not; they are there *only* for your child's good.

These laws apply to any child who is from the state of California, no matter where the commercial is actually shot. One Hollywood story has it that Linda Blair's casting in *The Exorcist* was due in some part to the fact that she was not a California child. If she had been, a studio teacher would have had to accompany her on the set, and the producers knew they would never have been allowed to put Blair through some of the stunts that they did. As one studio teacher put it, "Just reading the script would be morally injurious to a child."

California law is also adamant that no child is allowed to work in commercials (or any other branch of the entertainment industry) without a work permit. And the state is relatively strict when it comes to giving them out.

In order even to apply, a child must already have a promise of a job. In fact, the Application for Permission to Work in the Entertainment Industry is obtainable only from casting directors and movie studios. When you receive your child's application from the casting director of the commercial he has been hired for, you'll notice that she has filled in and signed the Statement of Studio or Casting Official, which attests to the employer's expectation of employing the child and requests that the work permit be granted.

Your part of the form, in addition to blanks for your child's name, address, school, grade level, and birth date, requires a signed statement affirming your desire that a work permit be issued to your child and guaranteeing that you will read the regulations governing the child's employment (printed on the back of the permit) and will "cooperate to the best of [your] ability in safeguarding his or her educational, moral, and physical interests."

Next you must take the application to your child's school, where the principal must fill in the blanks stating that your child is either satisfactory or unsatisfactory in citizenship and scholarship. He will then attach a copy of your child's most recent report card. If it shows less than a "C" average, your child will be denied a work permit.

Finally, you go to your own doctor and obtain his signature and statement that your child has been examined and found physically fit to work in the business.

When you have all these signatures, you take your child by hand *after school* (it's illegal to take a child out of school to do this) and proceed to the Division of Labor Standards Enforcement office in Los Angeles. This is the only office in the entire state that handles these work permits. So whether you live in San Francisco, Sherman Oaks, or San Diego, you must travel to Los Angeles with your child for the work permit. But only this first time; subsequent renewals can be handled by mail.

Then, if all the information on the application is in order, the correct signatures are where they belong, the physical exam and grade average are at or above the state minimums, your child will be given his work permit then and there. Most permits are valid for a six-month period, after which you must go through the whole process, except the trip to Los Angeles, again.

Compare all that to New York, where the laws that do exist are generally ignored for kids working in commercials. No minimum ages, no minimum hours, no mandatory parent or guardian, no teacher/welfare worker or other supervision. Protection of the child is left almost totally up to the parent and the integrity of the commercial-makers. Agents and managers know that often that's not enough.

Sandra Firestone gives a good example, about a little girl who had an 8:30 A.M. call for a commercial in Manhattan. "She lived quite far south in New Jersey, so you can imagine what time she had to get up to make her call. She was there on time but it wasn't until 4:30 that afternoon, *eight hours later,* that the director actually started shooting with her. And they didn't release her until midnight. She was a young child, yet they kept her sitting on that set for sixteen hours! That's wrong and it should never happen. *And* it's not an isolated case.

"Some sort of regulation is sorely needed here. We do have the Society for the Prevention of Cruelty to Children. You're supposed to get a work permit from them every time you do a commercial. But no one does, unless they're shooting with babies. The SPCC is supposed to be the agency that has jurisdiction over kids in the entertainment business. Once in a while they'll make a spot check, but the only time they have taken any action was when someone reported a case of child abuse on Broadway. It turned out to be a false report called in by an understudy who thought if he got the star taken out of the show by the SPCC, he'd get to go on. That is the *only* time I know of that the SPCC did anything."

The Screen Actors Guild has a rule in New York that allows SAG members to go onto a set where children are working to make sure that someone is with the kids. "That's a joke," laughs Xavier Rodriguez, a fifteen-year-old who has acted in commercials, on film, and on Broadway. "Half the time the union doesn't even know you're working because no one wants to rock the boat by telling them. And here in New York, they will work you on a commercial until all hours if you let them. I don't. If I get tired, I just say, 'That's it. Give me a break.'"

Kids like Xavier who are old enough and strong enough to take care of themselves are their own best protection. But the younger, more vulnerable child has only a parent—provided one of them is present—to defend him. Fathers tend to do a better job of it. "The mothers don't protect their kids that much," says Sandra Firestone. "They are terribly intimidated. You know, there have been so many stories about Stage Mothers that these women are really afraid to say anything on a set."

The lack of laws protecting kids in New York is the pet peeve of agents and managers alike. They *know* what can happen to a child on the set, and they know they are powerless to stop it. All of them are working in varying degrees for some sort of legislation to correct the situation. Until that happens, however, it is up to you, the parent, to do everything you can to take care of your child.

Laid-back L.A. versus Nervous New York

There's no doubt about it: The war between the Coasts—"Is there life after New York?" "Sure, in L.A."—is heating up in the commercial business. Each side contends that "their way" of doing things is the best. Mostly, that's a chauvanistic claim: New Yorkers are violently partial to New York and Angelenos are lazily partial to Los Angeles.

Their individual gripes—mostly from the New Yorkers—have to do with work style, none of which will affect a parent in either place. But there are several differences which, at the least, are interesting and, at the most, you should be aware of.

In Los Angeles, children's agents are available seven days a week; in New York, they shut up shop on weekends. This presents a problem because commercials are not always cast during normal working hours. Sometimes emergencies happen, a kid gets the measles, another must be found, and it's 9 P.M. on a Saturday night. If you live in Los Angeles and your child is wanted for an emergency casting session, there's no problem: The casting director will call the agent and you'll be notified immediately. In New

York, where there's no one to answer the agent's phone at 9 P.M. on that Saturday night—well, need I say more?

New York casting sessions tend more toward the "cattle call," mammoth events where every possible actor is present. In Los Angeles, cattle calls rarely, if ever, happen. "You don't have to wait so long to go into an interview in L.A.," says Xavier Rodriguez, who has worked in both cities. "And they're more straightforward with you in L.A. In New York, if you don't do a good job reading the copy, if you've gotten something wrong, they never tell you. But in L.A., they not only tell you, they give you another chance."

Another casting difference between the two cities is a very important one: First refusals do not exist on the West Coast. A first refusal is a tentative booking, a way of making sure that the first-choice actor doesn't take another job while the client makes his final decision. "When I'm interested in using someone in New York, I call up the agent and say I want a first refusal on them," explains Joan Lynn, casting director for Bob Giraldi Productions. "Most commercial actors here are commercial actors only. They go out for a lot of calls, so I have to make sure that they will be available for the day we're going to shoot. If I put a first refusal on someone and he does get another job for that same day, the agent will call me and give me the choice of booking that actor then—even though I don't have client approval—or releasing him to take the other job.

"In Los Angeles, it doesn't happen that way. They have something there called 'general availability,' which means that all the agent does is write down somewhere that I think I want the actor. If something else definite comes up, the actor can take that job without even notifying me. I had that happen to me in L.A. I had an actor on general availability for a Gino's Pizza commercial, but he got a TV movie. The agent called just to tell me that I'd lost him."

When all is said and done, the business of being a commercial kid isn't that different in the two cities. And certainly nothing about either place should make you think you need to pack your bags and move. If your child has talent in L.A., he has talent in New York. And if he's going to make it as a commercial child, he'll do it wherever he lives.

NEW YORK DIRECTORY

Unions

SAG, 1700 Broadway, 18th floor, New York 10019, (212) 957-5370

AFTRA, 1350 Sixth Avenue, New York 10019, (212) 265-7700

Agents

Michael Amato Theatrical Enterprises, 1650 Broadway #560, New York 10019, 247-4456

American International Talent Agency, 166 West 125th Street, New York 10027, 663-4626

Associated Talent Agency, 56 West 45th Street, New York 10036, 840-1909

Lola Bishop, 160 West 46th Street, Suite 301, New York 10036, 997-1836

*Bonnie Kid, 250 West 57th Street, New York 10019, 246-0223

*Rosemary Brian Agency, 50 East Palisades Avenue, Englewood, N.J. 07361, (212) 564-8616

‡Cup Stars, Inc., 527 Madison Avenue, New York 10022, 838-1163

Ford Talent Group, Inc., 344 East 59th Street, New York 10022, 688-8538

Jan J. Agency, 244 East 46th Street, New York 10017, 490-1875

*Joe Jordan Talent Agency, 400 Madison Avenue, New York 10017, 838-4910

*Sanford Leigh, 527 Madison Avenue, New York 10022, 752-4450

*Marge McDermott, 214 East 39th Street, New York 10016, 889-1583

Mary Ellen White, Inc., 370 Lexington Avenue, New York 10017, 889-7272

Fifi Oscard Associates, Inc., 19 West 44th Street, New York 10036, 764-1100

Palmer Talent Agency, 250 West 57th Street, New York 10019, 765-4280

Joel Pitt Ltd., 144 West 57th Street, New York 10019, 765-6373

Charles Vernon Ryan Agency, 200 West 57th Street, New York 10019, 245-2225

William Schuller Agency, 667 Madison Avenue, New York 10022, 758-1919

Tranum, Robertson & Hughes, 2 Dag Hammarskjöld Plaza, New York 10017, 371-7500

Gloria Troy Talent Agency, 1790 Broadway, New York 10019, 582-0260

Bob Waters Agency, 510 Madison Avenue, New York 10022, 593-0543

Ann Wright Representatives, 136 East 57th Street, New York 10022, 832-0110

Managers

Norma Belsky, 18 Fairway Drive, Lake Success, N.Y. 11020 (516) 487-0984

Cuzzins Management, 250 West 57th Street, Suite 2101, New York 10019, 586-1573

Kathy Dowd, 331 Madison Avenue, New York 10017, 661-4966

Barbara Jarrett, 220 East 63rd Street, Penthouse G, New York 10021, 355-7500

Muriel Karl, 888 Eighth Avenue, New York 10019, 245-3770

Selma Rubin, 104-60 Queens Boulevard, Suite 1D, Forest Hills, N.Y. 11375, 896-6051

Studio V Management, Inc., 200 West 57th Street, New York 10019, 586-4850

LOS ANGELES DIRECTORY

Unions

SAG, 7750 Sunset Boulevard, Los Angeles 90046, (213) 876-3030
AFTRA, 1717 North Highland Avenue, Hollywood 90028, 461-8111

Agents

*Iris Burton, 1450 Belfast Drive, Los Angeles 90069, 652-0954
Coralie, Jr. Agency, 4789 Vineland Avenue, ✗100, North Hollywood 91602, 766-9501
Lil Cumber, 6515 Sunset Boulevard, Los Angeles 90028, 469-1919
Dale Garrick, 8831 Sunset Boulevard, Los Angeles 90069, 657-2661
Gerritsen International, 8721 Sunset Boulevard, ✗205, Los Angeles 90069, 659-8414
Goldin-Dennis-Karg & Associates, 470 San Vicente Boulevard, Los Angeles 90048, 651-1700
‡Granite Agency, 1920 South La Cienega Boulevard, Los Angeles 90034, 934-8383
Greene's Creative Expressions, 439 South La Cienega Boulevard, ✗104, Los Angeles 90048, 278-9902
Beverly Hecht, 8949 Sunset Boulevard, Los Angeles 90069, 278-3544
*Junior Artists Unlimited, 4914 Lankershim Boulevard, North Hollywood 91601, 763-9000
*Toni Kelman Agency, 7813 Sunset Boulevard, Los Angeles 90046, 851-8822
Caroline Leonetti, 6526 Sunset Boulevard, Los Angeles 90028, 462-2345
‡Bessie Loo, 8746 Sunset Boulevard, Los Angeles 90067, 657-5888
Lovell & Associates, 1350 North Highland Avenue, Hollywood 90028, 462-2178

Hazel McMillan, 126 North Doheny Drive, Beverly Hills
    90211, 276-9823
*Mary Grady Associates, 10850 Riverside Drive, North Holly-
    wood 91602, 985-9800
*Michele Unlimited, 8060 Melrose Avenue, Los Angeles
    90046, 653-9610
Dorothy Day Otis Agency, 6430 Sunset Boulevard, Los An-
    geles 90028, 461-4911
Pacific Artists, 515 North La Cienega Boulevard, Los Angeles
    90048, 657-5990
Savage/Fishman Agency, 6212 Banner Avenue, Los Angeles
    90038, 461-8316
Don Schwartz & Associates, 8721 Sunset Boulevard, Los An-
    geles 90069, 657-8910
Dorothy Shreve, 13720 Burbank Boulevard, Van Nuys 91401,
    780-3022
Charles H. Stern, 9220 Sunset Boulevard, Los Angeles 90069,
    273-6890
Williamson & Associates, 932 North La Brea, Los Angeles
    90038, 851-1881
Wormser, Helfond & Joseph, 1717 North Highland Avenue,
    Hollywood 90028, 466-9111
Ann Wright Associates, 8422 Melrose Place, Los Angeles
    90069, 655-5040

Managers

Tami Lynn, 20411 Chapter Drive, Woodland Hills 91364,
    881-1511

*Specializes in children
‡Specializes in minorities

8

Beyond the Big Apple and the Big Orange

Contrary to anything that the experts on Madison Avenue and Sunset Boulevard will tell you, there are a lot of commercials being made all over the country by people who have never seen the inside of a Los Angeles sound stage or a Manhattan ad agency. While those two cities are the major markets and do get the lion's share of the work, they are being challenged by other cities throughout the United States that have thriving commercial fields, producing both local and national spots. In addition to these middle markets, there are the minor markets, cities that have several production companies kept busy making local commercials as well as the occasional national spot.

Where commercials are made, commercial children are needed. So no matter where you live, provided it is within driving distance of one of the middle or minor markets, your child can become a commercial kid. Although he may not make as much money or work as often as children in New York and Los Angeles, your child will have a career, one that provides all the benefits of a commercial career in the Big Two.

The Middle Markets

Chicago, Dallas, Miami, and Atlanta are the largest of the middle market cities. The business of making commercials in them has been well honed over a number of years. Consequently, getting your child started and the process involved in making him commercial is much the same as that in New York or L.A. You will need, first of all, to find an agent; in the middle market directory there is a comprehensive listing of the SAG-franchised agents in each area. Unless otherwise specified, these agents, most of whom handle kids as well as adults, prefer that you contact them in the normal manner: Send a picture accompanied by a résumé/letter and follow up with a phone call.

The smaller middle market cities are Denver, Detroit, Minneapolis, Phoenix, San Diego, and San Francisco. All of these cities have SAG-franchised agents, and you go the normal route to contact them. However, you may want to bypass the agents and freelance your child. The primary reason for doing this would be to enable him to work on nonunion commercials. It is sometimes the case that there are more nonunion jobs in these cities than union, but if your child is working through a SAG-franchised agent, he will only be put up for the union spots. Consequently, opportunities for work would not be as great as they would be if you opted for a nonunion career.

To free-lance your child in these smaller middle market cities, you must directly approach the casting directors, ad agencies, and production companies. Send each one listed in the directory (and those you discover on your own) a photo of your child and a résumé/letter like the one in Chapter 3, listing his abilities, talents, and the like. Follow this mailing with a phone call, just as you would for an agent. Don't expect anyone to get overly excited about your child. Most likely, they will put the photo and résumé on file and promise to call when a job comes up. Or they may tell you that they're not interested. Or they may ask you in for an interview. Unless it's the former, keep in touch with each contact you have made. Update your child's picture and résumé every six months or so. Call them every couple of weeks. Remind them that you are alive. When it comes to making it in these smaller markets, your tenacity in promoting your child will make all the difference.

MIDDLE MARKET DIRECTORY

ATLANTA

Union

SAG, 3110 Maple Drive NE, Suite 210, Atlanta 30305 (404) 237-0831

Agents

Atlanta Models & Talents, Inc., 3030 Peachtree Road NW, Atlanta 30305, 261-9627

Chez Agency, 1800 Peachtree Center and 230 Peachtree Street, Atlanta 30303, 688-7030

House of Cain, 996 Lindridge Drive, Atlanta 30324, 261-0727

Model's Touch, 2192 Campbelton Road, #105, Atlanta 30311, 753-5430

Cheryl Neal & Associates, 1401 Peachtree Street NE, Atlanta 30309, 892-2664

The Talent Shop, 550 Pharr Road NE, Atlanta 30305, 261-0770

CHICAGO

Union

SAG, 307 North Michigan Avenue, Chicago 60601, (312) 372-8081

Agents

AB Service Associates, Inc., 738 North La Salle Street, #100, Chicago 60610, 337-2726

Agency for Performing Arts, 203 North Wabash Avenue, Chicago 60601, 664-7703

A Plus Talent Agency, 666 North Lake Drive, Chicago 60611, 642-8151

Associated Booking Corp., 2700 North River Road, Des Plaines 60018, 296-0930

Larry Bastin Agency, 730 Waukegan Road, Deerfield 60015

Harris Davidson & Associates, 230 North Michigan Avenue, ⚔ 1325, Chicago 60601, 782-4480

Ebony Talent Associates, 7637 South Bennett Avenue, Chicago 60649, 978-6500

Ann Geddes, Inc., 2444 Hancock Center, Chicago 60611, 664-9892

Shirley Hamilton, 500 North Michigan Avenue, Chicago 60601, 644-0300

David Lee Models Central Casting, 936 North Michigan Avenue, Chicago 60611, 649-0500

Emilia Lorence, 619 North Wabash, Chicago 60605, 787-2023

Philbin Talent Agency, 2323 West Devon Avenue, Chicago 60659, 465-2490

Jimmy Richards Productions, 919 North Michigan Avenue, Chicago 60611, 644-1552

Norman Schucart, 1417 Green Bay Road, Highland Park, 433-1113 or 433-3233

DALLAS

Union

SAG, 3220 Lemmon Avenue, ⚔102, Dallas 75204, (214) 522-2080

Agents

Tanya Blair Agency, 2320 North Griffin Street, Dallas 75202, 748-8353

Kim Dawson Agency, 1143 Apparel Mart, 2300 Stemmons Freeway, Dallas 75247, 638-2414

The Norton Agency/European Crossroads, 2829 West Northwest Highway, ✶701, Dallas 75220, 357-6439

Peggy Taylor Agency, 4228 North Central Expressway, Dallas
75206, 827-7292

Joy Wyse Agency, 6318 Gaston Avenue, Dallas 75214,
826-0330

MIAMI

Union

SAG, 3226 Ponce de Leon Boulevard, Coral Gables 33134,
(305) 444-7677

Agents

A. Central Casting of Florida, Inc., 2451 Brickell Avenue,
Suite 4E, Miami 33129, 379-7526

Act I Casting Agency, 1451 South Miami Avenue, Miami
33130, 371-1371

Agency for Performing Arts, 7630 Biscayne Boulevard, Miami
33138, 758-8731

Camelot Talent Agency, 2233 Lee Road, Winter Park 33136,
644-0201

Travis Falcon, 17070 Collins Avenue, Miami Beach 33139,
947-7957

Florida Casting Agency, DuPont Plaza Center, 300 Biscayne
Boulevard Way, ✶310, Miami 33131, 358-3228

Florida Talent Agency, 2631 East Oakland Park Boulevard,
Fort Lauderdale 33306, 947-1931

Jean Henderson, 709 South Federal Highway, Pompano Beach
33062, 943-1291

International Creative Management, 111 NW 183rd Street,
Miami 33169, 652-9111

MarBea Agency, 104 Crandon Boulevard, ✶305, Key Biscayne 33149, 361-1144

Marks Talent Agency, 600 Lincoln Road, Miami Beach 33139,
543-2119

The Talent Agents, 1528 Northeast 147th Street, Miami
   33167, 940-7076

And now for the smaller middle markets.

DENVER

Union

SAG, 6825 East Tennessee Avenue, Suite 639, Denver 80224
   (303) 388-4287

Agents

Accents International Ltd., 470 South Colorado Boulevard,
   ✳15, Denver 80222, 399-2733
Barbizon Agency, 701 West Hampden Avenue, Englewood
   80110, 781-7828
J. F. Images, Inc., 1776 Jackson, Denver 80206, 758-7777
Light Company, 1443 Wazee Street, Denver 80202, 572-8363
The Talent Agency, 16 West 13th Avenue, ✳201, Denver
   80204, 893-1383
Vannoy Talent, 1100 East 16th Avenue, Denver 80218,
   832-7177

Advertising Agencies

Barickman Advertising, Greenwood Plaza, P.O. Box 9569,
   Denver 80209, 770-4500
Broyles, Allebaugh & Davis, Inc., 8231 East Prentice Avenue,
   Englewood 80110, 770-2000
Frye-Sills, Inc., 5500 South Syracuse Circle, Englewood 80110,
   773-3900
Sam Lusky Associates, 633 17th Street, Denver 80202,
   623-4141
Tracy-Locke, Inc., 7503 Marin Drive, Suite 2B, Englewood
   80111, 773-3100

Production Companies

Another Production Company, 1420 Blake Street, Denver 80202, 623-6616

Cinema Services, 2010 East 17th Street, Denver 80206, 320-5811

Image 9, 1089 Bannock, Denver 80204, 825-5288

JPI, Denver, 1420 Larimer Square, Denver 80204, 623-0167

Phelan Productions, Inc., 1621 York Street, Denver 80206, 399-4580

Summit Films, Inc., P.O. Box 129, Vail 81657, 476-5940

DETROIT

Union

SAG, 28690 Southfield Road, Lathrup Village 48076, (313) 559-9540

Agents

Advertisers Casting Service, 15324 East Jefferson, Grosse Pointe Park 48230, 823-1880

Afbony Models & Talent, 2310 Cass Avenue, ✷710, Lathrup Village 48201, 963-3962

Affiliated Models, Inc., 15920 West Twelve Mile Road, Southfield, 48076, 559-3110

Bettye Davis Modeling Agency, 19603 Mack Avenue, Grosse Pointe Woods 48236

Leslie Fargo Agency, 811 Fisher Building, Detroit 48202, 871-4445

Gail & Rice Talent, 18845 Mayfield, Livonia 48150, 427-9300

Patricia Stevens Modeling Agency, 1900 West Big Beaver Road, Troy 48084, 643-1900

Production Companies

National TV News, Inc., 13691 West Eleven Mile Road, Oak Park 48237, 541-1440

176 HOW TO GET YOUR CHILD

N/L Productions, Inc., 917 Fisher Building, Detroit 48202, 871-4225

The Tom Thomas Organization, Inc., 26600 Telegraph, Southfield 48034, 681-8600

Video Films Incorporated, 2211 East Jefferson Avenue, Detroit, 393-0800

Werthman Group, Inc., 1933 East Vernier, Grosse Pointe Woods 48236, 886-7686

PHOENIX

Union

SAG, 3030 North Central, #919, Phoenix 85012, (602) 279-9975

Agents

Bobby Ball Agency, 808 East Osborn Road, Phoenix 85014, 264-5007

G.A.F. Enterprises, P.O. Box 26208, Phoenix 85068, 264-9860

Hamco Personnel, 1802 North Central Avenue, Phoenix 85014, 257-1626

New Faces, Inc., 5108B North 7th Street, Phoenix 85014, 279-3200

Plaza Three Talent Agency, 4621 North 16th Street, Phoenix 85051, 279-4179

Red Wing American Indian Talent Agency, 711 East Palo Verde Drive, Phoenix 85014, 265-9703

Tor/Ann Talent & Booking, 3000 East Thomas Road, Phoenix 85016, 263-8708

Ad Agency

Jennings & Thompson, 3033 North Central Avenue, Phoenix 85012, 263-8588

Production Companies

Kucharo & Grad., Ltd., 57 East Osborn Road, Phoenix 85012, 263-5304

Linsman Film & Tape Productions, 7340 Scottsdale Mall, Scottsdale 85253, 949-9008

Marshall Faber Productions, 6412 East Desert Cove, Scottsdale 85254, 948-8086

Swartwout Productions, Inc., 6736 East Avalon Drive, Scottsdale 85251, 994-4774

Way Out West Productions, 4144 North 49th Street, Phoenix 85014, 959-5270

SAN DIEGO

Union

SAG, 3045 Rosecrans Boulevard, #308, San Diego 92110, (714) 222-3996

Agents

Commercial Artist Management Agency, 2232 Fifth Avenue, San Diego 92101, 233-6655

Crosby Talent Agency, 3611 Fifth Avenue, San Diego 92101, 291-2937

Tina Real, 3108 Fifth Avenue, San Diego 92101, 298-0544

SAN FRANCISCO

Union

SAG, 100 Bush Street, 26th floor, San Francisco 94104, (415) 391-7510

Agents

Brebner Agencies, Inc., 161 Berry Street, #1248, San Francisco 94107, 495-6700

Ann Demeter Agency, 2087 Union Street, San Francisco 94123, 567-5226

Grimme Agency, 214 Grant Avenue, ⚹302, San Francisco 94108, 392-9175

House of Charm, 157 Maiden Lane, San Francisco 94108, 421-0968

Panda Agency, 3721 Hoen Avenue, Santa Rosa 95404, (707) 544-3671

Ryden-Frazer Agency, 1901 South Bascom Avenue, ⚹344, Campbell 95008, (408) 371-1973

The Sabina Agency, 415 Merchant Street, San Francisco 94111, 788-3939

LaVonne Valentine Talent & Modeling Agency, 150 Powell Street, San Francisco 94102, 673-7965

San Diego and San Francisco, being part of the state of California, are bound by the stringent child labor laws there, in particular the one that insists that a child be signed with an agent. That means you don't have the option to free-lance your child in these two cities. However, you do have Los Angeles at your doorstep. There are a fair number of children from San Diego and San Francisco who commute regularly to Los Angeles for interviews and jobs. It's not cheap, and not all agents will agree to it. However, if your child is extremely commercial, starting him off in L.A. can certainly be worth your while.

The Minor Markets

The minor markets are easily defined as every city, other than the major and middle markets, where commercials are made. Some of the following areas are well on their way to qualifying as middle markets; others have only minimal commercial activity.

You can expect, as a rule, to have the easiest time getting your child started in those areas where commercial agents exist. They wouldn't be there if there weren't enough activity to justify their existence.

If you live in an area where there are no agents, check first to see if there is a nearby city—a commute within an hour and a half is considered nearby—that does list agents. If there is none, then you are truly on your own. You must be the agent. It's not difficult; it requires a lot of persistence, however. The rules are really the same as for free-lancing. Have professional photographs of your child taken, not just head shots but a variety of poses and moods. Select the best and have them made up into a composite, following the format set forth in previous chapters. A printer who does lithography will be able to do the paste-up and printing for you. With these composites you want to include a résumé/letter listing your child's vital statistics, special abilities, training, and any theatrical or modeling experience. Staple the résumé to the composite, making sure that your name, address, and telephone number are printed on both, and mail them to every ad agency and production company in your area and to those within commuting distance.

Wait a week and then call every one of those places you sent the composite. Be quick and polite; all you want to know is whether they expect someday to need children for their commercials. Whatever the answer, yes, no, or maybe, ask them to keep your child's photo on file, "just in case . . ."

From time to time, go through your list and make another round of phone calls, "just to check on the situation . . ." You may be considered a pest, but you will also be remembered if and when they do need to use a child on a job.

Getting that first job will be the most difficult; after that, your child will be known as a commercial kid, a proven professional to be called whenever the need arises. If your child's first job is on a union commercial, you would be wise to join immediately. In many areas where there are no agents, commercial-makers call SAG or AFTRA for the names of children available for work. Obviously, getting your child's name on that list is what you're aiming for.

MINOR MARKET DIRECTORY

ALABAMA

Production Companies

Arbus Films, 8005 Navios Drive SE, Huntsville 35802, (205) 881-8455

Metcalfe Film & Video Productions, 3709 Locksley Drive, Birmingham 35223, (205) 967-1661

ALASKA

Production Company

Films North, P.O. Box 2333, Anchorage 99510, 344-1026

ARIZONA

Agents

Dar Lu Modeling & Talent Agency, 2509 East Alta Vista, Tucson 85716, (602) 327-5692

Fosi's Talent Agency, 2777 North Campbell Avenue, Tucson 85719, (602) 795-3534

CONNECTICUT

Union

AFTRA, 117 Prospect Street, Stamford 06901

Agents

Connecticut Modeling Agency, 1326 Shippan Avenue, Stamford 06904, (203) 325-0576

Ridgefield Model Agency, 54 Main Street, Ridgefield 06877, (203) 438-7711

Production Companies

The Commercial Cannery, The Exchange, Suite 332, Farmington 06032, (203) 677-4853

Howard A. Kaiser, 602 Georgetown Woods, Deep River 06417, 526-9852

Owen Murphy Productions, Inc., 1 Turkey Hill Road South, Westport 06880, 226-4241

Sleeping Giant Films, Inc., 3019 Dixwell Avenue, Hamden 06514, 248-9323

Sound Concepts, Inc., 30 Hazel Terrace, Woodbridge, 397-1363

Many Connecticut children make the commute to Manhattan to pursue their commercial careers there.

DELAWARE

Production Company

Ken-Del Productions, Inc., 111 Valley Road, Wilmington 19804, (302) 655-7488

Depending on where you live in Delaware, you can also use Washington, D.C., and Philadelphia as your commercial centers.

FLORIDA

Agents

Dott Burns Model & Talent Agency, 478 Severn, Davis Island, Tampa 33606, (813) 251-5882

Production Companies

Peter J. Barton Productions, 1100 East Park Avenue, Tallahassee 32301, 224-3685

Chroma Color Corporation, P.O. Box 3241, Pensacola 32506, (904) 456-2804

Gordon-Kerckoff Productions, Inc., of New York, 1185 Cattlemen Road, P.O. Box 10235, Sarasota 33578, (813) 371-0013

Image Communications, Inc., 1700 North Westshore Boulevard, Tampa 33607, 872-6828

Glen Lau Productions, 3211 SW 27th Avenue, Ocala 32671, (904) 237-2129

M & M Photography, Inc., 1057 South Clearview, Tampa 33609, 251-5963

Patterson Studios, 600 Overlook Drive, Box 748, Winter Haven, (813) 324-3696

Michael Storms Productions, Inc., 10560 Jepson Street, Orlando 32817, (305) 277-2045

Hack Swain Productions, Inc., 1185 Cattlemen Road, P.O. Box 10235, Sarasota 33578, (813) 371-2360

United Film Productions, 2302 Diversified Way, Orlando 32804, (305) 422-4514

Casting Director

Sara & Woody Enterprises, 2405 North McRae Street 32803, Orlando (305) 898-4688

GEORGIA

Production Company

Filmit Productions, Inc., 18 East Macon Street, Savannah 31401, (912) 236-6361

HAWAII

Union

SAG, c/o Gregg Kendall, Hilton Lagoon, 2003 Kalia Road, Honolulu 96815, (808) 946-9577

Agents

Barbizon Agency, 1600 Kapiolani Boulevard, Honolulu 96814, 946-9081

B & B Talent Agency, 657 Kapiolani Boulevard, Suite 13, Honolulu 96813, 533-3583

Bob Busch, 47-136 Uakoko Place, Kaneahe 96744, 239-7373

Century Center, 1750 Kalakaua Avenue, Honolulu 96815, 955-2271

Independent Casting, Inc., 282 Opihikao Way, Honolulu 96825, 377-6036

Island Talent, 1833 Kalakaua Avenue, Honolulu 96815, 946-1606

JJ Productions, 1441 Kapiolani Boulevard, Honolulu 96814, 947-6871

Gregg Kendall & Associates, Inc., Ilikai Hotel, Suite 101, 1777 Ala Moana Boulevard, Honolulu 96815, 946-9577

John Robert Powers, 1314 South King Street, Suite 504, Honolulu 96814, 521-4908

Ruth Revere Talent Agency, 2708 Laniloa, P.O. Box 3079, Honolulu 96802, 537-3139

Saint John Studios of Hawaii, 1860 Ala Moana Boulevard, Honolulu 96815, 947-2822

Ad Agencies

Fawcett-McDermott Cavanagh, 1441 Kapiolani Boulevard, Honolulu 96814, 941-7722

Milici/Valenti Advertising, 700 Bishop Street, 12th floor, Honolulu 96813, 536-0881

Patt Patterson & Associates, Inc., 333 Queen Street, Honolulu 96813, 531-6431

Seigle Rolfs & Wood, Inc., 900 Fort Street Mall, Honolulu 96813, 531-6211

Production Company

Allison Productions, Inc., 1833 Kalakaua Avenue, Honolulu 96815, 955-1000

INDIANA

Unions

AFTRA, 606 Board of Trade Building, Indianapolis 46204
AFTRA, 1220 Victory Avenue, South Bend 46615

Agents

Wilhelmina Klinger, Box 36, Buck Creek 47924 (317) 589-3321

Production Companies

Film Productions of Indianapolis, 128 East 36th Street, Indianapolis 46205, 924-5163

Galbreath Media Group, Inc., 2920 Engle Road, Fort Wayne 46809, 747-6780

Kartes Productions, Inc., 9135 North Meridian Street, Suite B5, Indianapolis 46260, (317) 844-7403

Michaeljay Communications, Inc., 802 Wabash Street, Chesterton 46304, (219) 926-7615

Performance Productions, P.O. Box 68234, Indianapolis 46268, 291-6154

KANSAS

Production Companies

Centron Corporation, Inc., P.O. Box 687, Lawrence 66044, 843-0400

The Gilbert Group, 6801 West 76th Terrace, Overland Park 66021, (913) 642-9600

Meredith Video Productions, 4500 Johnson Drive, Fairway

KENTUCKY

Union

AFTRA, 410 South Third Street, Louisville 40202

Production Company

Louisville Productions, 520 West Chestnut, Lexington 40508, 582-7555

LOUISIANA

Union

AFTRA, 1110 Royal Street, New Orleans 70116, (504) 524-9903

Production Companies

Tom Buckholtz, 5900 Magazine Street, New Orleans 70115, (504) 891-0912

Charbonnet-Stroble, 3239 Dauphine Street, New Orleans 70117, 949-4040

Panorama Productions, P.O. Box 3297, Baton Rouge 70821, 766-8088

Brooks Read & Associates, 236 Napolean Street, Baton Rouge 70802, 343-1715

MAINE

Production Companies

Ballantine Films, Inc., RFD ⚹1, North Berwick 03906, (207) 676-4415

Foster & Associates, 40 Lincoln Avenue, Gardiner 04345, (207) 582-4607

MARYLAND

Production Companies

Academy Film Productions, Inc., 210 West 29th Street, Baltimore 21211, 338-0550

Doug Bailey Films, Inc., 140 Congressional Lane, Rockville 20852, 881-0200

BF&J Productions, Inc., 1742 Hillside Road, Stevenson 21153, 653-9373

Charlie/Papa Productions, Inc., 5813 Wicomico Avenue, Rockville 20852, 881-2420

Eastern Video Systems, P.O. Box 1324, Rockville 20852, 340-7873

Hallmark Films & Recording, 51 New Plant Court, Owings Mills 21117, (301) 363-4500

Monumental Films, Inc., 2160 Rockrose Avenue, Baltimore 21211, 462-1550

MASSACHUSETTS

Union

SAG, 11 Beacon Street, Room 1103, Boston 02108, (617) 742-2688

Production Companies

Applied Creative Arts, 55 Grace Street, Malden 02148, 322-4571

Bay State Film Productions, 35 Springfield Street, Agawam 01001, (413) 786-4454

Borden Productions, Inc., Box 520, Great Meadows Road, Concord 01742, 369-5030

Bostonia Productions, 390 Commonwealth Avenue, Boston 02169, 536-8270

W. H. Brown & Company, Inc., 873 Concord Street, Framingham 01701, 879-3336

Equinox-Boston Films, 50 Kearney Road, Needham 02194, 444-4479

Chester-Barley Films, Inc., 176 Newbury Street, Boston 02159, 267-0391

Cinemagraphics, 101 Trowbridge Street, Cambridge 02138, 491-0866

H. H. Fuller/Film Company, 54 Preston Road, Somerville 02143, 766-5632

Robert Gilmore Associates, Inc., 990 Washington Street, Dedham 02026, 329-6633

Steven Hansen Photography, 84 Berkeley Street, Boston 02116, 426-6858

Bruce Johnson Films, Inc., 1209 Boylston Street, Boston 02164, 267-9215 or 876-0707

Detrick Lawrence, Box 1722, Duxbury 02332, 934-6156

Midnight Sun Productions, Inc., 12 Porter Road, Cambridge 02140, 547-0477

Nightown Studios, Nourse Road, Bolton 01740, 779-2857

Peter S. Parker & Co., 2 Homans Lane, Canton 02021, 828-4923

Pike Productions of Boston, 47 Galen Street, Watertown 02172, 924-5000

September Productions, 17 Newbury Street, Boston 02116, 262-6090

Take 2 International, 59 Orchard Street, Belmont 02178, 484-1654

Videocraft Productions, Inc., 21 Brookline Avenue, Boston 02215, 267-7035

Vizwiz, 51 Sleeper Street, Boston 02210, 426-7776

D. J. Warnock Associates, Inc., 51 Melcher Street, Boston 02210, 482-7778

MINNESOTA

Union

SAG, 2500 Park Avenue, Suite A, Minneapolis 55402, (612) 885-2414

Production Companies

Fred Badiyan Productions, 2950 Metro Drive, Suite 310, Minneapolis 55420, 854-2946

The Filmakers, Inc., 430 Oak Grove Street, Minneapolis 55403, 870-8691

Low & Associates, Inc., 980 West 79th Street, Minneapolis 55420, 884-7524

Jim McGovern & Associates, 934 Hampden Avenue, St. Paul 55114, 644-2563

Markle-Goins, Inc., 127 North 7th Street, Minneapolis 55401, 338-7550

Northwest Teleproductions, Inc., 4455 West 77th Street, Minneapolis 55435, 835-4455

Reid Ray Films, Inc., 2269 Ford Parkway, St. Paul 55116, 669-1393

Sly-Fox Films, Inc., 1025 Currie Avenue, Minneapolis 55403, 336-3608

MISSOURI

Unions

AFTRA, 4530 Madison Upper Level, Kansas City 64111, (816) 753-4557

AFTRA, 818 Olive Street, Suite 671, St. Louis 63101, (314) 231-8410

Agents

Backstage Workshop Talent Agency, 8025 Ward Parkway Plaza, Kansas City 64114, (816) 363-8088

Jackson Artists Corp., 10000 West 75th Street, #122, Shawnee Mission, Kansas 66204, (913) 384-5353

Marquis Models, Inc., 9804 East 87th Street, Raytown 64138, (816) 356-8397

Production Companies

Celebrities Productions, 8229 Maryland, St. Louis 63105, 862-7800

Communico, 1315 North Highway Drive, Fenton, St. Louis 63026, 225-6000

Dix & Associates, Inc., 4501 Broadway, Kansas City 64111, 531-4455

Hardcastle Film Associates, 7319 Wise Avenue, St. Louis 63117, 647-4200

Fran Hunt Creative Services, 8911 Lou Court, St. Louis 63126, (314) 842-1686

Kleinman Productions, Inc., 7815 Milan Avenue, St. Louis 63130, 965-0714

Laclede Communications Services, Inc., 1345 Hanley Industrial Court, St. Louis 63144, 961-1414

Multimedia Forum, 2450 Grand Suite 400, Crown Center, Kansas City 64108, 274-8321

Versatile Television Productions, 324 Broadway, Cape Girardeau 63701, 335-8816

Dick Willis & Associates, 4138 Broadway, Kansas City 64111, 931-2100

Casting Director

The White House Studios, 229 Ward Parkway, Suite 5B, Kansas City 64112, (816) 031-3608

MONTANA

Ad Agency

Wendt Advertising, P.O. Box 2128, Great Falls 59403, (406) 452-8581

Production Company

Ronn Bayley Film/Tape, 202 Lindley Place, Bozeman 59715, 586-9656

NEBRASKA

Union

AFTRA, 3555 Farnam Street, Omaha 68131

Production Companies

Chapman/Spittler, Inc., 1908 California Street, Omaha 68102, 348-1600

Walter S. Craig Film Productions, 4315 Burt Street, Omaha 68131, 551-4400

NEVADA

Union

SAG, 2505 Mason Avenue, Las Vegas 89102, (702) 878-4875

Agents

Creative Entertainment Associates, 1629 East Sahara Avenue, Las Vegas 89104, 733-7575

Janssen/Baskow Agency, 732 South 4th Street, Las Vegas 89101, 384-0936

Jess Mack Agency, 1111 Las Vegas Boulevard South, Las Vegas 89104, 382-2193

Nevada Motion Picture Services, 3304 Spring Mountain Road, #30, Las Vegas 89104, 873-3317

Production Services of Nevada, 1111 Las Vegas Boulevard South, #208-C, Las Vegas 89104, 384-0692

Production Company

Larry Wood Productions, P.O. Box 11291, Las Vegas 89111, 739-7705

NEW HAMPSHIRE

Production Companies

Cineworks, 124 Great Bay Road, Greenland 03840, 431-4241

Merrimack Productions, 155 Myrtle Street, Manchester 03104,
    (603) 627-2599

David Quaid Productions, Inc., P.O. Box 698, Wolfeboro
    03894, 569-1818

NEW JERSEY

Agents

Jo Anderson Models, 400 Route 38, Maple Shade 08052,
    (212) 779-2447

Entertainment Associates, 6027 Prodigy Building, Route 130,
    Pennsauken 08110, (609) 662-3444

Production Companies

Allscope, Inc., P.O. Box 4060, Princeton 08540, (609)
    799-4200

Cinerex Associates, 11 Allison Drive, Englewood Cliffs 07632,
    (201) 567-9288

Creative Productions, Inc., 200 Main Street, Orange 07050,
    676-4422

Fiore Films, 128 Mallory Avenue, Jersey City 07304,
    432-4474

Leo Meister Productions, 321 River Road, Nutley 07110,
    (201) 667-2323

Performance Designs, Inc., 16 Allen Drive, Woodcliff Lake
    07675, (201) 391-8588

Samuel Lawrence Schulman Productions, Inc., 39 Elmhurst
    Avenue, Trenton 08618, 396-6913

Sounds & Images, 1480 Pleasant Valley Way, West Orange
    07052, 736-4310

Bob Thomas Productions, P.O. Box 1787, Wayne 07470, 696-7500

Zounds!, 224 Bellevue Avenue, Haddonfield 08033, (609) 429-4482

New Jersey is another state that feeds a lot of children into the Manhattan commercial business.

NEW MEXICO

Union

SAG, 410 Old Taos Highway, Santa Fe 87501, (505) 982-4296

Agents

Chaparral Talent Agency, 12105 Rosemont Avenue NE, Albuquerque 87112, 298-0106

Cinema Services of New Mexico, 712 Sundown Place SE, Albuquerque 87108, 255-7003

New Mexico Film Agency, 1710 Canyon Road, Santa Fe 87501, 983-8288

Territorial Talent Casting, 209 Second Street, Rio Rancho 87124, 897-0274

Universal Artists Ltd., 4001 Carlisle NE, Albuquerque 87107, 883-2848

Production Companies

Arlette Studio Film Productions, 1523 Elfego Baca Drive SW, Albuquerque 87105, 831-9615

Bandelier Films, Inc., 2001 Gold Avenue SE, Albuquerque 87106, 242-2679

SKS Productions, Box 2510, Santa Fe 87501, 983-7247

NEW YORK STATE

Unions

AFTRA, 341 Northern Boulevard, Albany 12204
AFTRA, 50 Front Street, Binghamton 13905
AFTRA, 615 Brisbane Building, Buffalo 14203
AFTRA, Suite 900 One Exchange, Rochester 14614
AFTRA, 1400 Balltown Road, Schenectady 12309

Production Companies

Lester Bergman & Associates, Inc., East Mountain Road, Cold Spring 10516, (914) 265-3656
Concepts in Communications, 1300 Statler-Hilton, Buffalo 14202, (716) 853-7477
ENT/Gates Films, Inc., 200 Chicago Street, Buffalo 14204 856-3220
Parameters Unlimited, 515 Broadway, Albany 12207, (518) 463-5366
Peter Pastorelle Productions, Inc., 50 West Street, Suite C9A, Harrison 10528, (914) 835-2930
Raul Da Silva & Other Filmmakers, 1400 East Avenue, Rochester 14610, 442-1373
WUTV-Channel 29, 951 Whitehaven Road, Grand Island 14072, 773-7531

NORTH CAROLINA

Production Companies

Martin Beck & Associates, P.O. Box 891, Boiling Springs 28017, (704) 482-0252
Jefferson Productions, 1 Julian Price Place, Charlotte 28208, 374-3823
Robert Rogers Productions, P.O. Box 3755, 1015 East Boulevard, Charlotte 28203, 377-3456

NORTH DAKOTA

Production Company

Bill Snyder Films, Inc., 1419 First Avenue South, Box 2784, Fargo 58103, 293-3600

OHIO

Unions

SAG, 1367 East 6th Street, Suite 229, Cleveland 44114, (216) 781-2255

AFTRA, 15 West Sixth Street, Suite 607, Cincinnati 45202, (513) 241-7332

AFTRA, 6600 Busch Boulevard, Columbus 43229

Production Companies

Actor's & Director's Studio, 2010 East Broad, Columbus 43209, 235-9831

Arocom Productions, 2680 West Market Street, Akron 44313, 867-7950

Bright Light Productions, Inc., 420 Plum Street, Cincinnati 45202, 721-2574

Cinecraft, Inc., 2515 Franklin Boulevard, Cleveland 44107, 781-2300

Cinema One Productions, Inc., P.O. Box 613, Edgewater Branch, Cleveland 44107, 228-1080

Film-Art Inc., 2436 Vine Street, Cincinnati 45219, 621-4930

Focus Unlimited, Inc., 5515 Southwyck Boulevard, Toledo 43614, 865-1341

Fox & Associates, Inc., 228 Standard Building, Cleveland 44113, 621-8520

Gaughan-Michitsch Films, 1706 Euclid Avenue, Cleveland 44115, 621-0599

Media Resources, 1441 North High Street, Columbus 43201, 291-3519

OKLAHOMA

Production Companies

KTVY Productions, 500 East Britton Road, Oklahoma City
73114, 478-1212

Prime Time Design, 1911 Classen Boulevard, Oklahoma City
73106, 521-8956

OREGON

Union

AFTRA, 111 American Bank Building, Portland 97205,
(503) 222-3986

Ad Agency

Petzold & Associates, 1800 SW 1st, Portland 97201, (503)
221-1800

Production Companies

Terry A. Hartman Studio, P.O. Box 40213, Portland 97240,
667-4613

Northwestern, Inc., 1224 SW Broadway, Portland 97205,
226-0170

Photo-Art Studios, 900 SW 13th Avenue, Portland 97205,
224-5665

PENNSYLVANIA

Unions

SAG, 1405 Locust Street, ✕811, Philadelphia 19102, (215)
545-3150

AFTRA, One Thousand, The Bank Tower, Pittsburgh 15222,
(412) 281-6767

Agents

Jolly Joyce, 2028 Chestnut Street, Philadelphia 19103,
564-0982
Main Line Models Guild, 160 King of Prussia Plaza, King of
Prussia 19406, 687-4759
Midiri Models, 1902 Chestnut Street, Philadelphia 19103,
561-5028
Models' Guild Philadelphia, 1512 Spruce Street, Philadelphia
19102, 735-4067
Joseph Rocco, 21 South Fifth Street, Philadelphia 19106,
462-2063 or 582-8040

Production Companies

Animation Arts Association, Inc., 2225 Spring Garden
Street, Philadelphia 19130, 563-2520
Aurvid Videor Productions, P.O. Box 413, Philadelphia
19105, 828-0502
Baker Productions, Inc., 1600 Walnut Street, Wayne 19087,
(215) 546-4634
Berghmans & Roberts Productions, Suite 338, Park City (West
Mall), Lancaster 17601, (717) 397-4869
Cine Dynamics, Inc., 2010 Josephine Street, Pittsburgh 15203,
381-9402
Hardman Associates, Inc., 213 Smithfield Street, Pittsburgh
15222, 281-4450
International Motion Pictures, Ltd., P.O. Box 3201, Erie
16508, 864-4908
Hal Kirn & Associates, 1700 Addison Street, Philadelphia
19146, 546-8887
The Latent Image, Inc., 247 Fort Pitt Building, Pittsburgh
15222, 261-5589
Leroy Motion Pictures Production Studios, 531 South Street,
Philadelphia 19147, 925-3769
The Media Shop, 7820 Spring Avenue, Chalfont 18914,
635-5885

Mode-Art Pictures, Inc., 3075 West Liberty Avenue, Pittsburgh 15201, 343-8700

Walter G. O'Connor Co., Box Y, Hershey 17033, 534-1000

Hartwick Przyborski Productions, 100 Ross Avenue, Pittsburgh 15221, 765-3910

Schulman Berry Kramer Co., Inc., 711 Montgomery Avenue, Narbeth 19072, 667-7171

The Seventh Art, Box 190, RD 2, Malvern 19355, 647-2562

Tel-Fax, Inc., 4654 Airport Road, Bath 18014, 837-1600, 837-1861

TPC Communications, 445 Melwood Street, Pittsburgh 15213, 682-2300

Visions, 1079 Summerwood Drive, Harrisburg 17111, (717) 652-4937

RHODE ISLAND

Production Company

Studio 12, 2 Needham Street, Johnston 02919, 943-2333

SOUTH CAROLINA

Production Company

Tri-Comm Productions, Inc., Sea Pines Circle, Hilton Head Island 29928, (805) 785-5920

TENNESSEE

Union

SAG, 1014 17th Avenue South, Nashville 37212, (615) 256-0155

198

HOW TO GET YOUR CHILD

Production Companies

Continental Film Productions Corp., 4220 Amnicola Highway,
Chattanooga 37406, 622-1193

DMK Films, Inc., 713 Melpark Drive, Nashville 37204,
383-3044

Fotovox, Inc., 752 South Sommerville, Memphis 38104,
774-4383

Ami Ron Productions, 206 Elmington Avenue, Nashville
37205, 269-9778

Scene 3, 1813 8th Avenue South, Nashville 37203, 385-2820

TEXAS (other than Dallas)

Agents

Gerri Halpin Agency, 911 Kipling, Houston 77006, 526-5749

Mad Hatter Inc., 1400 South Post Oak, ✳1501, Houston
77056, 621-3770

Production Companies

Channel Six Productions, 2955 IH-10, Beaumont 77702,
892-6622

Englander/Take Two, 2708 French Place, Austin 78722,
476-6338

Film House, 800 West Avenue, Austin 78701, 478-6611

Bob Green Productions, Inc., 7950 Westglen, Houston 75074,
977-1334

KMCC McAlister TV Enterprises, 84th & Avenue L, Lubbock
79408, (806) 745-2828

MCI Productions-Houston, 10 Greenway Plaza, Houston
77046, 627-9270

Media Masters, Inc., 2640 Fountainview, Houston 77057,
977-8626

MFC Film Production, Inc., 5915 Star Lane, Houston 77057,
781-7703

Texas Coast Productions, 4021 Austin, Houston 77004, 528-8209

Texas National Productions, Inc., 543 Brooklyn Avenue, San Antonio 78215, 226-5077

Casting Directors

Austin Actors' Clearing House, 501 North IH-35, Austin 78702, 476-3412

The Casting & Production Group, Inc., 702 Windrock Drive, San Antonio 78239, 653-5794

Interart Works, 108 West 8th, Austin 78701, 472-7099

New Gary Griffin Productions, 12667 Memorial Drive, Houston 77024, 465-9017

UTAH

Agents

JF Images, 350 South 4th East, Salt Lake City 84111, (801) 364-1976

McCarty Casting, 150 West 500 South, Salt Lake City 84107, 359-9294

Ad Agency

Gillham Advertising, 15 East 1st South, 5th floor, Salt Lake City 84111, 328-0281

Production Companies

Osmond Commercial Productions, 1420 East 800 North, Orem 84059, 244-4444

Michael Utterback Productions, 918 East 900 South, Salt Lake City 84105, 531-7767

VERMONT

Production Companies

Cambridgeport Film Corp., Box 72, Roxbury 05669, 485-8428
Resources, 116 South Champlain Street, Burlington 05401,
    862-0550
Vermont Studio, RFD 2, Putney 05346, 257-0859

VIRGINIA

Production Companies

Ads A-V Production, Inc., 115 Hillwood Avenue, Falls Church
    22046, 536-9000
Colony Productions & Studios, 311 West Franklin Street, Rich-
    mond 23220, 643-3571
Screenscope, Inc., 1022 Wilson Boulevard, Arlington 22209,
    527-3555
Stuart Finley, Inc., 3428 Mansfield Road, Falls Church 22041,
    820-7700
Studio III, 1905 Colonial Avenue, Norfolk 23517, 623-0214

If you live in Northern Virginia, you can add Washington, D.C. to
your commercial territory.

WASHINGTON

Union

SAG, 158 Thomas Street, Seattle 98109, (206) 624-7340

Ad Agencies

Cole & Weber, Inc., 3100 South 176th Street, Seattle 98188,
    433-6200

McCann-Erickson, Inc., 2300 Seattle First National Bank Building, Seattle 98154, 682-6360

Ricks-Ehrig, Inc., 4th & Vine Building, Seattle 98121, 623-6666

Production Companies

George Carlson & Associates, Arcade Building, Seattle 98101, 623-8045

Coffin & Company, 1941 Aurora Avenue North, Seattle 98109, 282-1941

DeCourcey Associates, Inc., 2120 West Barrett, Seattle 98199

WISCONSIN

Union

AFTRA, WRJN Sentry Broadcasting Co., Racine 53405

Production Companies

Ash Film Productions, 5018 Milward Drive, Madison 53711, (608) 271-2848

Lemorande Production Co., 207 East Michigan Avenue, Milwaukee 53202, 271-3358

Moynihan Associates, 1717 South 12th Street, Milwaukee 53204, 645-8200

Nelson Productions, Inc., 3929 North Humboldt Boulevard, Milwaukee 53212, 962-4445

WASHINGTON, D.C.

Union

SAG, Chevy Chase Center Building, Suite 210, Washington, D.C. 20015, (202) 657-2560

Production Companies

Astrafilms, Inc., 530 Eighth Street SE 20003, 543-1011

Audio Visual Specialties, 2637 Connecticut Avenue NW 20008, 462-6078

Georgetown Productions, 1428 Wisconsin Avenue NW 20007, 337-1487

Hermes Films, Ltd., 3218 39th Street NW 20016, 244-3942

Screen Presentations, Inc., 309 Massachusetts Avenue NE 20002, 546-8900

TWII Productions, Inc., 1611 Connecticut Avenue NW 20009, 265-4433

Visual Images, 2637 Connecticut Avenue NW 20008, 387-0831

Voice & Vision Productions, 1833 Kalorama Road NW 20009, 483-1700 (mostly Spanish-speaking commercials)

Washington Filmakers, 2233 Wisconsin Avenue NW 20007, 333-0700

Worldwide Films, Inc., 514 Tenth Street NW 20004, 628-3727

If you live in one of the six states not listed in this directory, or if your state shows only one or two production companies, don't be discouraged: The making of commercials goes on virtually all over the country. In many towns and cities, it is the local television stations who produce the commercials. Call all the stations in your area and find out which ones have a production department that services their local sponsors. Then send them the photograph/résumé package you've made up for your child. Don't ask in advance if they'd be interested in using your child; they won't know that they are until they see how terrific he is.

Do the same for all the advertising agencies listed in your Yellow Pages. Even the smallest probably has one or two accounts, local businesses most likely, for whom they produce commercials.

And finally, while you have the phone book out, check to see if there's a category called Theatrical Agents, or some similar wording. Most of the agents in this book are union-franchised but there are many all over America who are legitimate operators even though they're not affiliated with SAG or AFTRA. Call them all, but be aware always of the unscrupulous ones who are looking to make money from your ambitions for your child. Remember the rule: If they ask you for payment—for their time, their drama lessons, their photographs, whatever—you ask for the door. Legitimate agents, union or otherwise, earn their income *after* they get your child work, not before.

9

The Model Child: A Primer on Print

Name a dream, any dream . . . No, make it your first dream, the one you held dearest as a child. To be a model, right? To wear an organdy dress with a full skirt, your hair, somehow golden instead of its normal mousy brown, rolled in ringlets and tied back with a kiss-me bow. Standing, all childhood beauty and innocence, smiling out of the pages of the Rotogravure. And admit it: Somewhere, deep inside you, that dream still exists. If not for you, then for your child.

The genesis of children in advertising was the printed picture; specifically, a painting of a yawning child in pajamas holding a candle in one hand and a huge tire in the other. It was 1906, and Fisk's "Time to Re-Tire" ad become one of the most widely known trademarks in America.

As our country moved on into the sophisticated realm of advertising, and as technology improved, painted children made way for photographed children and the world of model kids was born.

For years photographic modeling, or "print work," as it's called, reigned supreme in the world of advertising. But the advent of television, and with it commercials, has relegated print work to a second-fiddle status. The potential for fame and fortune is just not the same for the child who does only print work as for the commercial kid.

However, that doesn't mean it's easier to get your child into modeling or that the requirements are any lower. The field, which encompasses all photographic ads in magazines, newspapers, billboards, and catalogues, demands the same level of professionalism as commercials. "The average concept is that all a person has to do in print work is go stand in front of a camera and be photographed," says Jeanette Walton, head of the print department at the Wormser, Helfond & Joseph Agency in Los Angeles. "Well, that's just not so. It requires more than just a look. You can't take just any kid off the street and make him a model.

"That was made very clear when California extended their child labor laws to cover the print field. A lot of photographers thought they'd get real smart and get around the legal requirements by bringing in their nephews and nieces and neighbors to be their models. But inevitably I'd get a call from them a week or so later. 'I have to reshoot that job,' they'd say. 'I need one of your kids.'

"That happened because they had amateurs. Not only did the sessions take three or four times as long to shoot, but they just didn't come out good. You know, if you get, say five hundred amateurs in front of you, *maybe* you'd come up with three or four really great kids. There's a certain talent involved in modeling; it's not just a nothing job."

Talent/Temperament/Type

The talented model child isn't that different from the talented commercial kid. The basics for both are an outgoing, friendly personality with no fear of strangers. "You can have the most beautiful child in the world," says Walton, "but if he's shy and he's going to put his head down and his thumb in his mouth and hold onto Mother's leg, he's not going to accomplish much in still photography."

The truly superb model kids bring another quality to their work. It's indefinable, says top children's photographer Elyse

Lewin. "The best kids throw a little extra of themselves into the picture. They'll do exactly what I tell them to and then some. Like that little girl over there." Lewin points to a photograph of a small girl sitting in a big chair. "I said to her, 'I just want you to sit there and put your finger in your mouth.' She did it, and then instinctively her foot went out a certain way and her little finger extended. That's nothing you can teach a child to do; it's just being a natural at still photography."

Model kids must also have the temperament so important in commercials. They must be able to take direction, to do exactly what the photographer asks. And they must have a good attention span, one that is better, in fact, than a commercial child's. It isn't rare for the print child to be asked to hold a pose for a long period of time. And if you think that is easy, try to sit or stand in one place without moving at all for even a minute.

Go back to the quiz in Chapter 2. If you haven't done so already, take it. The results will go a long way toward telling you if your child has the talent and temperament to be a model child.

The area where there's a real difference between the model child and the commercial child is in type. Print work does not allow for the same wide range of types that commercials do. "Kids who do commercials can be extreme Character types and therefore not very attractive," says Jeanette Walton. "But children who do print must be quite good-looking. Sometimes I will get a call for a Norman Rockwell type or a pixie look. But it doesn't happen that often, and it is almost always for a product ad. For fashion photography, they seldom if ever will take anything but a Beautiful child."

For the full spectrum of print work, agents look for the very attractive child, particularly when it's a baby or a girl. "The acme in girls is blue eyes, blond hair, and the all-American, girl-next-door look," says Walton. "That's the image I get the most requests for. Boys don't have to be so beautiful, but they must be appealing and wholesome-looking."

As is the case in commercials, the ethnic child is not in as much demand. And minorities even less so. "We do try to have a certain number of black, Spanish, and Oriental children on our books,"

Walton continues, "but the requests for them are maybe ten out of every ninety calls I get."

More important than the child's type, however, is whether or not he is photogenic. "Some kids aren't that pretty, but they're terrifically photogenic," Walton explains. "And some kids are gorgeous but they take an awful picture. Usually the ones who aren't photogenic don't like having their pictures taken. They can't relax in front of a camera, and it shows in the shot."

Elyse Lewin agrees. "The most important thing parents can do to determine if their child is right for this business is to see if he likes having his photo taken. Children who do make wonderful models. They feel secure, attractive, confident, and they will do anything in front of the camera. But the kids who don't like having their pictures taken—well, their parents can just forget about a career."

More important than anything in determining if your child can do print work is whether he wants to. Looks, temperament, talent all pale in the child who doesn't want to be a model. "I've learned a lot about this business, and I now feel that the only real requirement is that the child really wants to do it," insists Jeanette Walton. "I tell the parents who bring their kids to me. 'This activity *has got* to be determined 100 percent by whether or not your child wants a career in print.'"

Getting An Agent

Today there are not many agents who handle children just for modeling. Generally, the agency will have a specific department for print work. Or, if it's a small agency, the children's agent will handle both commercials and print.

Consequently, your first move will be to find out which agents in your city represent children for modeling. Go to your local Screen Actors Guild and get a list of their franchised agents. Although SAG doesn't franchise print agents, their list will tell you which commercial agents handle print as well. Moreover, any of the commercial agents will be able to tell you of their counterparts who only handle print work. Don't, repeat, *don't* answer one of those come-on ads in your newspaper promising to "Make Your Child a Model!" No self-respecting, honest agent advertises; only those wanting your money for no return do.

Print agents, like commercial agents, won't see kids before they've screened their photographs. "If I saw everyone who calls me without first having checked out their pictures, I would be doing nothing else all day long," says Walton.

She advises that the pictures you send show your child smiling and looking straight into the camera—in other words, a head shot. Forget profiles and artsy serious shots. This is the time to show the sparkle in your child's eyes and that wide grin. If this year's school photos are really good—and face it, few are—you can send them. Otherwise, get out your camera and start shooting yourself, at close range. Actually, doing it yourself serves a double purpose: If your child balks at sitting still for you, if his eyes glaze over and his smile becomes set, you know his chances of making it as a model are slim.

The cover letter you send with the photographs should be short and to the point. You can use the sample in Chapter 3 as an example. Make sure you include your child's clothing sizes. In print work, they are not so much interested in how old children are but in what sizes they wear. Ask a photographer what the most popular ages are for kids in the print field, and the answer turns out to be the most popular sizes—3 to 6X and size 10 and size 12.

Once the agents receive your photographs, if they like what they see, you and your child will be called in for an interview. "I *have* to see the youngster in person," says Walton. "I can look at a picture and pretty much know whether the child qualifies as far as looks go. But these pictures are usually taken by a parent or grandparent in the child's own home surroundings. They're all smiles and love and happy there. But it's not uncommon that when they come in here, I find they are very shy outside the familiar territory."

The agent's interview for print is not so involved as the one for commercials. A short chat is all the agent needs to determine if a child has the personality and temperament to be a model. His

speech and reading ability are of no concern. Nor is the agent
going to put him through an improv. But in some way a good
agent will still find out if the career is the child's idea or the parents'. "I don't use any tricks," explains Walton. "I just say to the
child, 'Are you interested in going to a studio and meeting a photographer and having him take your picture, and then later you'll
see your picture in the newspaper or a magazine? Does that sound
like fun to you? Is it something you'd like to do?'

"I can spot the pushy parent who is forcing his or her child into
it a mile away. And I don't want any part of them. To me, that is
cruel—and self-serving."

Once an agent agrees to represent your child, she will explain
how she works and what you are expected to do. Generally, this
part of the interview does not differ at all from a commercial
agent's interview. Ten percent is the standard agent's fee, and
most will ask that you sign a contract. The agent will put your
child's name and vital statistics in the agency's book and, in most
cases, send you out to have professional photographs taken.

"If the child is very young, under four, we don't suggest having
composites made," says Jeanette Walton. "They change too fast at
that age, and it doesn't seem right to put the family to that kind of
expense and effort. Once they're four or five, however, I do suggest the parent take them to a photographer. I don't push it right
away, though. First, I try as best I can to get them one or two
jobs, just to see if they're going to be able to work. It's possible to
do that without pictures because I cast a lot of the jobs myself.
But I can't really do a selling job on them without photographs. I
get requests every day from photographers saying 'Please send me
pictures of boys, size 8 to 10, or girls, size 6X.' I send the pictures
and the initial casting is made from them. But if I don't have
photos of a particular child to send—well, that negates the possibility of that child getting that job."

Photographs for print work are almost always composites: a
head shot on one side and several different poses on the other.
Most agents have large loose-leaf notebooks containing the composites of all the children they represent. They give these notebooks to every photographer and advertising agency that uses

children for print work, and much of the initial casting is done from them.

The Casting Session

Print ads are most often cast by the photographer who is shooting the job rather than a casting director. "Normally when I'm casting, I will call the various agencies that I deal with—and there are only about three or four of them—and I either ask for a kid that I've already worked with or I ask to see new children of the right coloring and size," says Elyse Lewin. "I only have one agent who I know is so good that I don't even have to see the child before the job. I'll describe what I'm looking for and the agent will either send me the perfect kid for the job or she'll say, 'I'm sorry; I don't have anyone for that.'

"If I can, I prefer to work with children I've used before. Once I find a child who appeals to me, I'm a little bit in love with him and I use him all the time. I have a group of kids, some of whom I started using when they were six months old. Today they're six and seven and they're still my number one children.

"But for some jobs I can't use them because they're not the right size. Like one job I do every year for a blue jean manufacturer. I have to have a blond surfer type who is a size 12. But a size 12 child only lasts one year—kids do grow—and so every year I have to find a new one.

"In those cases where I don't know a child who is the right size or type, I have a casting session. I try not to make them cattle calls, but sometimes the agents force you into it. I'll tell them I want a blonde and they'll throw in a couple of redheads and a brunette. Their reasoning is that it's a good opportunity for me to see the child so I can keep her in mind for the next job. But from my point of view, it's a waste of time. The most I like to see in one casting session is about twenty kids."

Lewin sees the children after school, staggering their appointments so they don't arrive all at once. "I try to arrange to have the kids from agency number one arrive from, say, 3 to 4 P.M., those from agency two, from 4 to 5 P.M., and so on. I don't think it's fair to keep the kids and their parents hanging around for a long time, especially when they've made a long trip to the session."

For most print casting, the interview is very simple. A Polaroid is taken of each child, the photographer talks to them for a few minutes to get an idea of their personality and temperament and then has a look at the composites to see how they photograph.

For Elyse Lewin, the casting choice is a personal thing. "I just have to fall in love with the child. I prefer the kids who have spunk. The ones I don't like are the ordinary kids, the typical commercial child. And the little girl who has ringlets and is trying to look like Shirley Temple. She stands there and says, 'I-take-tap. I-take-baton.'"

The final casting decision is usually made by the client. "Sometimes they leave the decision up to me," says Lewin. "But most of the time, I pick the two or three children who I think are best and send their Polaroids to the client. They choose the one they want from the pictures. But if they don't like any of my choices, I have to start the casting process again from scratch."

Since casting is based so much on a personal connection between the photographer and the child, there isn't that much you can do to help your child's chances. However, Lewin does suggest you try and find out in advance what the job is and dress your child accordingly. "If they're casting kids to be in a birthday party picture, then the parent should bring the child dressed in a party outfit. If it's going to be a little farm girl shot, for example, bring her in blue jeans and pigtails. If you do that then right away the photographer can say, 'Oh, I could see her in the picture.'"

Shooting the Ad

If a photographer has "seen your child in the picture," he or she will call your agent and make a booking. Your agent will then call you with all the pertinent information as to time and place. Sometimes you will be asked to bring some of your child's clothes along to use in the shoot. Elyse Lewin, however, rarely asks parents to provide any part of the wardrobe. "I just don't trust them to have anything that's going to be what I need. I plan everything very specifically in my photographs. For instance, if I'm doing a picture of a little girl wearing a pink dress, I want a precise shade of pink. I can't describe that to parents or expect them to hit by chance on exactly what I want. So I almost always dress the kids myself. Sometimes, with babies, I'll ask that they bring their own diapers. Or I'll tell the parents to bring the child's shoes. Let's say I want a girl to wear Mary Janes. I'll ask the parent to bring them, and if the child doesn't have any, I'll tell them to buy a pair, we'll split the cost, and the child gets to keep the shoes."

Depending on the type of work being done, you can expect the shoot to last an hour or a day. "When I'm doing a catalogue," explains Lewin, "I'm shooting all day long because we do eight to ten pictures a day. But a single ad—well, even before we bring the child in, we've worked on it sometimes for a day and a half. We've gotten the wardrobe, found the location, done the necessary tests of the film. Then we go to the location ahead of time, so that we're all set up and ready to shoot by the time the child arrives. In those cases, the children only work about an hour.

"Of course, with babies it's much less than that. No baby can work more than fifteen or twenty minutes without getting tired. So we usually get two babies for the job and keep switching them back and forth until we get the shot done."

Your rules of conduct for the shooting session are the same as those for parents of commercial kids. Number one: Don't bring anyone with you. The photographer does not need—nor does your child—a cheering section on the sidelines. Besides, the set will be crowded enough, particularly when an ad agency is involved in the shoot. The same complement of agency people that hang around at commercial shoots are likely to be at these print shoots.

Rule number two: Keep your opinions to yourself. Part of the photographer's expertise is the ability to work with children. Advice from you is superfluous and can be detrimental to the session.

Lewin's method of dealing with children is to "treat them with

respect. I look them right in the eye when I talk to them. I don't
talk down or treat them like they're animals. I say, 'Now listen, I
want you to sit down there. Oh, you're going to look so wonderful. Just trust me; you're going to look perfect.' Kids may be little, but they still have a lot of pride and ego. If you tell them
they're going to look wonderful, they'll get happy and do whatever you want."

But if a parent is hovering all around, hissing "Smile!" and
straightening clothes, the child will likely end up a rigid bundle of
nerves.

If the shoot is a short one, and you'll be told in advance of the
expected duration, you only have an hour or so to sit on the sidelines. If it's to be an all-day affair, come prepared. Bring a book,
needlepoint, or your checkbook to balance—anything that will
keep you occupied all day. Don't worry about eating, however;
the same royal feasting takes place on print shooting sessions as
on commercial shoots. "We have a catered lunch and snacks all
day long," says Lewin. "But I have learned one thing: Don't give
the kids candy or sweet things. I've found they get a sugar high
that makes them really hyper. So now I give them nuts and pret-
zels. Even the littlest baby gets a pretzel to suck on."

Once the session ends and your child is released, that job is
over. Say goodbye to the photographer like you'll never meet
again; in other words, don't start pressing to have your child used
again. If that photographer is going to call on your child again, it
will be because she thinks the kid is terrific, not because you say
so. If you've got to rave to someone, do it to your child. He's the
one who needs to know how great you think he is.

The Law, Unions, and Money

Most of the child labor laws that apply to commercial kids cover
model children as well. Social Security cards are mandatory, and
the requirements for work permits vary from state to state. Your
agent is the expert on these subjects and will advise you of exactly
what your state demands before your child can work in print.

The only thing to say about unions and print work is that there aren't any—and most people think that's a shame. Without a union to represent them, people who do print work have no protection other than their agent. And where they most need that protection is in the pocketbook.

"Right now every job I do is negotiable," says Jeanette Walton. "My kids get a straight $75 an hour. But that's not standard. There are a lot of agents out there who undercut my prices. They send their kids out for $50 an hour."

Sometimes a child can end up making more than his flat session fee because the job is upgraded. "If the ad has been contracted for magazines only and then the advertiser decides he wants to make a billboard of it, we renegotiate the fee," explains Walton. "The ad agency will call me and say, 'Okay, we want to use this ad for billboards, and we'll pay the child an extra $300.' That happens relatively frequently."

But you can only count on your child getting the straight session fee, and since the rates vary from agent to agent, one question you should have answered to your satisfaction *before* you sign with an agent is what your child's hourly rate will be.

Obviously, you're not going to make a fortune from your child's modeling work. "It certainly can't compare to the money a child earns doing commercials," says Walton. "Over a long period of time, *maybe,* if they saved it all, the money would help to put a kid through college. But that would take an awfully long time. About the only way a family can really make a lot of money from print work is to have a number of children all doing it at the same time. I have a couple of families like that, and they take in anywhere from $100 to $400 a week."

Walton would like to see a union for print models not only to standardize the pay rates but also to act as a watchdog ensuring that her clients actually get their money. "I spend an awful lot of my time, blood, sweat, and tears getting the model's money. The accounts pay up when they feel like it rather than on a schedule. And it isn't necessarily the tiny photographer on the corner who is the worst offender when it comes to paying the bill. I have just as much trouble getting the money due a client out of a big ad agency. Actually, the large advertising agencies are the worst offenders, not only because no one is really worried about paying the print model, but because of their computer systems. They're set to pay on sixty- and ninety-day cycles. If something goes wrong and the client doesn't get paid, I finally track someone down at this big company and say, 'Listen, this person worked three months ago on one of your ads. Everyone but him has gotten paid.' Well, there's no way that the agency person can go and take a check out and write it out and send to me. They have to put the whole thing into the computer again.

"If there were a union, that would never happen. It doesn't when these agencies are doing commercials. You know damn well that the money is paid on time, because the agency is going to get a fat fine from SAG if it isn't.

"I think the most important facet of my activities these days is trying to raise the level of respect for this medium. Right now we're low man on the totem pole, and it's all a matter of money. If we had a union that would predetermine the session fees and the times of payment, the reputation of the business would suddenly improve."

Where the Work Is

Everywhere. In varying degrees, there is some potential for making your child a model in every city in the United States. The markets are categorized in the same way as for commercials— major, middle, and minor—with the same cities in each category.

New York, of course, is Mecca for models. There is more print work done there than anywhere else in the United States. And there are more model kids there than anywhere else. That makes the good news the tremendous work and earning potential New York model children have; the bad news is the intense competition.

Much of the print work done in New York by children is done by commercial kids. They work both fields, using the same agent. There are fewer children doing just print work, and they must find an agent willing to represent them for that alone. Not all agents will, because they can make more money for the same effort handling only commercial children. "I will get kids out on print jobs to get them some experience," says Jean Walton of Ann Wright Associates. "But the only time I will actually concentrate on a print career for a child is when I have one who is very pretty and poised but who can't deliver lines. And even then, I'll only send them out for print jobs until they get rid of their New York accent or learn to read a script."

That being the case, if you are only interested in modeling for your child, you are going to have to be a bit more selective when it comes to contacting agents. A list of those New York agents who do represent children for print work is at the end of this chapter. But before you go to the effort of sending them photographs and setting up interviews, call and ask if they will represent your child for print work only.

Los Angeles, the other major market, never used to be much of a town for modeling. However, the opportunities there are ever-increasing now, largely because of the influx of major advertising agencies that are setting up branch offices that are responsible for their own national advertising campaigns. Moreover, much of the catalogue work for stores in the western states is done in Los Angeles. And then there is the constant run of daily newspaper ads for L.A. department stores, always a good source of work for model kids.

The situation regarding agents is much the same in L.A. as it is in New York: Some agents only handle print work for clients who also do commercials; others will take a child just for print. Check with the agents in the list that follows to see which is which.

The middle markets, particularly the big four, also have thriving print fields. According to Lynne Hamilton of the Shirley Hamilton Agency in Chicago, a full 50 percent of their business for children is photographic modeling. The situation is similar in Atlanta, Dallas, and Miami. In fact, as a general rule, you will have an easier time getting your child into print than commercials in all of the middle markets: There is simply more photographic advertising done there than commercial.

That is even more true of the minor markets. Just look at your local newspapers. See any ads for stores down the street? Any children in those ads? Chances are that they're local kids. Those stores, which can afford to advertise in a newspaper, don't have the money to spring for commercials.

Because print work accounts for so much of their business, agents in the middle and minor markets are not picky about handling kids just for modeling. So go back to Chapter 8 for a list of agents in your area, then proceed with your inquiries as detailed earlier in this chapter.

If there are no agents listed for your area, that only means you'll have to work harder to get your child started. The two best sources for print work are advertising agencies and photographers, both of which you'll find listed in your local Yellow Pages. Get their addresses and proceed as if you were contacting an agent.

You may find, as you go through the phone book, that there are some modeling agencies listed for your town. By all means, call them. But—and it cannot be repeated too often—if they promise your child work in exchange for your money, head the other way. No agent can make that kind of promise: They're empty words that can end up costing you a lot.

NEW YORK PRINT AGENTS
(see Chapter 7 for addresses)

Associated Talent Agency
Ford Talent Group, Inc.
Sanford Leigh
Marge McDermott
Fifi Oscard Associates, Inc.
Palmer Talent Agency
Joel Pitt Ltd.
Charles Vernon Ryan Agency
William Schuller Agency
Gloria Troy Talent Agency
Ann Wright Representatives

LOS ANGELES PRINT AGENTS
(see Chapter 7 for addresses)

Iris Burton
Lil Cumber
Gerritsen International
Beverly Hecht
Caroline Leonetti
Hazel McMillan
Mary Grady Associates
Dorothy Day Otis Agency
Pacific Artists
Dorothy Shreve
Williamson & Associates
Wormser, Helfond & Joseph
Ann Wright Associates

10

Your Role: Stage Parent or Career Protector

Stage Parent: It's not a description, it's an insult, a label that is an instant synonym for greedy parent, abusive parent, predatory parent—bad parent. And it's a label that is stamped on you, automatically, as soon as you start your child's career.

"Please," begged the woman, her arm around her daughter. "Please put a kind word in your book about us parents."

"Yes," said another. "Tell them we're not all Stage Parents."

So I'm telling you: They're not. The majority of parents of commercial kids are loving, caring people. Their ambition for their children is healthy, their attitude toward the career is realistic, their involvement is that of facilitator, not dictator. But these parents are quiet about what they do and their stories don't make good copy, so no one ever hears about them. Like the Ugly American, it's the Stage Parent who makes the news, and unfortunately there are enough of them around to fuel the fires that started way back in the mid-1880s, when the first era of kid stars was born.

The goldmining camps of the Wild West were their training

ground. Primarily little girls, they danced and sang on stages, tables, and bars, straight into the hearts of lonely miners starved for family warmth and love in obscure mining towns all over California. Little Lotta Crabtree, Little Elsie Janis, Baby Gladys Smith—"fairy stars" they were called, these first child stars. And behind them were their mothers, Mary Ann Crabtree, Ma Janis, Charlotte Smith, always plotting and prodding, hustling and haranguing, justly earning them the title of the First Stage Parents.

Eventually these fairy stars moved out of the West into grinding cross-country tours. They shimmied and warbled on the vaudeville stages or died nightly in the pseudo-Dickensian tragedies that were then the rage. And that is all they did. The theater and mother, that was their life. And for mother, it was the theater, daughter—and the money.

With the coming of film, there was a new medium for the child stars to try. Baby Gladys beat them all when she moved from Broadway to the Biograph, became D. W. Griffith's new star, and took another name: Mary Pickford.

But all this was just the warmup for the real heyday of the child star. It began in the 1920s, when Charlie Chaplin hired a little boy called Jackie Coogan to appear in his new film, *The Kid*. Audiences went crazy over Jackie's tearful performance. The film was declared a masterpiece, Chaplin made $1.5 million from it, and all over Hollywood directors started looking for their own pint-sized moneymakers. The great tide of the child star craze had begun.

The kids who came to fame then and throughout the entire period, which ended with World War II, are legendary. Mickey Rooney, Judy Garland, Shirley Temple, Jackie Cooper—their names are household words. But their fame didn't just happen; behind each was a mother or father who saw gold in their child's grins and did whatever they had to to mine it.

During that twenty-year period, Hollywood was teeming with would-be child stars. It is estimated that hopeful parents with child in tow arrived in the city at the amazing rate of one hundred every fifteen minutes. Although only the smallest fraction of them actually made it into the movies, it isn't hard to understand what motivated these parents to abandon their lives in small towns all over the country for the unknown orange groves of Southern California.

The United States was in the midst of the Depression then. The movie business in Hollywood was the only place in the country where Americans saw hope and success. For those not already beaten by the times, the magic of the movies seemed their one chance to make something of their lives. The fact that they tried to use their children to do it was nothing new. Diana Serra Carey, who as Baby Peggy was one of the first great child stars, points out in her book, *Hollywood's Children:* "Since antiquity, the children of rich and royal house alike were deployed as pawns by ruthlessly ambitious parents who betrothed them in infancy, dispatched them to distant wars, or consigned them to the cloister, whatever best advanced the family's financial or political ends. The progeny of Europe's poor faced an even crueler fate." To save their families from starvation, children were sold as beggars, hustled to the mines, chained in factories, or bartered as the lowest of household help.

But we are in different times now, and the forces that influence a parent to push a child toward stardom are far gentler than they once were. The motivations still rest on ambition and money, but it is the rare child who becomes a sacrificial lamb.

Yet the reputation still remains, and there are enough hustling, greedy, insensitive parents out there to ensure that every generation of parents with kids in the business has its rotten apples.

Actually there are three types of parent in the Stage Parent category: The Ruthless Child Ravager, who, being the archtypical Stage Parent, needs no explanation; the Blind Zealot, the parent whose ambition overrides his or her natural humanity; and the Naive Offender, the parent who innocently steps over the boundaries from good parenting to Stage Parenting. Often what differentiates one from the other is not the heinousness of their act but the intentions behind it.

Throughout this book there is advice, outright and implied, about how to avoid earning the title of Stage Parent while you move your child through the various stages of making him a commercial kid. But there is nothing that teaches so well as example.

Ruthless Child Ravagers

There is a little girl in the business who has done an awful lot of jobs in an awful lot of years, more years, in fact, than most kids stay active in commercials. The reason is that she's very small and she never seems to grow very much, so she remains eligible for all those parts in the six- to eight-year-old range, even though she's now close to twelve. Word has it that she doesn't grow because her parents don't feed her very much—so that she won't grow very much. They give her enough to maintain her strength and see her through her long days at work. No one would be any the wiser except for one thing: Put her at an audition where there's food around and her concentration is immediately broken. The script, the camera, the interview itself are all forgotten as she eyes the apple or doughnut or even a soda cracker and hesitantly, fearfully almost, asks, "May I have that?"

Right now her parents are reaping only rewards from her career. She's bright, she's cute, she's very, very talented. But she's nearing the end. Though her body is still tiny, her face is growing older and harder. The camera picks that up, and so do the commercial-makers. On a recent interview, she almost got the job until the director reviewed her tape. "I don't know," he said, shaking his head. "I thought she was perfect but there's something in her eyes I didn't see before. She looks, well, she looks too old. I just don't understand it."

I do; as the commercial says, "You can't fool Mother Nature."

Another child, another interview, this time for a commercial in which six girls would do a soft-shoe number. The casting call was for ten- to twelve-year-olds who had some dancing experience. The choreographer was at the interview, carefully demonstrating the steps the children would do in the audition.

She took them in groups of six, ran through the dance once on her own and then led them through it several times until they were sure of themselves. It wasn't a particularly complicated number, provided a child had had some dancing lessons.

Standing on the sidelines, next to her mother, was an eleven-year-old with new tap shoes on her feet and fear in her eyes. The choreographer demonstrated the number and then said, "Okay, girls, let's all try it together."

The eleven-year-old turned to her mother. "Please, Mommy, I don't want to do it."

Her mother said nothing, ignoring the child as if she hadn't spoken.

The girl knew what the silence meant. "Please don't make me." She was close to tears.

Through clenched teeth, her mother answered, "Get out there."

"Plea—" She never got the words out of her mouth. Her mother's right hand flashed up and cracked across her daughter's cheek; her left shoved the child hard onto the dance floor.

The choreographer missed none of it. "Take your daughter home," she told the mother. "If she doesn't want to do it, no one will make her. Go."

These are not isolated incidents, nor are they the grossest stories of child abuse perpetrated by the worst of the Ruthless Child Ravagers. Not unheard of is the casting couch for commercial kids. Generally, however, it's their mothers who are offering their services in return for contracts. But one casting director knows of a fourteen-year-old commercial kid whose mother has been promoting her for the past two years. "Her mother makes the contacts for her," says the casting director. "Not for just any old job, though. She's past that point. Now she's out for the top of the line —an exclusive contract to be the spokesperson for a product."

Then there are the parents, a number of them, according to industry sources in several cities, who know exactly what kind of child the commercial business is looking for. Blond, blue-eyed, the all-American kid next door. Only problem is that genetically, these parents could never produce such a child. So they adopt. They start with one and groom that adopted child for a commercial career. Once he's on his way, they adopt another. Groom that child, get him started, and adopt another. They end up with a regular assembly line of commercial kids, all adopted, of various ages: a lifetime guarantee of a nonstop income.

Do these stories sound too fantastic to believe? Well, believe them; they're true. The Ruthless Child Ravagers earn their name. You will recognize them readily once your child starts working, and you will learn in time that nothing you hear about them is *too* fantastic to be true.

The Blind Zealots

There are probably more Stage Parents in this category than the other two. They aren't essentially cruel people as the Ruthless Child Ravagers are. Nor are they innocently stupid, as are the Naive Offenders. Blind Zealots are so intent on their child's career that they don't see their actions as abusive.

Like the mother of a seven-year-old commercial kid who called her agent from a callbox on the freeway. "We were on our way to the interview, but we've just been in a five-car accident," she excitedly told the agent. "Don't worry, though. Ginny's all right and her dress didn't get ruined at all. We can still make it to the interview; a taxi is on the way."

"My God," the agent exploded. "Forget about the interview. Take Ginny home. That's where she belongs right now."

"Oh no, we'd never even consider that. We're professionals. This business is our life. I'm just calling to make sure that it's okay if we get there a little late."

Agents say that one of the tip-offs to Blind Zealots is that they start talking about the career as *"Our* career" or *"My* career." This inclusion of themselves into something that is strictly their child's is a sure sign that the parent's ego is inextricably tied up with the child. What their child does is a direct reflection on them: If he succeeds, they are successful; if he fails, they are failures. Since no one wants to be a failure, these parents will do everything they can to ensure their child never fails.

A very talented commercial kid, a nine-year-old boy from New York, was due at an interview for a soft drink spot that had a big dance number in it. But the boy was appearing in a Broadway musical, his matinee ran late, and by the time he and his mother got to the audition, the choreographer had gone. The casting director, because she knew the child was a really good dancer, told his mother, "Come back tomorrow when I have the girls' audition and I'll let your son try out then."

That should have been the end of the story, at least until the next afternoon. But this mother wasn't taking any chances. She knew the choreographer was working in another show on Broadway. So she hiked her child down to that theater and told the stage manager in no uncertain terms, "We must see Martha, the choreographer. This is an emergency."

The stage manager didn't question her. He went for Martha, who came running, not knowing what could possibly be wrong. Instead of some distraught person, however, she was confronted by a very calm mother who said, "We're auditioning tomorrow for that soft drink commercial. I'd like you to show us the dance steps so we can prepare."

Martha's mouth dropped. "I can't believe you're asking me that. I am really shocked that you'd come here like this for that reason." She turned and left the mother and son standing alone.

Later Martha called the casting director and told her what had happened. The casting director was furious and called the boy's agent, telling her to cancel his interview. The agent was furious and called the child's manager. The manager was furious and called the mother. The mother was in hysterics. She called the casting director back. "You can't do this to my son," she cried. "Please don't embarrass him like that."

The casting director was stoney. "You should have thought of that before you pulled your little trick. I don't want to see you or your son at this interview."

"We're coming anyway," the mother insisted. "You can't stop us. And you better make sure you put my son's interview on tape."

The casting director wasn't going to argue. She'd said her piece; now she hung up. But the next afternoon when mother and son showed up, she ignored them. They sat in the waiting room until every other child had been seen. Finally, the casting director called the boy in. The choreographer showed him the dance and the casting director pushed the Record button on the videotape. Then, almost before he was out the door, she pushed Erase. It was all done very quietly and the mother never knew. Just as she never knew two months later why her son was fired from his Broadway show. Everyone else knew, however; the producers got rid of the child because they couldn't take his pushy mother.

Blind Zealots often ruin their kids' careers. Agents, managers, and casting directors watch them work, know the outcome will be disastrous for the child's emotional well-being and refuse to participate in the process. It is not only their unwillingness to be involved with such parents that makes them withdraw their services and shut the child out of interviews, but the knowledge that in so doing they are protecting him in the only way they can—by slowly squeezing him out of the business, the arena of his destruction.

Bonnie Schulman of the Bonnie Kid agency remembers the day she called one of her clients in for a "checkup chat." He was one of her most successful children, a perfect commercial kid with blue eyes and blond hair. When he came walking into her office with his mother, Schulman noticed something she had never seen before: His blond hair was still beautifully golden, but there was a fine line of dark brown showing at the roots. She sent him out to the waiting room and turned to his mother. "Are you dyeing his hair?" she demanded.

"Well, I'm lightening it a little," the mother admitted.

"Don't." Schulman was short and sure.

"I think it's more his look to be blond," the mother said, defensively.

"Then I think you better find yourself another agent."

Schulman had no illusions that her action would then and there end the child's career and thereby save him from his mother. In fact, he did go on and find another agent. But eventually, that agent too will get his mother's number and send them on their way. To another agent and another and another. "But eventually," says Evelyn Schultz, "these parents run out of agents."

Blind Zealots are also the parents who run into trouble with the commercial-makers. They're the ones who are kicked off sets and banned from locations by directors furious at their intervention. Like the mother of an eight-month-old baby, one of fifteen hired to crawl their way through a bank commercial. "I couldn't believe this one mother," exploded the director. "She took a bead on where the camera was aimed and kept running into the shot to push her kid right in front of it. We asked her a number of times to stay out of the way, but that woman was determined her kid was going to star. Finally, we had to kick her out. It solved the problem for us that day, but can you imagine what life is going to be like for that child as he grows up in the business?"

Once a parent is thrown off a set, the chances of that particular director or production company using the child again is just about nil. And word travels fast in the small world of commercials. "Don't use that kid; his mother's a pain." Eventually, the child's circle narrows: Agents won't handle him, casting directors won't call him, production companies won't hire him. Soon this child who had such a promising career has no career. A has-been, never-was at six or eight or ten. And the parent who was grimly determined to make sure the child turned out a winner is left with a silent phone and a stack of composites. And no idea of what went wrong.

But even before that happens, the child may burn out from the constant parental pressure. "I've had some dynamite children that were totally ruined by their mothers," says Tami Lynn, the Los Angeles manager. "They put constant pressure on their kids. 'Do this, do that, brush your hair, smile, why didn't you get that job, what did you do wrong?'

"They're constantly yapping at the child instead of just taking them on their interviews, bringing them home, giving them dinner, and letting them play till bedtime. And it's not just on interviews. Seven days a week they're putting the pressure on the kid. The mother isn't a mother anymore; she's the agent, the manager, the dictator. The child starts getting uptight. He's always worrying if he's going to be able to accomplish what Mama wants. And once that happens, he starts messing up on interviews. He's too anxious to be able to go in and be himself, talk to the director with any ease. And then it's not too long before this great little kid has been turned into a neurotic.

"I've tried to stop it when I see it going on. I've called parents in and told them, 'Please, let up on your child. You love him; that's more important than whether he gets the job. You've got to tell him that.'

"But it doesn't work. Nothing is going to stop that kind of parent. They just go in like bulls, and all I can do is sit back and watch."

Naive Offenders

Naive Offenders mean well. Their dastardly deeds, or even their mildly provocative ones, spring not from a desperate personal need for their child's success but from their earnest attempts to Help, to Do Things Properly.

In their most benign state, Stage Parents who are Naive Offenders bother only the agent. "They're the parents who call you all the time," says Evelyn Schultz. "They're worried about this, they have a question about that. Or they heard at an interview that such and such a commercial is being cast and why isn't their child being sent up for it. What that parent doesn't know is that maybe I've already submitted their child's pictures and the casting director turned him down. Or maybe the kid is the wrong size or coloring or age and that's why I haven't called him for it. I try to be always available to my parents and responsive to their needs, but with that kind I'll stand for their nudging only once or twice before I say, 'Maybe you'd be happier with another agent.' Those parents don't stay with us too long."

Sometimes the Naive Offender's eagerness leads to the same crimes that the Blind Zealot perpetrates. Often with the same disastrous results.

Joan Lynn, the casting director for Bob Giraldi, tells of one Naive Offender who brought her daughter to callbacks for a commercial where a number of girls were going to be at a slumber party. During the taping of the interviews, Lynn left to go to the ladies room. Scurrying behind her was the Naive Offender. She waited until Lynn was at the sink, washing her hands, before she held out a hundred-dollar bill. "What's that for?" Lynn asked in surprise.

"Please—my daughter has been auditioning for a year now and she hasn't gotten one commercial yet," the mother's voice held a pleading note. "Please use her in this one."

Lynn stared at her. "I'm very insulted that you're doing this. And I want to tell you something: I have nothing to do with whether your child gets this job or not. Moreover, she's a talented girl. You should let her do it by herself."

Nothing more was said until several days later when the mother called Joan Lynn. "You were right," she said softly. "My daughter got the job. And I'm so very embarrassed about what I did. I realize now that that sort of thing just isn't done."

A bribe—it usually smacks of the Blind Zealot. The difference in this case is that the mother meant well. Most Naive Offenders, when their behavior is corrected or even pointed out to them as wrong, are shocked to see what they've been doing. They never dreamed their actions were even mildly abusive. The Blind Zealots, on the other hand, would deny their actions were wrong or harmful—or they wouldn't care. But with the end results of both kinds of Stage Parents so similar, and because intent is so personal and rarely disclosed, it is often difficult to tell the Blind Zealot from the Naive Offender.

The casting call was for a commercial to be aired in the summer months. They needed boys and girls, six to eight, all sizes, shapes, and colors—a regular United Nations call, as it's known in the business. One mother, having found out in advance that the commercial would be set at a picnic, brought her seven-year-old daughter dressed in shorts and T-shirt. Nothing wrong with that; it's never a bad idea to "costume" a child for an interview. But this was Chicago; it was thirty degrees outside and snowing. Was that mother a Naive Offender, obliviously playing the game by the book? Or a Blind Zealot, who thought nothing of sacrificing her child's physical comfort and health for a better chance at the job?

Another day, another mother, this one intently combing hei

son's auburn Dutch boy into smooth perfection. He sat patiently, never uttering a word, his eyes red and bleary, his nose streaming, his color high with an obvious fever. Blind Zealot, not caring her kid had a cold? Or Naive Offender, not knowing she should turn down the interview?

In the end, it makes no difference. The child suffers equally, whatever the parent's intent. And the parents, despite their different titles, are ultimately both Stage Parents.

All Stage Parents are not mothers. True, most of them are, but that's because more mothers take the active role in their child's career than fathers. But when Dad does get involved, say the professionals, watch out! Agents, casting directors, commercial-makers agree: The only thing worse than a Stage Mother is a Stage Father.

"Fathers who get involved in their kids' careers are the biggest pain there is," says manager Sandra Firestone. "They are much worse than any mother. They're much more demanding, much more pushy. In fact, the only two times I've broken a contract with a child I represented was because I couldn't take the father's interference."

Why are fathers so awful? Evelyn Schultz says it's because "they think they know it all. The mothers at least let you direct them and advise them. But the fathers—they're sure that because they're out there in the business world, they know exactly what their child should be doing and how the career should be handled."

Not only that, but consider that the world of commercials is run, to a great degree, by women. And that, according to casting director Sheila Manning, is what makes Stage Fathers so terrible. "They have all the negative qualities of Stage Mothers *plus* the whole macho trip they lay on you."

Like Stage Mothers, Stage Fathers come in the three varieties. It was a Stage Father of the first degree, a Ruthless Child Ravager, who turned a set upsidedown, left his child in tears and the director sputtering with rage on one commercial shoot. He told the director how to direct, the kid how to act, he screamed about the pay, the food, the commercial itself. He made, says the child's agent, "such a stink that the director just shrieked, 'Get him out of here! I don't care how you do it but get him out!'" Needless to say, that child will never work for that director again.

It was a Stage Father, one of the Blind Zealots, who sent his son into an interview with this message for the director: "Dad says to tell you that if I get this commercial, you can have the condo in Mammoth for the weekend."

And it was a Stage Father, a Naive Offender, who called his daughter's agent late one night about the commercial call she had the next day. "How Oriental do they want her to look?" he asked in a worried tone.

The agent was astonished. "What do you mean how Oriental? What are you planning to do—give her rice and chopsticks and carry her in on a rickshaw?"

The Career Protectors

It is easy to go on at length about the crimes of Stage Parents. Outrage is inspiring. It is not so easy to sing the praises of good parents, the Career Protectors, if only because their actions are not extraordinary when viewed day by day. How much can one say about the parent who takes her child for a consolatory Coke after an interview that didn't go so well? Not nearly so much as one can say about the parent who cracks her kid across the face after such an interview. So enough of defining Stage Parents of all types; time now to define the Career Protectors.

The Career Protector's child is in commercials for one reason only: Because it is something the *child* wants to do. That doesn't mean to say that every child of Career Protectors has at some time or other gone to them and said, "Help me get into TV commercials." It is true that some do. After all, kids today are products of television. Their fantasy life, to a great extent, revolves around it. So after hours of sitting in front of the set, admiring the kids who seem no different than he, it isn't unusual for a child to think, "Hey, I could do that." From there, it is one short step to: "Hey, Mom, I want to do that."

However, some children aren't that verbal. Some children aren't that aware of their feelings. And face it, at the age some children enter the commercial business, they don't even know how to talk yet.

All of this is to say that *you* can be the one who brings up the subject. You can plant the seeds of desire in your child's mind. But before you do, ask yourself one question, and be totally honest: Do you want your child to be a commercial kid because it will benefit you or because it will benefit him? Do you see it as a source of money, of prestige, of power for you, or a source of fun for him? These are really the same question, asked two different ways. But there is only one right answer.

If your motives are the good ones, i.e., if you answer the question correctly, you cannot help but ensure that your child's career is, from start to finish, what it should be, an enjoyable learning experience. Children are extremely sensitive to their parents' feelings and needs. Scratch the surface and you'll find most kids live to please mommy or daddy. Your child will never feel it is important whether he wins or loses a role, will never feel he has failed or done wrong, will never feel pressure to do or be or perform except as he naturally is *only* as long as you never feel any of these things.

Starting out in the business with the correct mindset is the major part of being a Career Protector. The other part, the source of your title, is in protecting him from his career.

The commercial business is a grownup business, run by and for adults. No part of it is oriented to a child's tender sensibilities or nascent ego. Consequently, the child who is not protected can end up being crushed by the build-up of day-to-day occurrences that wouldn't faze an adult.

Remember that and watch your child closely for signs that the career is too much for him. Is he nervous before all his interviews? Is he upset or unusually quiet when they're over? Both of those are good signs that the rejection aspect of the business is getting to him. Jeanette Walton, the print agent at Wormser, Helfond & Joseph, has a daughter who did commercials. Until one day when they were driving home from an interview and Walton looked over to see her child silently crying. "What's wrong?" she asked.

"Oh, Mom, I'm just so ashamed that I didn't get the job. I'm so sorry and I feel so bad because I blew it."

Walton comforted her as best she could. And later that night she said to her husband, "Wendy's commmercial career has just come to a sudden end. There is no way that I want any part of something that could make her cry and feel bad like that."

Your child may not be so overt about his feelings. Your only clue may be his sudden unwillingness to go on interviews. Or that your normally bubbly child is turning rather solemn. If you suspect he's unhappy, talk to him. Ask him if he likes what he's doing or if he'd rather forget the whole thing. And let him know it makes no difference to you whichever way he answers.

Let's say, however, that your child is quite able to accept the inherent pressure and rejection of the business. You still have to work to ensure that outside influences—friends and neighbors— don't produce a negative effect. Myra Unger says that there is nothing about either the people or the pressure of the commercial business that has ever been a problem for her two kids; it's always been the attitude of outsiders that has bothered Abe and Judy. The Unger's solution, once they recognized the problem, was to put their children into a school for professional children.

Kara Olsen's mother, on the other hand, anticipated trouble when her daughter first began working. "I felt the problems would come when Kara's school peers became jealous of the money she was making. So we dealt with that in the beginning by design. Kara gets a normal allowance, but no more than that. Because she doesn't have any money to flash around and because she doesn't brag about her career to her friends, the kids aren't jealous and she has had no problems."

Mrs. Olsen, like all Career Protectors, keeps in constant contact with Kara's teachers. You should do the same. Ask the teacher to watch for signs of trouble with your child's classmates, or some change in his classroom behavior. Don't wait for a report card filled with low grades and bad citizenship reports to tell you that your child is in trouble.

And finally, don't ever forget that, no matter his ambition and no matter his success, your child is, first and foremost, a child. All of the things, large and small, that are important to childhood must still be his. "Children have very important things going on in their lives," says agent Jean Walton. "Little League and football, Scouts and birthday parties. You have got to allow them to do these things, even though it may mean they miss out on interviews. It's the only way their careers will really work well—if their lives are balanced."

And a commercial child's life cannot be balanced unless the parent works hard to see that it is. Which brings us full circle to the fact that whatever his abilities—his talent, his looks, his own personal ambition—your child's success ultimately depends on you. "The truth of the business," says Walton, echoing every other agent, manager, casting director, and commercial-maker, "is that the best kids, the most successful ones, have the best parents. It's funny, but that's just the way it works out."

About the Author

Jane Gassner Patrick graduated from the University of Pittsburgh with a degree in theater arts and philosophy. She moved to London in the late sixties and began her journalistic career in production at the BBC Television News. After seven years in England, she returned to the United States, worked as a news reporter and documentary producer for Pacifica Radio in Los Angeles, and in 1975 was appointed Associate Editor of the Los Angeles *Free Press*.

Jane Patrick is now a free-lance journalist and writer. Her articles, ranging from humorous personal accounts to major investigative news features, have appeared in a number of local and national magazines, including *Los Angeles, Playgirl, Emmy, New West,* and *New Times.*

Index

242   INDEX

White, Mary Ellen, 36
White Agency, Mary Ellen, 9, 47,
   73–74, 148, 165
White House Studios, the, 189
Wild spots, 141–42
William Schuller Agency, 39, 165,
   218
Williamson & Associates, 167, 219
Willis & Associates, Dick, 189
Wisconsin, 201
Withholding taxes, 127–28
Wood Production, Larry, 190
Worker's Compensation, 130
Work permits, 76, 112, 113

application, 126
California, 159–60
modeling, for, 214
revocation, 118
Worldwide Films, Inc., 202
Wormser, Helfond & Joseph
   Agency, 13, 167, 206, 219
Wright Associates, Ann, 167
Wright Representatives, Ann, 5,
   44, 149, 165
modeling, 217, 218, 219
WUTV-Channel 29, 193
Wyse Agency, Joy, 173

Zounds!, 192